WordPress 3 Site Blueprints

Ready-made plans for 9 different professional
WordPress sites

Heather R. Wallace

BIRMINGHAM - MUMBAI

WordPress 3 Site Blueprints

First published: August 2010

Production Reference: 1280710

Published by Packt Publishing Ltd.
32 Lincoln Road
Olton
Birmingham, B27 6PA, UK.

ISBN 978-1-847199-36-2

www.packtpub.com

Cover Image by Vinayak Chittar (vinayak.chittar@gmail.com)

Credits

Author
Heather R. Wallace

Reviewers
Andreas Wenning
Dominique-Alain Jan

Acquisition Editor
Usha Iyer

Development Editor
Mehul Shetty

Technical Editor
Aditya Belpathak

Indexer
Hemangini Bari

Editorial Team Leader
Aanchal Kumar

Project Team Leader
Lata Basantani

Project Coordinator
Jovita Pinto

Proofreader
Lesley Harrison

Production Coordinator
Aparna Bhagat

Cover Work
Aparna Bhagat

About the Author

Heather R. Wallace is an author, WordPress consultant, and web developer who has been building websites since 1997. She has developed and managed several different websites and blogs; many of which have been powered by WordPress.

While Heather manages several websites, it's at `WPBlogBot.com` that she offers her consultation services on a wide variety of WordPress-related tasks such as installation, customization, troubleshooting, and more.

About the Reviewers

Andreas Wenning is a Bachelor in IT and Telecommunications from Denmark, and is skilled in programming concepts, network routing and security, mobility, mobile networks, and wireless transmission. These skills are getting enhanced further with his studies for a Master's degree in Telecommunication.

He has been working for a web hosting company and has extensive experience with web applications from making them easily deployable. From supporting those applications he also knows the caveats and pitfalls when deploying.

He is also involved in the Kubuntu/Ubuntu Linux community, and has been appointed "Master of the Universe" with commit rights to community-supported packages. Here he has also been providing security updates for some of the included web applications.

Through his own company `Awen.dk` he has been and is providing services and consulting within these experiences; this also includes server deployment and custom integration of systems built on open source technologies.

Dominique-Alain Jan is a long time technologist who started with IT at the age of 16, programming his first Commodore 64 and then his Apple II and Macintosh in the eighties.

He has a Bachelor's degree in Economics and Law of the Fribourg's University (Switzerland), a Master's degree in Computer Science of the University of Lausanne (Switzerland), and he is finishing a Master of Art in Distance and Open Education from The Open University (UK).

As an educator and consultant in communication for his political party during the last election, Dominique-Alain has a wide experience with Wordpress, Wordpress MU, and blogging in general.

Nowadays, he is sharing his time as e-learning consultant in the UK, France, and Australia, as a technology teacher at a High School, and at the Teacher Training School in the Canton of Vaud in Switzerland.

I would like to dedicate this book to my mother, Lucinda. Thank you for all of your love, friendship, and support. You are, without a doubt, the best mother, and friend, that I could have ever hoped to have.

Table of Contents

Preface

Sure, WordPress can be used for blogging, but this powerful software is capable of so much more. With the right combination of plugins, themes, customizations, and configurations WordPress can be transformed into a community portal, an e-commerce site, and more. There's very little that WordPress can't do — if you can image it, then it's probably possible with WordPress.

While some books merely talk about the capabilities of WordPress in general and then leave you to figure out how they apply to your situation, WordPress 3 Site Blueprints takes a different approach. As you follow along, you will learn by doing, because each of these nine chapters shows you how to build a WordPress-powered site from start to finish.

Each chapter provides easy-to-understand, step-by-step instructions, along with screenshots, to make it easy for you to follow along. In addition, detailed information is provided to help you optimally configure each and every plugin and theme mentioned in this book, so that you can get the most out of each of these sites. By the time you reach the end of each blueprint, you will have succeeded in creating a fully-functional website that's ready for use as is or that you may customize further, if you so desire.

What this book covers

Chapter 1, Project 1: Migrating a Static Website to WordPress shows you how to migrate from an existing static HTML website to a WordPress blog. This includes important information, such as how to transform your HTML template into a WordPress theme and how to move the content from your previous website into WordPress.

Chapter 2, Project 2: Building a Community Portal details how you can transform a typical WordPress installation into a community portal by first performing certain configurations on WordPress, so that its network functionality is useable. From there, this chapter then details how to further enhance the functionality of your site through the usage of the **BuddyPress** and **bbPress** plugins.

Chapter 3, Project 3: Building an E-Commerce Website covers the creation of an e-commerce store that's built using the **WP e-Commerce** plugin. Once you reach the end of this chapter, you will have a full-fledged e-commerce website that's capable of selling various products, managing inventory, and integrating with a number of popular payment processors.

Chapter 4, Project 4: Building a Local Classified Ads Website provides details on using the **ClassiPress** theme to build a classified ads website centered around a particular locality. This chapter also shows you how to improve upon ClassiPress by adding private messaging capabilities to your site.

Chapter 5, Project 5: Building a Consumer Review Website guides you through the creation of a consumer review website using the **WP Review Site** plugin. Once this project is complete, you will have a website where visitors can post their opinions about various products and/or services.

Chapter 6, Project 6: Building a Job Board Website shows you how to use the **JobPress** theme to create a job board where employers can post listings for prospective employees to browse. As you read, you will be shown how to create a stand-alone job board as well as how to run JobPress alongside an existing site.

Chapter 7, Project 7: Building a Microblogging Website provides information on using the **P2** theme to build your very own microblog. As this project progresses, you will be shown how to perform enhancements in order to make your microblog private and to make it so that it's possible for your users to mark certain conversations as favorites.

Chapter 8, Project 8: Building a Local Business Directory covers the creation of a directory where potential clients can browse member profiles submitted by local businesses. The various plugins, custom pages, as well as configurations and edits detailed in this chapter will all help you to complete this project.

Chapter 9, Project 9: Building a Membership Website guides you through the creation of a membership site using the **WishList Member** plugin. Once this site is complete, you will be able to sell subscriptions of various types, add content, configure membership options, and collect subscription fees using the payment processor of your choosing.

Appendix A, provides a small collection of plugins that can be used to improve just about any website that was built with WordPress.

Appendix B, offers guidance on the installation of WordPress themes and plugins using various methods. So, if you're new to WordPress, then getting started will be easy using the instructions provided here.

What you need for this book

In order to build the projects detailed in this book, you will need the following:

- A text editor
- A web browser
- A web hosting account
- An installation of WordPress 3.0 or greater
- PHP version 4.3 or greater
- MySQL version 4.1.2 or greater

Specific chapters have their own unique requirements. Here are the various themes and plugins that you will need in order to build each of the projects detailed in this book.

The following are required for *Chapter 1, Project 1: Migrating a Static Website to WordPress*:

- The Import HTML Pages plugin 1.21 or greater
- The Redirection plugin 2.1.25 or greater
- The Google XML Sitemaps plugin 3.2.3 or greater

The following are required for *Chapter 2, Project 2: Building a Community Portal*:

- The Buddypress plugin 1.2.3 or greater
- The Slide2Comment plugin 1.4.13 or greater
- The SI CAPTCHA Anti-Spam plugin 2.5.2 or greater
- The Simple Trackback Validation plugin 2.1 or greater
- The BuddyPress Profile Privacy plugin 0.2-alpha or greater
- The BuddyPress Template Pack plugin 1.0.2 or greater

The following are required for *Chapter 3, Project 3: Building an E-Commerce Website*:

- The WP e-Commerce plugin 3.7.6.2 or greater
- The NextGEN Gallery plugin 1.5.3 or greater
- The WP e-Commerce NextGEN BuyNow plugin 1.1.0 or greater
- The WP e-Commerce Gold Cart and Grid Module or greater
- The WP e-Commerce DropShop or greater
- The WP e-Commerce MP3 Audio Player or greater
- The WP e-Commerce Members Only Module or greater

The following are required for *Chapter 4, Project 4: Building a Local Classified Ads Website*:

- The ClassiPress theme 3.0.2 or greater
- The WP Private Messages plugin 1.0.1 or greater
- The New User Email Setup plugin 0.5.2 or greater
- The SexyBookmarks plugin 3.2.3 or greater
- The User Photo Plugin plugin 0.9.4 or greater
- The WP-EMail plugin 2.52 or greater
- The WP-Print plugin 2.50 or greater

The following is required for *Chapter 5, Project 5: Building a Consumer Review Website*:

- The WP Review Site plugin 3.1 Alpha or greater

The following is required for *Chapter 6, Project 6: Building a Job Board Website*:

- The JobPress theme 2.0 or greater

The following are required for *Chapter 7, Project 7: Building a Microblogging Website*:

- The P2 theme 1.1.3 or greater
- The Sidebar Login plugin 2.2.10 or greater
- The Absolute Privacy plugin 1.3 or greater
- The WP Favorite Posts plugin 1.5.1 or greater

The following are required for *Chapter 8, Project 8: Building a Local Business Directory*:

- The Register Plus plugin 3.5.1 or greater
- The User Photo plugin 0.9.4 or greater
- The Exclude Pages plugin 1.8.3 or greater
- The WP htaccess Control plugin 1.5.3 or greater
- The Members List plugin 2.9.8 or greater

The following is required for *Chapter 9, Project 9: Building a Membership Website*:

- The WishList Member plugin 2.20.435-2 or greater

In addition, if you would like to add to the functionality of your completed websites, then you will need these plugins, which are the subject of *Appendix A*.

- The Akismet plugin 2.3 or greater
- The WP-DB-Backup plugin 2.2.2 or greater
- The WP-reCAPTCHA plugin 2.9.7 or greater
- The Maintenance Mode plugin 5.2 or greater
- The WP Hide Dashboard plugin 2.0 or greater

Who this book is for

If you're a self-learner or a WordPress consultant who, instead of being content with using WordPress out-of-the-box, is interested in exploring all that this open source software has to offer, then this book is for you. The clear instructions provided in each chapter will guide you through the process of creating a varied collection of WordPress sites for either yourself or a client.

While some experience with WordPress is required to get the most from this book, if you can install themes and plugins, you should be able to follow these easy-to-understand WordPress blueprints with no problem. Some knowledge of CSS and HTML will be beneficial, but experience with PHP isn't required.

Conventions

In this book, you will find a number of styles of text that distinguish between different kinds of information. Here are some examples of these styles, and an explanation of their meaning.

Code words in text are shown as follows: " You already began to make the switch over to your new website when you reverted index.php back to its original name and renamed index.html."

A block of code is set as follows:

```
<title>
  <?php wp_title('&laquo;', true, 'right'); ?>
  <?php bloginfo('name'); ?>
</title>
```

When we wish to draw your attention to a particular part of a code block, the relevant lines or items are set in bold:

```
<title>
  <?php wp_title('&laquo;', true, 'right'); ?>
  <?php bloginfo('name'); ?>
</title>
```

New terms and **important words** are shown in bold. Words that you see on the screen, in menus or dialog boxes for example, appear in the text like this: " If you want to browse through a massive collection of free themes, then the **Install Themes** screen should be your first stop."

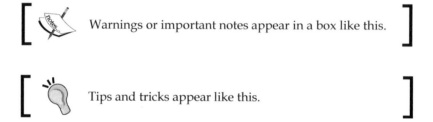

Warnings or important notes appear in a box like this.

Tips and tricks appear like this.

Reader feedback

Feedback from our readers is always welcome. Let us know what you think about this book—what you liked or may have disliked. Reader feedback is important for us to develop titles that you really get the most out of.

To send us general feedback, simply send an email to feedback@packtpub.com, and mention the book title via the subject of your message.

If there is a book that you need and would like to see us publish, please send us a note in the **SUGGEST A TITLE** form on www.packtpub.com or email suggest@packtpub.com.

If there is a topic that you have expertise in and you are interested in either writing or contributing to a book, see our author guide on www.packtpub.com/authors.

Customer support

Now that you are the proud owner of a Packt book, we have a number of things to help you to get the most from your purchase.

Downloading the example code for the book

You can download the example code files for all Packt books you have purchased from your account at http://www.packtpub.com. If you purchased this book elsewhere, you can visit http://www.packtpub.com/support and register to have the files e-mailed directly to you.

Errata

Although we have taken every care to ensure the accuracy of our content, mistakes do happen. If you find a mistake in one of our books—maybe a mistake in the text or the code—we would be grateful if you would report this to us. By doing so, you can save other readers from frustration, and help us to improve subsequent versions of this book. If you find any errata, please report them by visiting http://www.packtpub.com/support, selecting your book, clicking on the **let us know** link, and entering the details of your errata. Once your errata are verified, your submission will be accepted and the errata added to any list of existing errata. Any existing errata can be viewed by selecting your title from http://www.packtpub.com/support.

Piracy

Piracy of copyright material on the Internet is an ongoing problem across all media. At Packt, we take the protection of our copyright and licenses very seriously. If you come across any illegal copies of our works, in any form, on the Internet, please provide us with the location address or web site name immediately so that we can pursue a remedy.

Please contact us at copyright@packtpub.com with a link to the suspected pirated material.

We appreciate your help in protecting our authors, and our ability to bring you valuable content.

Questions

You can contact us at questions@packtpub.com if you are having a problem with any aspect of the book, and we will do our best to address it.

1
Project 1: Migrating a Static Website to WordPress

Many websites start out being created with nothing more than HTML, CSS, and a few images. For some, that will always be enough and there will never be any need to change. For others, however, there will come a time when more is required. The individuals responsible for maintaining these websites might one day need the extra convenience that comes with publishing content with the push of a button or they might require the extra bells and whistles that can only be incorporated with ease thanks to a wide array of plugins. Whatever the reason, they will ultimately decide that they need to migrate their static website to something more robust and many will realize that now is the time to make the transition to WordPress.

This chapter is designed specifically for those who find themselves in this situation. At first, the prospect of making this transition might seem daunting and you might wonder where to begin. Rest assured that there's no need to feel overwhelmed because this chapter covers the process from beginning to end so that you will never get lost along the way.

In this chapter, you will learn how to:

- Prepare for the transition
- Temporarily keep your new website hidden from both visitors and search engines
- Transfer the content from your old website into WordPress
- Create a theme using your current template or select a new theme
- Protect your website's position in the search engines
- Make sure that your new website is error-free
- Entice the search engines to update your listings once your completed website is online

Preparing for the transition

Before going any further, it's extremely important for you to create a backup of all of the files that currently make up your static website. That way you can ensure that none of the data from your original website is lost. This is important for two reasons. The first being that it's always best to keep a copy of every version of your website because you never know when you might need to refer back to it for one reason or another. Secondly, during the transition, you will need your static website to remain online and functional until your WordPress website is ready to go live. Should one of the files from your current website accidentally get deleted before the transition is complete, you can easily upload a replacement copy from your computer to get things back in working order.

After backing up all of the necessary files, you will next need to document the name of each of your web pages and its web address. This is best done using a spreadsheet. Open your spreadsheet program and then label the first column **File Names**. Next, label the second column **URLs.** Visit your website and then begin recording this information in your spreadsheet. Once you've finished, your spreadsheet should look similar to the one shown below.

	A	B
1	File Names	URLs
2	index.html	http://example.com/
3	about.html	http://example.com/about.html
4	services.html	http://example.com/services.html
5	contact.html	http://example.com/contact.html

This step is important because, before your WordPress website is made visible to the search engines, you will need to use this spreadsheet, along with the **Redirection** plugin, to create several 301 (moved permanently) redirects so that the previous URL for each of these web pages points to its new location online.

Installing WordPress

Now it's time to install WordPress on your server. You should be able to do this automatically, since many web hosts provide their users with a **cPanel** control panel that includes the **Fantastico De Luxe** autoinstaller. With Fantastico De Luxe, you will be able to automatically install several different applications, including WordPress.

Even if your web host doesn't offer cPanel with Fantastico De Luxe, it still may be possible for you to automatically install WordPress. To find out if automatic WordPress installation is possible, contact your web host and ask them if they provide an autoinstaller with their service. If you're lucky, then you just might find that they do offer something comparable to Fantastico De Luxe.

If your web host doesn't offer an autoinstaller, then you will need to install WordPress manually. At the WordPress website, you will find instructions for what they call the **Famous 5-Minute Install**. So, even if you do have to install the software manually it shouldn't take more than a few minutes if you follow the instructions found at http://codex.wordpress.org/Installing_WordPress#Famous_5-Minute_Install.

Hiding your new WordPress installation

Normally, after installing WordPress, you would get right to installing a theme, configuring the software to your liking, and then adding content. In this case, however, additional steps need to be taken to ensure that your WordPress installation temporarily remains hidden. Secrecy, at this point, is important for two reasons:

1. When migrating from static HTML to WordPress, it's important that you continue to direct visitors to your original website for as long as possible. This measure will avoid a great deal of inconvenience and confusion that your visitors might otherwise suffer.

2. While creating the WordPress version of your website, you don't want it to be prematurely indexed by the search engines because, at this point, it's still a work-in-progress.

So, the first thing that you need to do to keep your new website temporarily under wraps is locate the index.php file located in the main folder of your WordPress installation and then rename it to 1index.php. Adding the number one to the beginning of the file name will make it easier to locate when it comes time to return this file to its original name since the it should appear at the top of your file list just under .htaccess. Renaming index.php guarantees that your index.html file will continue to act as your website's home page for the time being.

Having done that, your WordPress website is now hidden from visitors. Now you need to take steps to ensure that it's also hidden from the search engines crawlers. To do this, begin by logging in to your WordPress **Dashboard**. Once there, click on **Settings | Privacy**. In this section, you will find the **Privacy Settings** screen that contains the **Site Visibility** settings for WordPress.

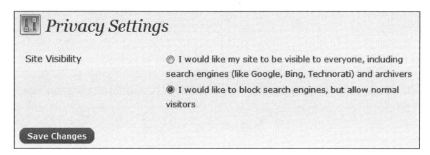

In this area, you can choose to make your site visible or invisible to the search engines. Since you don't want the crawlers to index these pages just yet, tick the radio button next to **I would like to block search engines, but allow normal visitors**. Then, click **Save Changes**.

This setting doesn't guarantee that search engines won't crawl WordPress since websites with this option selected have been indexed. Taking this measure does, however, at least reduce the likelihood of your WordPress website appearing in the search results until you're ready to reveal it to the crawlers.

Two methods for migrating content

There are two ways to get all of the content from your static website over to WordPress. The method that you choose will be determined by the number of pages in your current website as well as the availability of PHP5 on your server because the plugin used to automatically import content specifically requires this version.

As you might have guessed, a website with only a few pages is ideal for the manual method, while a website with several pages is better suited to the automatic method. Once you've determined which method to use, you can then begin the process of importing content into WordPress.

The manual method

If your static website consists of only a few pages, then the simplest option for getting the content from your static website over to WordPress is to just copy it from your old site and then paste it into the new one. Since the content on your old website existed as pages, it should do so on your new site as well.

Walking through this process will give you a feel for how it's done. For this example, suppose that you're recreating a page from your static site called **Services**. To do this, navigate to **Pages | Add New**. On this screen, enter **Services** as the title of this page. Then, paste all of the content that was previously included in the body of your static **Services** page into the text area. Now, click **Publish** to add this page to your site.

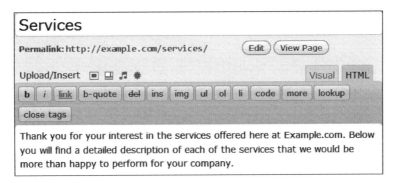

Repeat this process for each of the web pages found on your static website until all of your content has been transferred over to WordPress.

The automatic method

If your website contains several pages, then it's possible for you to avoid the tedious process of copying and pasting each one. Instead, you can import your content automatically. To do this, you will need to use the **Import HTML Pages** plugin available at `http://wordpress.org/extend/plugins/import-html-pages/`. As previously mentioned, in order for this plugin to function, your server must offer PHP5.

After installing and activating the plugin, go to **Settings | HTML Import**. On this page, you will find the **HTML Page Import Options** screen. The plugin should function as desired with many of these options left at their default settings. There are, however, two options that should be discussed.

In the textbox labeled **Beginning directory** enter the location of the folder that contains the pages from your static website.

Beginning directory:

/home/example/public_html/

This should be a full path from the server root, on the same server where WordPress is running now.

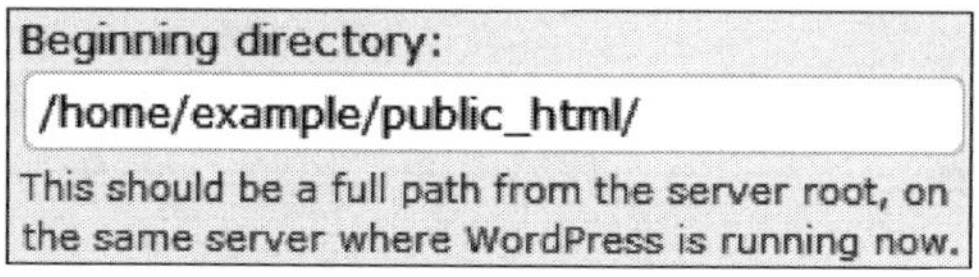

Next, scroll down until you see a textbox labeled **Phrase to remove from title page**. If you included the name of your website in the title tags of your static site, then enter that name into the textbox. Failure to follow this step could result in your website's name appearing twice in the title bar.

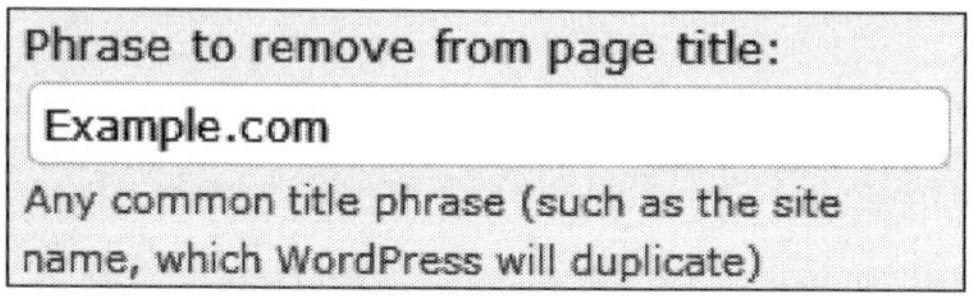

Phrase to remove from page title:

Example.com

Any common title phrase (such as the site name, which WordPress will duplicate)

Click **Import using these options** and the content from your static website will be imported into WordPress automatically.

This screenshot shows what the **Services** web page from the static website looked like before being imported.

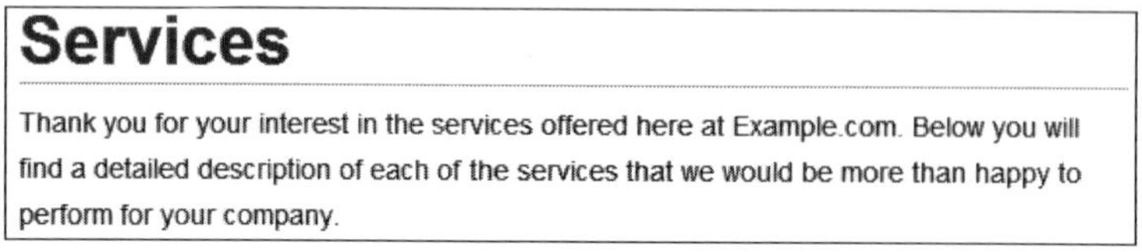

Services

Thank you for your interest in the services offered here at Example.com. Below you will find a detailed description of each of the services that we would be more than happy to perform for your company.

In this screenshot, you can see what the newly created **Services** page looks like after being imported into WordPress with the **Twenty Ten** theme activated.

Services

Services

Thank you for your interest in the services offered here at Example.com. Below you will find a detailed description of each of the services that we would be more than happy to perform for your company.

As you can see, this page wasn't imported perfectly. The two main problems are that the title is being displayed twice and that the text is being wrapped in to a narrow column. A look at the **Services** page from the administration area quickly reveals the cause of these problems.

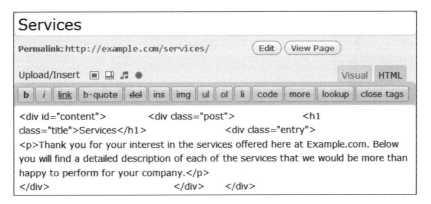

When the page was imported, several unnecessary HTML tags were included along with the page's text. The only way to remedy this problem is to delete all of these unnecessary elements.

So, while the automatic method does save time versus the manual method, it isn't perfect. When using this method, various edits will still need to be made to these pages so that the content on your site will be displayed properly.

Partially revealing WordPress

At this time, you will need to locate `1index.php` on your server and then return it to it's original name of `index.php`. Next, find `index.html` and then rename it to `1index.html`. Both of these steps must be taken at this point because, once your theme is activated, you will need to be able to access your WordPress home page in order to proceed. With `index.php` in place and `index.html` renamed, your WordPress website will now be visible to visitors, but it will still be hidden from search engine crawlers.

Turning your current template into a theme

You may think that migrating to WordPress means that you will also have to give up your current website design. This, however, doesn't have to be the case. If you're happy with the way your website looks now, then it's entirely possible to continue using your current design. To do this, you will need to convert your static HTML/CSS template into a WordPress theme.

 Your static website may have been designed so long ago that it was created with a deprecated version of HTML or it may not include a stylesheet (CSS). If that's the case then you should first update your design, so that it's compliant with the latest web standards. This will make the process of converting your template much easier and will allow you to create the best theme possible. After your update is complete, you can then proceed with converting your template into a theme.

Inner workings of WordPress

WordPress is unlike static websites in that a great deal of the information displayed onscreen isn't hardcoded into the web page. Instead, template tags are placed in various template files where hardcoded information would normally appear. These template tags send queries to the database, retrieve information, and then incorporate the results into the web page. For example, when building a static website you would include the page title by using the following HTML code:

```
<title>Packt Publishing - About Us</title>
```

For every page of a static website, you need to manually include a unique title. With WordPress, however, the website name and title for each web page is dynamically generated by two template tags. In this way, WordPress can display a unique title for each page by querying the database. As you can see, an updated WordPress-compliant title looks very different from a static HTML page title.

```
<title>
  <?php wp_title('&laquo;', true, 'right'); ?>
  <?php bloginfo('name'); ?>
</title>
```

Once you've finished creating your theme, the output shown in your browser's title bar will look similar to the following screenshot. The exact title displayed in the title bar will, of course, depend upon which web page you're currently viewing.

A WordPress page is the sum of its parts

When designing a static website, a different file must be created for each page. Within these files, the header, content, sidebar, and footer are all present. WordPress differs from this in that each section of a WordPress web page is contained within its own template file. WordPress then assembles each of these pieces on the fly to generate a complete web page.

Now that you understand how WordPress themes work, it's time to begin building your template files.

Beginning of a theme

Think of a name for your new theme. Once you've decided what you would like to call it, create a new folder on your computer with this name. Copy the images folder from the backup of your static website that you created earlier and then paste it into your theme's folder.

Open your text editor, create the following blank files, and then save them to your theme folder.

- functions.php
- header.php
- index.php
- single.php
- page.php
- sidebar.php
- footer.php

Copy the stylesheet used on your original site and then paste it into the theme folder for your WordPress theme. Next, rename the stylesheet that you just pasted into your new theme folder so that it's now called style.css.

Open `style.css` in your text editor so that a stylesheet header can be added at the top of the file. This information is required because, without it, your theme won't appear on the **Manage Themes** screen located within WordPress. The following is an example of what a well-formatted stylesheet header should look like. You will, of course, need to customize it with information that's appropriate to you and your theme.

```
/*
Theme Name: Your Theme's Name.
Theme URL: Your Theme's URL
Description: A few sentences describing your theme.
Author: Author's Name
Author URL: Your website address.
Version: The current version number for your theme.
*/
```

After adding the stylesheet header to this file, be sure to save the changes that you've made.

Segmenting the template from your previous site

Segmenting the HTML template used on your static site is the next step in this process. Your aim will be to separate the template into four sections. Open a page from your site's original HTML template and then think about which content would best be placed in each of the `header.php`, `sidebar.php`, and `footer.php` templates.

Begin by surrounding the header section of your template with the following comment tags:

```
<!-- BEGIN HEADER -->
<!-- END HEADER -->
```

Even though this content will be located in `header.php`, that doesn't mean that the final comment tag for this section should be placed immediately after the closing head tag. Instead, it should be placed just before the area where the page content begins. For example, if your original site template contains a logo area and a horizontal menu, then the ending header tag would need be placed just after that.

If your template has a sidebar, then its beginning and ending should be marked with the following comment tags:

```
<!-- BEGIN SIDEBAR -->
<!-- END SIDEBAR -->
```

Next, the footer should be surrounded by these comment tags.

```
<!-- BEGIN FOOTER -->
<!-- END FOOTER -->
```

There will now be a section of code located in the center of your template that hasn't been designated with comment tags. Surround this section with the following:

```
<!-- BEGIN MAIN CONTENT -->
<!-- END MAIN CONTENT -->
```

Now that the HTML template used on your static website has been segmented into sections, it's time to begin building the individual files that will comprise your WordPress theme.

Creating the functions file

Before building the templates that will comprise your theme, you should first work on creating the `functions.php` file. This file allows you to add additional functions to WordPress in order to further extend the functionality of your WordPress site.

With the code that you're about to add to `functions.php`, along with the code that you will be adding later on to your various template files, you will be able to do things such as implement a widget-ready sidebar on your site as well as take advantage of many of the new features that are now offered in WordPress 3.0.

A sidebar isn't much of a sidebar if it isn't widget-ready. So, the first piece of code that you need to add to `functions.php` will be responsible for enabling this functionality on your site.

Open `functions.php` and then enter the following code. What this code does is tell WordPress that your theme includes a widget-ready sidebar.

```php
<?php
if ( function_exists('register_sidebar') )
    register_sidebar(array(
    'before_widget' => '',
     'after_widget' => '',
     'before_title' => '<h2>',
     'after_title' => '</h2>',
     ));
```

Now, add the following code that will allow you to make various changes to the background of your site without editing your stylesheet. When you would like to make changes, navigate to **Appearance | Background** where you will find the **Custom Background** screen.

```
add_custom_background();
```

Place the following line of code into `functions.php`, so that feed links will automatically be added to your theme's header:

```
add_theme_support( 'automatic-feed-links' );
```

Now, add the following PHP closing tag to the end of this file:

```
?>
```

With the creation of `functions.php` complete, you can begin work on your theme's first template file.

Creating the header template

Copy the code in the segmented HTML template file that's located between the two header comment tags and then paste it into the blank `header.php` template that's located in your WordPress theme folder.

When building a WordPress theme, it's important to include a DOCTYPE because it tells browsers which version of HTML or XHTML you're using and makes it easier for browsers to render your web page correctly. Its presence is also important because any theme lacking this information won't pass validation testing.

 Validation testing services check websites to ensure that they don't contain errors. This is important because if a site doesn't validate it may not appear as the designer intended it to when it's viewed in various browsers.

If your header doesn't already have a DOCTYPE statement, add the following line of code at the very beginning of the `header.php` template.

```
<!DOCTYPE HTML PUBLIC "-//W3C//DTD XHTML 1.0 Transitional//EN"
"http://www.w3.org/TR/xhtml1/DTD/xhtml1-transitional.dtd">
```

Next, replace `<html>` with the following. The purpose of the template tag that's included within this `<html>` tag is to tell the browser which language you're using to create your web page.

```
<html xmlns="http://www.w3.org/1999/xhtml" <?php language_
attributes(); ?>>
```

From there, remove the opening and closing head tags as well as everything in between them. With the original `<head>` tag gone, a new one has to be added to take it's place. This one, however, won't be exactly like the old one. That's because it contains additional information to tell browsers that your site supports XFN.

 To learn more about XFN, you can visit the XFN: Introduction and Examples page found at `http://www.gmpg.org/xfn/intro`.

Here's the new opening head tag that you need to add to your template:

```
<head profile="http://gmpg.org/xfn/11">
```

This next piece of code should look familiar since it was presented earlier. As you will recall this code is used to dynamically display your blog name and a unique title for each of your web pages.

```
<title>
<?php wp_title('&laquo;', true, 'right'); ?>
<?php bloginfo('name'); ?>
</title>
```

Next, enter the following code to include meta information for your website:

```
<meta http-equiv="Content-Type" content="<?php bloginfo('html_type');
?>; charset=<?php bloginfo('charset'); ?>" />
```

This next line of code is used to provide a link to the stylesheet for your theme.

```
<link rel="stylesheet" href="<?php bloginfo('stylesheet_url'); ?>"
type="text/css" media="screen" />
```

The following code must now be added so that threaded comments will function properly on your website:

```
<?php if ( is_singular() ) wp_enqueue_script( 'comment-reply' ); ?>
```

Next is what is known as an **Action Hook** template tag. Action Hooks must be included in order for some aspects of WordPress to operate properly. For example, without this Action Hook, some plugins won't function. That's why you must now add it to `header.php`.

```
<?php wp_head(); ?>
```

With all of that code in place, you can now add `</head>` to close this section.

The next line of code that you need to enter will depend upon whether your site currently displays a text title or a logo image. Either way, you will first need to locate the section of code that's currently responsible for displaying this information.

If your website has a text title, then replace the placeholder title with the following code:

```
<a href="<?php bloginfo('url'); ?>/"><?php bloginfo('name'); ?></a>
```

If your site uses a logo, then replace it with the following line of code:

```
<a href="<?php bloginfo('url'); ?>"><img src="<?php
bloginfo('stylesheet_directory'); ?>/images/logo.png" alt="Logo"
style="border: none;" /></a>
```

You will, of course, need to replace `logo.png` with the appropriate name for your image in order for it to appear. You should also replace `"Logo"` in the `alt` attribute with the name of your website.

Whether you add either of these next two template tags will depend upon how your current web design is laid out. If your header section contains a navigation bar, then one of the two following template tags will be required.

To place either of them, first locate the unordered list responsible for displaying your navigation bar and then remove all of the list items.

Place the following template tag where your list items were previously located if you would like to display links to your pages:

```
<?php wp_list_pages('title_li='); ?>
```

If, instead, you would like the navigation bar to display links to your categories, then this template tag should be entered where your list items previously appeared.

```
<?php wp_list_categories( $args ); ?>
```

After adding this last template tag, save `header.php`. With this template complete, it's time to create the `index.php` template for your theme.

Creating the index template

Return to your HTML template file, copy the code located between the two main content comment tags, and then paste it into the `index.php` template for your WordPress theme.

In order for WordPress to assemble your template files into a complete web page, you need to include template tags to call the other sections of the site. The first section that you need to call is the header. To do this, enter the following template tag at the beginning of `index.php`.

```php
<?php get_header(); ?>
```

The `sidebar.php` and `footer.php` templates also need to be called. To do this, enter these template tags at the bottom of `index.php`.

```php
<?php get_sidebar(); ?>
<?php get_footer(); ?>
```

With those in place, it's now time to concentrate on adding **The Loop** to `index.php`. In WordPress, The Loop is responsible for displaying content on your website. Without it, your site would display the header, sidebar, and footer with nothing in between.

The Loop contains several lines of code that perform many different functions. Once again, each section will be added individually, so that you will have a clear understanding of the action that each piece of code performs.

Find the section of your site where your content normally appears. Then, place this code, which is responsible for beginning The Loop, just after the `<div>` tag that begins your content area.

```php
<?php if (have_posts()) : ?>
<?php while (have_posts()) : the_post(); ?>
```

The next template tag that you're about to place will be responsible for displaying a linked title to the content published on your site. So, locate the area where your content heading appears. It will, most likely, be surrounded by headings tags. Once you find it, remove the placeholder headline and then replace it with the following template tags. If the headline was surrounded by heading tags, then make sure that these template tags are encapsulated in them too.

```php
<div id="post-<?php the_ID(); ?>"><a href="<?php the_permalink() ?>"
rel="bookmark" title="<?php the_title(); ?>"><?php the_title(); ?></
a></div>
```

Now you need to add code so that the area known as the post metadata section will be displayed. It's important that the postmeta data is added to your template because this section typically includes information on the author, category, post date, and comment count, as well as a link to edit the post if you're logged in. This information is displayed by placing the following code into your template.

```
Posted in <?php the_category(', ') ?> by <?php the_author() ?> on
<?php the_time('F jS, Y') ?> | <?php edit_post_link('Edit', '', '
| '); ?><?php comments_popup_link('No Comments', '1 Comment', '%
Comments'); ?>
```

Next is the template tag responsible for displaying your page's content. This should be placed in the section that currently contains the placeholder content for your site. If this placeholder content is surrounded by <div> tags, or any other tags, then be sure to encapsulate this template tag in them as well so that the appropriate styles will be applied.

```
<?php the_content('Continue Reading...'; ?>
```

Finally, enter the following line to end The Loop:

```
<?php endwhile; ?>
```

The Loop may have ended but that doesn't mean that you're finished building the index.php template just yet. That's because a few more lines of code still need to be added for index.php to be complete.

If your blog is set to display a certain number of posts per page, then your visitors will need a way to navigate between those pages so that they can access all of your content. Add the following template tag to index.php and navigation links will appear on your index, category, archive, and search pages.

```
<?php posts_nav_link(); ?>
```

Should a visitor arrive at a post or page that doesn't exist (404 error), you will need a way for WordPress to handle the situation. You can also make things more convenient for visitors by adding a search box, so that they can attempt to locate the content they were hoping to find. This can be done with the following lines of code. Just add this code to index.php and it will act as a combination 404/search page should the need arise.

```
<?php else : ?>
<h2>Not Found</h2>
<p><?php _e("Sorry, no posts or pages could be found. Why not search
for what you were trying to find?"); ?></p>
<?php get_search_form(); ?>
```

With that code in place, visitors who navigate to a non-existent page will now see a screen similar to the one shown in the following screenshot:

At this point, you just need to add the next line of code to index.php and then this template will be completely finished.

```php
<?php endif; ?>
```

Now, save index.php, so that you can begin work on your theme's single.php template.

Creating the single template

To create this template you need to open single.php and index.php in your text editor. Copy all of the content from index.php and then paste it into single.php. With that content in place, single.php is almost complete. Before it's finished, however, you will need to make some edits and additions to this template.

To begin, you need to edit this page so that the post title is no longer linked. To do this, look for the following code:

```html
<div id="post-<?php the_ID(); ?>"><a href="<?php the_permalink() ?>"
rel="bookmark" title="<?php the_title(); ?>"><?php the_title(); ?></
a></div>
```

Then, replace the preceding with the following.

```html
<div id="post-<?php the_ID(); ?>"><?php the_title(); ?></div>
```

Now, look for the following template tag that's responsible for displaying the content on your page.

```php
<?php the_content('Continue Reading...'); ?>
```

Since single.php displays the full post, 'Continue Reading...' doesn't need to be included in this tag. So, replace the preceeding template tag with this one.

```php
<?php the_content(''); ?>
```

Look for the following template tag that's used to display navigation links on your non-single pages.

```
<?php posts_nav_link(); ?>
```

Once you locate that tag, replace it with the this code that's used to display navigation links on single post pages so that visitors can easily move backward and forward between your posts.

```
<?php previous_post_link('&laquo; % link', '%title'); ?> <?php next_
post_link('%link &raquo;') ?>
```

Now, look for the end of The Loop. When you find it, place the following template tag above it so that visitors will be able to leave comments on your posts.

```
<?php comments_template(); ?>
```

Then, remove all of the code used to display the 404/search box, since this code only needs to be present in the `index.php` template.

With those changes made, you can now save `single.php` before beginning work on your theme's next template.

Creating the page template

Now it's time to create the template that will be used to display the pages on your site. Building this template couldn't be easier since it's almost an exact duplicate of `single.php`.

To begin, open `single.php` and `page.php` in your text editor. Copy the content from `single.php` and then paste it into `page.php`.

Now, you only need to perform one edit. Look for the following code and then remove it from this template.

```
<?php previous_post_link('&laquo; % link', '%title'); ?> <?php next_
post_link('%link &raquo;') ?>
```

Save `page.php` and then you can begin work on building a widget-ready sidebar for your site.

Creating the sidebar template

In the template file for your HTML website locate the section of code between the two sidebar comment tags and then paste it into `sidebar.php`. Delete any content while leaving the tags responsible for styling the sidebar in place. Then, add the following code between the styling tags.

```php
<?php if ( !function_exists('dynamic_sidebar') || !dynamic_sidebar() )
: ?>
<?php endif; ?>
```

After those lines of code have been added, save `sidebar.php`.

If you have widgets enabled in WordPress, this piece of code, along with the previous entry that you added to `functions.php`, will make it possible for widgets to display in your sidebar. If there are no widgets in use, then the sidebar will display nothing.

Now, you're probably wondering what you're supposed to do with all of the content that was previously located in your sidebar. Well, there's little point in hardcoding it into the `sidebar.php` template. Instead, you should take all of that content and incorporate it into WordPress using widgets. If you previously had a list of categories in your sidebar, then place them in your new sidebar with the **Categories** widget. Perhaps you had a paragraph containing contact information. That can be included using a **Text** widget. Anything that your sidebar previously contained can easily be added to your site with the use of widgets.

Now that the `sidebar.php` template is finished, work can begin on the final template that you need to build for your WordPress theme.

Creating the footer template

Once again, open the template file for your original HTML website. This time, copy all of the code located between the footer comment tags. This should then be pasted into the `footer.php` template. Other than that, only one piece of WordPress-related code needs to be added to this template file. Once again, you will need to include an Action Hook so that certain plugins will function properly. The following Action Hook should be placed at the top of `footer.php`.

```php
<?php wp_footer(); ?>
```

With that, the `footer.php` template is complete, so save it before moving on to the final step that you will need to complete before you can upload your WordPress theme to your server.

Adding comments templates

Prior to the release of WordPress 3.0, themes could use template tags to call files without the theme actually containing those files. For example, a theme could call `comments.php` without the theme including that particular template.

In that instance, WordPress would simply substitute the `comments.php` template from another theme. Since the developers of WordPress have updated the default theme to Twenty Ten, this will no longer be an acceptable practice. Instead, WordPress themes will be expected to contain all of the files that are called via template tags.

You've already created many of the templates required in order for your theme to comply with these new standards, but there are still two that are missing. They are `comments.php` and `comments-popup.php`. Without these templates, your theme won't be fully compliant.

The easiest way to go about adding these files to your theme is to copy them from the default theme that was used on version 1.5 through 2.9 of WordPress.

This theme can be obtained from the WordPress **Free Themes Directory** at `http://wordpress.org/extend/themes/default`. Once there, download the **Default** theme to your computer. Next, unzip the ZIP file and then paste `comments.php` and `comments-popup.php` into the folder containing your theme.

With the addition of those two files, your theme now contains all of the necessary templates. So, upload the folder that contains your theme to the `wp-content/themes` directory located on your server.

Polishing your newly created WordPress theme

Now that your WordPress theme has been uploaded, it needs to be activated. To do this, log in to the **Dashboard** and then navigate to **Appearance | Themes**. Now, click the **Activate** link for your theme.

After your theme has been activated, you might notice that it looks very much like your old template, but that certain elements aren't exactly right. This is likely to occur since new elements have been introduced into your website. Since these elements didn't previously exist in your original HTML template there's nothing in your stylesheet to dictate how they should look.

Welcome

Posted in <u>News</u> by hwallace on May 10th, 2010 | <u>Edit</u> | <u>No Comments</u>

Thank you for visiting the new WordPress version of our site. We will be updating this site frequently with news about our services as well as special offers, so stop back often.

For example, the post-metadata section will be a new addition to your website, so you may find that the content in this section isn't formatted properly. The preceding screenshot provides an example of a post metadata section without special styling. As you can see, its appearance is identical to that of the post which causes the post metadata section to become distracting.

After an entry is added to the stylesheet to govern the formatting of the post metadata section, it then blends in nicely with the overall appearance of the website.

Welcome

Posted in <u>News</u> by hwallace on May 10th, 2010 | <u>Edit</u> | <u>No Comments</u>

Thank you for visiting the new WordPress version of our site. We will be updating this site frequently with news about our services as well as special offers, so stop back often.

If you find an element of your website that doesn't look right after building your theme, then create a new entry in your stylesheet to format the layout of that section. This process of making additions or edits to your stylesheet will need to be undertaken for any areas that don't look quite right. Once this process is complete, your theme should look nearly identical to your original HTML template with the only difference being the addition of the new WordPress-specific elements.

Adding a screenshot for your theme

When you activated your theme, you may have noticed that its title and description were displayed but that an image wasn't visible. That's because you need to create a screenshot of your new theme in order for it to appear on the **Manage Themes** screen.

To do this, take a screenshot of your site's home page. Now, you need to shrink this screenshot down to the right size, so open your image editing program and then paste the contents of your clipboard as a new image. Crop out any unnecessary elements (such as your browser) and resize the image so that it measures 300 x 255. Save the image as `screenshot.png` and then upload it to your theme folder.

Now a screenshot of your site's new theme will now be visible on the **Manages Themes** screen.

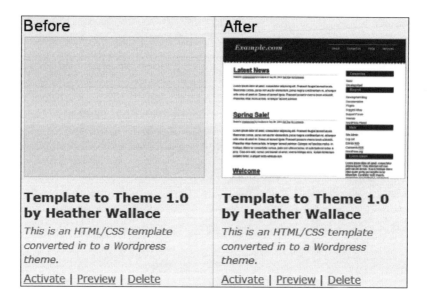

Starting fresh with a new theme

Perhaps you don't want to keep your old website design and would prefer to make a completely fresh start. If that's the case, then a new WordPress theme is in order. When selecting a new design, there are certain things that you will need to consider. Do you need one, two, or three columns? Is the theme that you're considering widget-ready? Is the stylesheet easy-to-read, so that you can make customizations if needed?

It's best to take the time to find a high-quality theme that you will be happy using for years to come, rather than choosing a sub-standard theme only to discover a few months later that it doesn't meet your needs.

There are a myriad of free and premium themes on the Internet, and it can be a bit of a chore to find the best ones if you don't know where to look. So, rather than aimlessly searching for a theme, you should begin your search at the following sites.

Free themes

If you want to browse through a massive collection of free themes, then the **Install Themes** screen should be your first stop. You can reach this screen by navigating to **Appearance | Themes**. Then, click on the **Install Themes** tab. Using the **Feature Filter**, you can search for themes that match a variety of criteria. For example, you could specify that you only want to browse for blue themes that contain two-columns. On this screen, you can also search for themes by keyword, author, or tag.

Smashing Magazine frequently partners with the Internet's top web designers to release some of the highest-quality freely available WordPress themes. Unfortunately, the themes aren't placed into a category of their own. Instead, you must visit the site at `http://www.smashingmagazine.com/` and then browse through the **Freebies** category in order to locate all of the free themes that are available for download. This minor inconvenience is, however, more than worth the trouble because the themes available at this site are among some of the best that you will find.

Premium themes

ThemeForest claims to be the "biggest marketplace of its kind" and, judging by their selection, this certainly seems to be the case. The site, located at `http://themeforest.net/`, is filled with a large collection of premium website templates and CMS themes, so there's no shortage when it comes to selection. Each design is inspected by a reviewer before it appears on the website to ensure that only quality templates and themes are offered for download.

Elegant Themes, which can be found at `http://www.elegantthemes.com/`, is a subscription service that allows its members access to WordPress themes for a nominal yearly fee. The site already contains a collection of previously released designs and new themes are added on a regular basis. In addition, members have access to a support forum where a responsive staff offers assistance for any technical issues that might arise.

Premium Themes, located at `http://templatic.com/`, is basically a combination of the two previous sites in that you can buy individual themes or sign up for one year to become a member of **The Premium Themes Club**. Membership in the club grants you access to download all of the designs in their collection.

Maintaining search engine ranking

During the process of migrating from a static website to WordPress you will be adding new pages and posts. You will also eventually delete all of your original HTML pages since they will become unnecessary and redundant. This means that your previous content will now exist on pages that are located at completely different web addresses. If nothing was done, then your website would lose its search engine ranking and **PageRank** for each of those deleted pages. Another consequence would be that anyone clicking those outdated links would arrive at 404 pages rather than the web pages that they hoped to visit.

This is a less than desirable situation and, luckily, it can be avoided by installing the Redirection plugin found at `http://wordpress.org/extend/plugins/redirection/`. With the help of this plugin, when the search engines arrive to crawl your website, they will be sent to the updated location for all of your old web pages. These redirects will also be beneficial should a visitor happen upon an outdated link since they will also be redirected to the page's new location.

Introducing Redirection

The Redirection plugin is primarily designed to manage 301 redirects. This functionality is especially useful when migrating from a static website to WordPress as many 301 redirects will be needed in order to direct the search engine crawlers and visitors to your new web pages. In addition, this plugin also has the ability to track 404 errors. This will prove useful as it will allow you to monitor your website for errors and to ensure that everything is performing as it should be.

In order for this plugin to operate properly, permalinks need to be enabled on your site. You should, therefore, configure that WordPress setting before installing and configuring the Redirection plugin, so click on **Settings | Permalinks**. On this screen, in the **Common settings** area, choose any of the available options other than default. Then, click **Save Changes**.

Common settings

⊙ Default	`http://example.com/?p=123`
⊙ Day and name	`http://example.com/2010/05/21/sample-post/`
⊙ Month and name	`http://example.com/2010/05/sample-post/`
⊙ Numeric	`http://example.com/archives/123`
⊙ Custom Structure	`/%postname%/`

Setting up and configuring Redirection

After installing and activating the plugin, go to **Tools | Redirection**. This will take you to the first page of the **Redirection** settings and configuration area. It's on this screen that you will enter all of the necessary 301 redirects.

To do this, open the spreadsheet that you previously created. Copy the URL of the first static page listed in the spreadsheet and then paste it into the **Source URL** textbox. Next, enter the new URL for that web page into the **Target URL** textbox. Then, click **Add Redirection**. Repeat this process for each of your static web pages.

Clicking **Groups**, **Modules**, and **Options** will take you to additional settings screens for this plugin. These remaining options can, however, be left at their default settings and everything should run smoothly.

Completing the switch to the new website

You already began to make the switch over to your new website when you reverted `index.php` back to its original name and renamed `index.html`. With your 301 redirects in place, it's time to complete the transition. The first thing that you need to do is delete all of the files that comprised your original website.

Next, return to the **Privacy Settings** screen by clicking on **Settings | Privacy**. Once there, tick the radio button next to **I would like my site to be visible to everyone, including search engines (like Google, Bing, Technorati) and archivers**. With that, your website will now be visible to both human visitors and search engine crawlers.

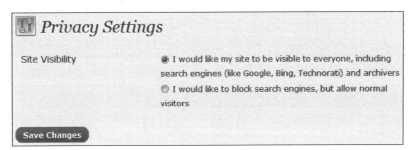

Testing your new website for errors

Now you must ensure that your new website is free from errors. To do this several quality-control measures will need to be taken. With the help of the following tools, you can virtually guarantee that your website will run smoothly.

W3C validators

Much of your quality-control checking will be done on the W3C website. At this site, you can check the markup, links, and CSS of your WordPress website.

Link checking

Begin by using the **W3C Link Checker** located at `http://validator.w3.org/ checklink`. As the name implies, this utility crawls your WordPress installation to test your links, so that you can be sure that they all function properly.

When you arrive at the W3C Link Checker, type the URL for your home page into the textbox and then click **Check**.

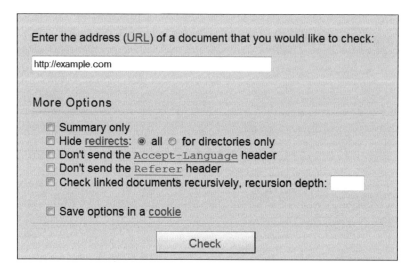

Once your website has been processed, you will receive a set of results that will either detail any problems that were encountered or inform you that your website is free from linking errors. Should you find that linking errors do exist, correct the troublesome links and then run the utility again until your website receives good results.

MarkUp Validator

Next, check the validity of the markup used in your WordPress theme by visiting the **W3C MarkUp Validator** at `http://validator.w3.org/`.

Once there, enter the URL for your home page into the **Address** textbox and then click **Check**.

After the utility checks your website, you will be shown a results screen that will either detail errors and warnings or inform you that your website has passed inspection. If you discover that your theme contains markup errors, you will need to fix these problems, and then run the validator again until your website is found to be error-free.

CSS Validator

The last of the WC3 validators that you will need to run is the **CSS Validator** found at `http://jigsaw.w3.org/css-validator/`. As you might have guessed, this utility will check your site and stylesheet for possible errors.

Enter the URL for your home page into the **Address** textbox and then click **Check**.

Once your CSS has been checked, you will be taken to the results screen, which will either present you with information detailing the errors that were encountered, or inform you that your CSS is error-free. If problems were found, you will be shown these errors and warnings along with a section containing valid CSS information that you can use to help you correct these issues. After correcting these problems, run the utility again until no errors are found.

Cross-browser compatibility

A website isn't much good if it doesn't display properly in all the major browsers. That's why cross-browser compatibility is so important. A visit to the **Adobe BrowserLab** at `https://browserlab.adobe.com/`, will provide you with an exact rendering of your website as it appears on all major browsers.

Should you discover that your website doesn't display properly in one of the major browsers, then you will need to make changes to your design in order to correct the issues. Continue tweaking your design and subjecting it to cross-browser compatibility testing until everything displays properly.

Content inspection

Now that you've verified that your website is technically sound you next need to ensure that all of your content appears correctly. To do this, visit your website and inspect each page. Has all of the content transferred as you intended? If not, visit the **Dashboard** to manage the offending posts and/or pages.

Submitting a sitemap to the search engines

Just because you've updated your website that doesn't mean that the search engines will crawl all of your web pages. That means that the search engine listings for some of your web pages could be updated quickly while others remain outdated for quite some time. There is, however, something that you can do to encourage the search engines so that they will be more likely to give your website a thorough crawling.

What is needed, in this situation, is a site map. Luckily, it's possible to create a site map for your entire website with the help of the **Google XML Sitemaps** plugin.

Introducing Google XML Sitemaps

This plugin, which can be found at `http://wordpress.org/extend/plugins/google-sitemap-generator/`, is designed to generate an XML site map for your website. A site map is useful because it will provide a road map for the crawlers so that they can easily find the new locations for all of your website's old pages as well as discover any new pages or posts that you might have added.

With this plugin, you will only need to customize a few settings and then click a link in order to generate a site map of your entire website.

Setting up and configuring Google XML Sitemaps

After installing and activating the plugin, go to **Settings | XML-Sitemap**. From this page you can configure all of the settings for this plugin as well as generate your site map.

At the top of the screen, you will see a message informing you that the site map for your website hasn't been generated yet. That's fine. This message should just be ignored for the time being. You need to focus on configuring some of these settings first.

> **The sitemap wasn't generated yet.**
>
> The sitemap wasn't built yet. Click here to build it the first time.
>
> If you encounter any problems with the build process you can use the debug function to get more information.

In the **Basic Options** section, under **Sitemap files**, deselect **Write a normal XML file (your filename)**. All search engines support compressed site maps, so there's little point in wasting the disk space that would be used by creating an uncompressed site map.

The options in the **Building mode** section should be left at their defaults, so move on to **Update notifications** where you can select which search engines you want to notify about updates to your website. By default, all of the search engines are selected, except for Yahoo! Add a checkmark next to **Notify YAHOO about updates of your Blog**, so that this search engine is also selected.

In order for Yahoo! to receive notifications you will need to provide an API key. If you already have a Yahoo! API key, enter it into the textbox shown in the following screenshot:

> ☑ Notify YAHOO about updates of your Blog
> Your Application ID: [   ]
> Don't you have such a key? Request one here! (Web Services by Yahoo!)

If you don't have an API key, right-click **Request one here** and then open that link in a new browser window. Doing this will direct you to a Yahoo! Login screen. Once there, either log in or create a new Yahoo! account. Once you've logged in, you will then be taken to a **Developer Registration** page. Provide the necessary information and then click **Continue**. You will then be provided with an application ID. Copy this string, return to the settings screen for Google XML Sitemaps, and then paste your API key into the **Your Application ID** textbox.

All of the settings under **Advanced options** should be left at their defaults. You can also scroll past the **Additional pages** area until you reach the **Post Priority** section of the screen. At this point, since your WordPress website is new, your posts won't have any comments so it doesn't make sense to leave this set to the default option that uses the number of comments to calculate the post priority. Instead, tick the radio button next to **Do not use automatic priority calculation**.

All of the remaining settings should be left at their defaults, so scroll to the bottom of the screen and then click **Update options**. After the screen refreshes, click the link at the top of the page to generate your site map. The plugin will work to build your site map and, when it's complete, a screen that details the results of the build will appear.

> **Result of the last build process, started on May 10, 2010 9:31 pm.**
>
> Your sitemap was last built on **May 10, 2010 9:31 pm**.
>
> Your sitemap (zipped) was last built on **May 10, 2010 9:31 pm**.
>
> Google was **successfully notified** about changes.
>
> YAHOO was **successfully notified** about changes.
>
> Bing was **successfully notified** about changes.
>
> Ask.com was **successfully notified** about changes.
>
> The building process took about **0.5 seconds** to complete and used 14.5 MB of memory.
>
> If you changed something on your server or blog, you should rebuild the sitemap manually.
>
> If you encounter any problems with the build process you can use the debug function to get more information.

Summary

By now, the transformation will be complete and your previous site will have successfully evolved from static HTML into a fully-functional, dynamic WordPress website. You could consider this to be the end of this project or you could look at it as being just the beginning.

WordPress is capable of doing so much. With skill, imagination, and plugins your website could grow even further. Now that you have the power of WordPress at your disposal, why not make the most of it and explore the possibilities?

In this chapter, you learned the steps required to transfer a static HTML website over to WordPress. With this information, you now know how to make this transition seamlessly. You also learned how to redirect site visitors and search engine crawlers so that no traffic is lost as a result of the changes that have been made to your site.

In the next chapter, you will learn how to build a community portal where members will be able to build personal profiles and interact with their fellow members.

2
Project 2: Building a Community Portal

The Internet certainly has come a long way from the early days when static websites were the norm. Back then, users would visit a website, read its content, and then leave because there was nothing else for them to do. There was no way for them to interact with other users or feel like they were a part of something bigger. As the years progressed, social networking came onto the scene and changed the face of the Internet. Today, community portals such as **Facebook**, **LinkedIn**, and **MySpace** are among some of the most popular destinations online. With social networking having become such an integral part of so many people's lives, you may be wondering how you can take advantage of its phenomenal popularity and build a community portal of your own.

In this chapter, you will learn exactly what you need to know to do just that. You may want to build a niche community portal to serve a particular segment of Internet users or you might have your sights set a bit higher having decided to take on the big boys by going for broad appeal. It doesn't matter if you're thinking big or small. With the instructions provided in this chapter you can take your community portal in either direction.

To accomplish your objective, you will first enable the network feature that's been added to WordPress 3.0. You will then throw **BuddyPress** and **bbPress** into the mix. By the time you've concluded this project, you will have a well-rounded, fully functional community portal that's just waiting to be discovered by the citizens of the Internet.

In this chapter, you will learn how to:

- Determine whether `mod_rewrite` is enabled on your server
- Enable the **Network** menu in WordPress
- Complete the network installation process

- Set up and configure BuddyPress
- Integrate bbPress into BuddyPress
- Protect your community portal from bots and spammers
- Protect the privacy of your community members
- Give your portal a new look
- Offer your members more theming options
- Ensure that your portal is fully functional before launch

Once this project is complete, you will have succeeded in creating a site that's similar to the one shown in the following screenshot:

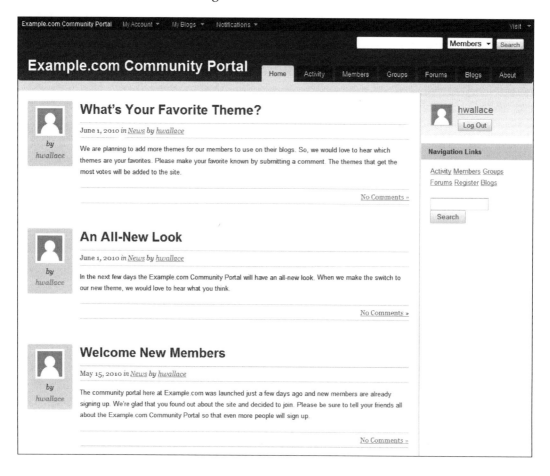

Integrating WordPress, BuddyPress, and bbPress

Prior to to the release of WordPress 3.0, if you wanted to build a community portal, you had to install Wordpress MU. With the latest release of this application, however, WordPress and WordPress MU have merged. As a result, the process involved with building a community portal is now a lot easier.

The multi-site version of WordPress alone is quite robust, but even with all that it can do, it can't create a community portal on its own. With the multi-site feature activated in WordPress, you will just have the functionality required to build a blog network. What you also need, however, is something capable of adding the social networking aspect to your website. That's where BuddyPress comes in. This plugin/theme bundle is specifically designed to take a network-enabled version of WordPress to the next level. Features that you would expect to see on any social network are included such as member profiles, private messaging, groups and more.

With only WordPress and BuddyPress it's entirely possible to have a very powerful community portal, but your website can be further improved by adding bbPress into the mix. With bbPress installed, your members will be able to create their very own forums.

WordPress, BuddyPress, and bbPress really do come together to create one features-filled community portal. Now that you know the components required to build a community portal that has the potential to rival all others; it's time to get started with the installation, integration, and configuration process.

Checking for mod_rewrite

Before doing anything else, you must first run a check on your server to see if `mod_rewrite` is enabled. The network-enabled version of WordPress needs `mod_rewrite` to function, so it's important to know early on what you're dealing with, so that you can either dive right in or deal with the problem before proceeding. Nearly all web hosts have `mod_rewrite` enabled, so this shouldn't be a problem, but you need to check just to be sure.

To perform this test, begin by opening your text editor. Then, enter the following lines into a blank document:

```
Options +FollowSymLinks
Redirect /redirect.html http://www.packtpub.com
```

Save this file as `.htaccess` and then upload it to your server.

 When naming the `.htaccess` file, make sure that you have included a dot at the beginning of the file name as this is easy to overlook.

Once the file is sent to your server, check if it has a `.txt` extension. If it does, rename it so that it's simply `.htaccess`. Now, open a new browser window and then visit the main page of your site.

If you're redirected to the homepage for Packt Publishing, then `mod_rewrite` is enabled. If you aren't redirected, then your server doesn't have `mod_rewrite` enabled, which poses a slight problem. In that case, you will need to send a support ticket to your hosting provider to ask them to enable `mod_rewrite` on your server. Hopefully, you won't have to wait too long to receive a reply back from your hosting provider telling you that the issue has been resolved.

There's one last thing that you need to do before beginning this project and that's to delete the `.htaccess` file from your server. With the `mod_rewrite` test complete and the `.htaccess` file deleted, it's now time to visit the network installation screen, so click on **Tools | Network**.

Enabling the WordPress Network menu

After installing WordPress, you may have noticed that the **Network** menu was no where to be found. That's because network settings aren't activated in the default installation of WordPress. This means that before you can create your community portal, you will have to enable the **Network** menu on your installation of WordPress.

To do this, open `wp-config.php`, which can be found in the directory that contains your WordPress installation. Then add the following line to this file.

```
define('WP_ALLOW_MULTISITE', true);
```

Save `wp-config.php` and then upload it to your server.

Now, when you log in to the **Dashboard**, you will find that a link to the **Network** settings screen has been added to the **Tools** menu.

Network installation

The first thing that you will probably notice when you visit this screen is the message found near the top that tells you to make sure that the Apache `mod_rewrite` module is installed since it will be used at the end of the installation. Since you already dealt with the issue of `mod_rewrite`, this message can be ignored.

Take a moment to think about how you want the web addresses for the blogs in your network to be formatted. Be sure to carefully consider this decision, since it can't be changed later.

If you want them to be formatted as subdirectories, which means that they would look like this `http://example.com/sitename`, then no changes need to be made since the **Sub-directories** setting is already selected by default. If, however, you would like to use a subdomain format, which would look like this `http://anything.example.com`, then you need to do two things. First, enable the **Sub-domains** setting. Next, add a wildcard subdomain in your web hosting control panel.

To add a wildcard subdomain, open a new browser window and then navigate to the control panel provided by your web host. Now, you must create a subdomain as you normally would, but, this time, enter an asterisk in the box where you would typically type your subdomain. After this subdomain has been created, everything will be in place for your community portal to offer blogs that are accessible at subdomain web addresses.

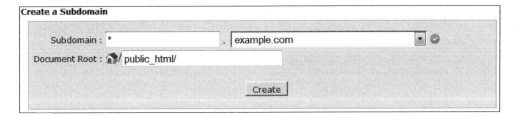

Return to the network installation screen, where you will now be configuring the settings found in the **Network Details** section. In the **Network Title** textbox, enter the name that you would like to assign to your network.

Then, enter your email address into the **Admin E-mail Address** textbox before clicking **Install**.

Enabling the network

After clicking **Install**, you will arrive at a screen that contains three steps that must be performed in order to enable your blog network. Before any of those steps are taken, however, you should heed the warning found at the top of the screen that recommends that you save your site's existing `wp-config.php` and `.htaccess` files. If an `.htaccess` file doesn't exist, just save a copy of `wp-config.php`.

> **Caution:** We recommend you backup your existing `wp-config.php` and `.htaccess` files.

Now, you need to create the directory where the uploaded media for your additional sites will be stored. So, navigate to `/wp-content`. Once there, create a directory named `blogs.dir`. Then, change the permissions on this directory so that it's writeable by the web server.

For this next step, you need to make some changes to `wp-config.php` and `.htaccess`, if it was previously saved. The alterations that must be made will, of course, depend upon whether you opted to use subdomains or subdirectories on your site.

You already saved a copy of `wp-config.php` and, possibly, `.htaccess`, to your computer, but you shouldn't perform these changes on those files since they're your backup in case anything goes wrong. So, make another of copy `wp-config.php` and `.htaccess`, if you were previously able to make a copy of it.

Open one of the copies of `wp-config.php` in your text editor and then add the lines from the first text area located in step two on the **Enabling the Network** screen. When adding these lines, be sure to place them above the line that reads **/* That's all, stop editing! Happy blogging. */**

```
define( 'MULTISITE', true );
define( 'VHOST', 'no' );
$base = '/';
define( 'DOMAIN_CURRENT_SITE', 'example.com' );
define( 'PATH_CURRENT_SITE', '/' );
define( 'SITE_ID_CURRENT_SITE', 1 );
define( 'BLOG_ID_CURRENT_SITE', 1 );
```

If you previously opted to use subdomains, then you will next need to add a set of unique authentication keys to `wp-config.php`. These authentication keys, which are found in the second text area located in step two, should now be copied. Then, paste them into `wp-config.php`. These should, once again, be added just before the line that reads **/* That's all, stop editing! Happy blogging. */**.

 The second text area, containing these authentication keys, will only appear on this page if the subdomain option was selected earlier.

You're finished making edits to `wp-config.php`, so save this file before proceeding.

If you were able to save an `.htaccess` file from your server, open one of your copies now. Then, replace any pre-existing WordPress rules with the content found in the last text area located on the **Enabling the Network** screen. Now, save the changes that you've made to `.htaccess`.

If an `.htaccess` file didn't exist on your server, you will need to create one now by opening a blank document in your text editor. Paste the content from the last text area into your blank document and then save it as `.htaccces`.

Upload your updated copies of `wp-config.php` and `.htaccess` to the directory on your server where your installation of WordPress is found.

After those files have been uploaded, navigate to the **Dashboard**. As you can see, a new **Super Admin** menu has been added to your screen.

Setting up and configuring Super Admin

Now that the **Super Admin** menu is available, you can get started configuring these network-specific WordPress settings. No actions need to be taken on the **Admin** screen, so click on **Super Admin | Sites**.

Sites

Since this is a network-enabled version of WordPress, it's important to ensure that additional blogs can, in fact, be created on the site. You can easily verify that this functionality is working by creating a test blog. On the **Sites** screen, you can add additional blogs to your network.

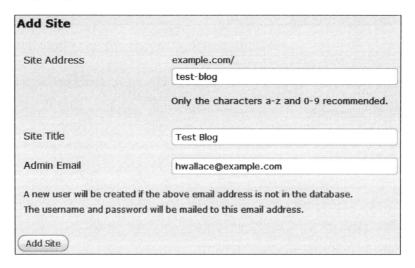

To do this, scroll down to the **Add Site** area of your screen. In the **Site Address** textbox, enter a text string to serve as the subdomain or subdirectory for this blog. Next, type a name for this blog into the **Site Title** textbox. In the **Admin Email** textbox, enter the same email address that you used when you installed WordPress. Then, click **Add Site**.

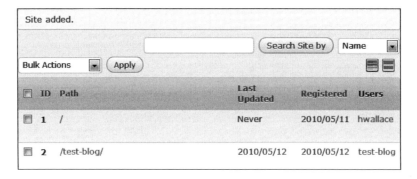

Once this site is created, it will be added to the top portion of your screen. Hover near the link for your test site. From the now visible set of links, right-click **Visit** and then open this link in a new window. If all went well during this test phase, you will be taken to the home page for this blog.

 If you encounter difficulties while performing this test, then an error may have occurred during the WordPress or network installation process. In that case, you should delete WordPress, as well as the database that was associated with this installation, from your server. Reinstall everything and then try this test again. Once you're able to successfully create a site on your network, you can move on to the next step of this project.

This test blog has served its purpose and is no longer required, so return to the **Site** settings screen and, once again, hover near the link for this blog. When the set of links appears, click **Delete**. Then, when the confirmation screen appears, click **Confirm**.

With this test successfully completed, click on **Super Admin | Users** to visit the next screen found in this settings area.

Users

Since you're the only user on the network at the moment, you don't need to perform any actions on this screen. You should, however, have a look around so that you will be familiar with this area when it comes time for your site to go live.

Once your site goes live and members begin populating it, you will be able to visit this screen to edit the accounts of your users as well as delete them from your site.

You don't need to visit the **Themes** screen just yet, so click on **Super Admin | Options** to be taken to that settings area instead.

Options

Operational Settings is the first settings area found on this screen. The **Network Name** and **Network Admin Email** found in this area can be skipped since these textboxes already contain the information that you provided during the network installation. **Global Terms** is next and you can either leave this setting at it's default or enable it depending upon your own preferences.

The **Dashboard Settings** area follows. The **Dashboard Site** textbox is empty and can be left as is. **Dashboard User Default Role** is set to **Subscriber**, which is ideal, so you can move on to **Admin Notice Feed**. If you would like to display the latest post from your main site's RSS feed on all site dashboards, enter its URL into the textbox. If you don't want this feed to be displayed, leave this textbox empty.

Next, is the **Registration Settings** area where you will see a section labeled **Allow new registrations**. By default, registrations are disabled. There isn't much point to a community portal if it's impossible for people to become a part of the community, so you need to change this setting. To do this, you need to tick the radio button next to **Both sites and user accounts can be registered**.

Registration notification is up next and this setting is currently enabled. With this setting enabled you will receive an email every time someone registers at your website. If you would prefer not to receive these notifications, disable this setting. Next is the **Add New Users** setting, which is currently disabled. Once again, it's up to your preference whether you want to allow site administrators to add new users to their blog.

Most of the remaining settings found on this screen can be left as is so scroll down until you reach the section marked **Upload Settings**. If you would like to give your users the ability to upload images, videos, or music, place a checkmark next to the appropriate setting.

 Some themes (including **Twenty Ten**) support Featured Images. Users, however, will be unable to use this feature unless image uploads are enabled.

Changes don't need to be made to the remaining settings found in this area, so you can move on to **Menu Settings**.

In a network-enabled version of WordPress you have a couple options when it comes to managing plugins. You can choose to allow your users access to the plugin management screen, which will give them the ability to enable or disable certain plugins, or you can opt to retain a considerable amount of control by completely restricting their access to this screen. If you would like to let your users access the plugin management screen then enable the **Plugins** setting. If not, just leave this option as is since it's disabled by default.

Next, click **Update Options** to save the changes that you've made. There's just one more screen to visit in the **Super Admin** settings area, so navigate to **Super Admin | Update**.

Update Network

At this point you don't need to do anything other than familiarize yourself with the **Update Network** screen. When you want to update all of the sites in your network, however, you will need to return to this page.

With the **Super Admin** settings configured, you now have the capability of running a network using WordPress, but this is just one aspect of your community portal. Now you need to install BuddyPress to add the social networking aspect to your website.

Activating the BuddyPress Default theme

After installing and activating BuddyPress, an alert will appear at the top of your screen to tell you that the functionality offered by BuddyPress isn't available on your website just yet. For these features to be made available to your members, you will need to install a BuddyPress-compatible theme.

> **BuddyPress is ready**. You'll need to <u>activate a BuddyPress compatible theme</u> to take advantage of all of the features. We've bundled a default theme, but you can always <u>install some other compatible themes</u> or <u>upgrade your existing WordPress theme</u>.

You have a few options when it comes to themes. You can activate the default BuddyPress theme, install a different compatible theme, or upgrade your existing theme so that it can be used with BuddyPress. For now, it's easiest to keep things simple, so begin with the default BuddyPress theme. Later on, you can change to a new theme after you've finished installing and configuring everything.

Activating this theme is a two step process. First, navigate to **Appearance | Themes** and then click **Activate** for the **BuddyPress Default** theme. Next, click on **Super Admin | Themes**. Tick the radio button labeled **Yes** for the BuddyPress Default theme and then click **Apply Changes**. Now the BuddyPress Default theme will be in use on your site and available for usage by your users.

Setting up and configuring BuddyPress

After activating the plugin, you might have noticed that a new **BuddyPress** menu appeared. Click on **BuddyPress | General Settings** to access the **BuddyPress Settings** screen.

BuddyPress Settings

There are only two settings on this screen that you need to concern yourself with; the rest can be left at their defaults settings. The first option that you need to alter is located at the top of the screen and is labeled **Base profile group name**. As you can see, this is currently set to **Base**. This text appears in a couple of places. First, when your users go to **My Account | Profile | Edit Profile**, they will see **Editing 'Base' Profile Group**.

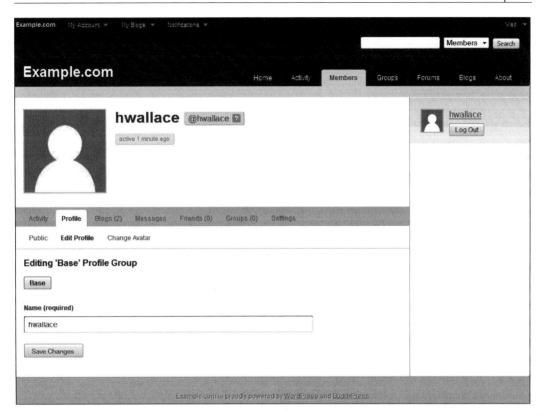

The second place that this text can be found is on the BuddyPress **Profile Field Setup** screen where it's used as the name of the default field group.

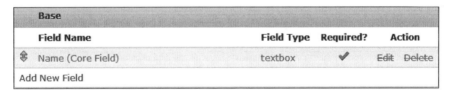

In both instances, something less enigmatic would be beneficial. Think of a descriptive label that would be useful in both situations and then enter it into the **Base profile group name** textbox.

You will find the other setting that you need to configure located at the bottom of your screen, so scroll down until you see the **Default User Avatar**. In this area, select the type of avatar that you would like to display for users without a custom avatar and then click **Save Settings**.

Component Setup

Now, click on **BuddyPress | Component Setup** to be taken to the **BuddyPress Component Setup** screen. By default, all of the components found on this screen are enabled. How you choose to configure the majority of these settings will depend upon your preferences and the features that you would like to make available on your website. It should be noted, however, that both the **bbPress Forums** and **Groups** components should remain enabled if you plan on integrating bbPress into your community portal. Also, the **Extended Profiles** component should be left set to **Enabled**, so that your members can have more detailed profiles attached to their accounts.

Profile Field Setup

Skip the **Forums Setup** screen for now, and instead click on **Profile Field Setup**. On this screen, there are three actions that you can take. You can add additional field groups, add new fields, and then choose the location for each of these fields within their group.

At present, your installation of BuddyPress has one default field placed within one default field group which now bears the name that it was given when you changed it from **Base** on the **BuddyPress Settings** screen. Any fields located in this default field group will appear on the signup screen under the heading of **Profile Details**.

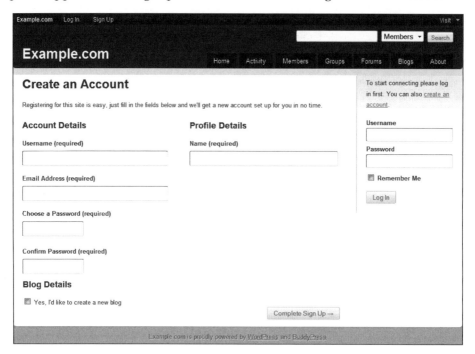

This field group also appears on the screen that your users see when they go to edit their profile.

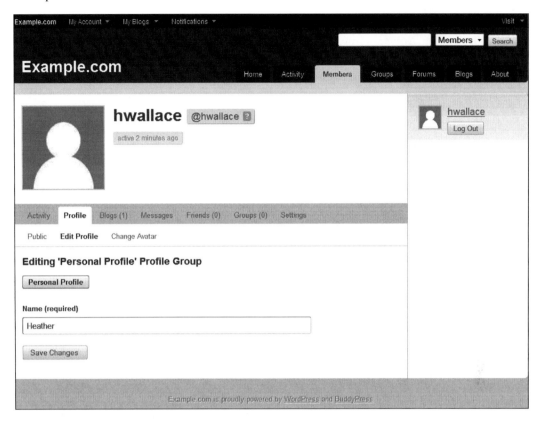

Any additional field groups that you add will only be visible to users when they wish to edit their profile. As things stand, your users will have a profile that consists of nothing more than their name. Since that doesn't make for much of a profile you need to add some additional field groups and fields. With the addition of these new groups and fields, it will be possible for your members to build a robust profile page.

Begin by adding fields to the default field group. This section should include the standard information that you might expect to see on any signup form. Suppose that you want to add a drop-down menu for registrants to select their gender. To do this, click on **Add New Field**. In the **Field Title** textbox, enter **Gender**. In the **Field Description** textbox you have the option of providing explanatory information about this field. In this case, the purpose of this field is pretty obvious, so no description is necessary. Next, you have the option of making this a required field. The last setting is a drop-down menu labeled **Field Type**. With this setting you can choose from many different field types. **Drop Down Select Box** seems to be the most obvious choice, so select that from the list.

Upon selecting that option, a new options area will appear. Here you can enter options for this field. First, select how you would like your drop-down selections to be ordered. Next, enter **Female** into the textbox labeled **Option 1**. Click **Add Another Option** and then enter **Male** into that textbox. Don't select either option as a default value. Click **Save**, and this field will now be included in your default field group.

Continue adding any additional fields that you would like to include within this group before moving on to creating a new field group.

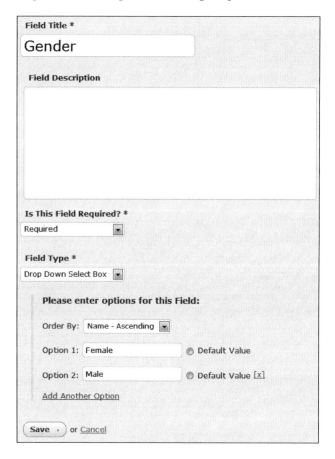

Now that you've customized your default field group, it's time to think about the information that you would like users to be able to provide on their profile pages. Think about the field groups and fields that are appropriate to the theme of your community portal. For example, if you're planning on creating a community portal geared toward sports fans, you might add a field group called Favorite Teams. Within this field group you could place textboxes for your members to enter their favorite baseball, football, basketball, or soccer teams.

Once you have a clear idea of the fields that you would like to include, you should next consider how those fields might be organized. You might find it helpful to construct an outline to depict the organizational layout of your field groups and fields. This will help you to decide how everything should appear onscreen, the field groups that will hold certain fields, and the type of entry method appropriate for each field.

Once again, suppose that you're creating a sports-related community portal. If that were the case, then your organizational outline might look similar to the following:

- Favorite Teams
    - ° Baseball — textbox
    - ° Basketball — textbox
    - ° Football — textbox
    - ° Soccer — textbox

- Favorite Sports to Play
    - ° Baseball — checkbox
    - ° Basketball — checkbox
    - ° Football — checkbox
    - ° Soccer — checkbox

With your outline handy, begin by adding the first of your new field groups. To do this, click the button labeled **Add New Field Group**. On this screen, enter the name of your first field group into the textbox labeled **Field Group Name** and then click **Add New Field Group**.

The **Profile Field Setup** screen will now contain both your default field group and the new one that you just created. There will also be an **Add New Field** link located within each of these field groups.

Click the **Add New Field** link located within the field group that you just created. Then, create the first of the new fields within this field group. Continue this process until all of the fields within this group have been created.

Favorite Teams			Edit	Delete
Field Name	**Field Type**	**Required?**	**Action**	
Baseball	textbox	--	Edit	Delete
Basketball	textbox	--	Edit	Delete
Football	textbox	--	Edit	Delete
Soccer	textbox	--	Edit	Delete
Add New Field				

Continue creating a field group and adding fields to it until you've reached the end of your outline. Once this process is complete, you can then change the location of any fields within their group. This can be done quite easily by just dragging and dropping the field to a new location. Keep in mind that fields can't be dragged from one field group to another. If you decide that you would like a field to appear in a different group, then you will need to create the field within that group and then delete it from its original group.

As you will recall, you previously skipped over the **Forums Setup** screen. Well, now it's time to visit that screen so that you can install and integrate bbPress into your website.

Allowing your users to create forums

With the combination of WordPress and BuddyPress, your users will have quite a few features available to them. There is, however, one thing that these two prices of software can't do and that's provide your members with the ability to add forums to their groups. For that, you need bbPress.

Installing and integrating bbPress

The process for installing bbPress and then integrating it with BuddyPress couldn't be easier. To begin, click on **BuddyPress | Forums Setup**. Since you're creating a new website, you won't have a current installation of bbPress to concern yourself with, so click the button labeled **Set up a new bbPress installation** and then, on the **New bbPress Installation** screen, click **Complete Installation**. You should now see a screen telling you that the installation has been completed.

> *Forums Setup*
>
> All done! Configuration settings have been saved to the file `bb-config.php` in the root of your WordPress install.

The process that you just completed not only installed bbPress, it integrated it with BuddyPress as well. You can see evidence of this by, once again, clicking on **BuddyPress | Forums Setup**. As you can see, this screen now provides you with a message telling you that the bbPress forum integration with BuddyPress was a success.

> bbPress forum integration in BuddyPress has been set up correctly. If you are having problems you can re-install

Activating plugins across your portal

With the multi-site function enabled on your installation of WordPress, you will be able to activate plugins across your entire network. With network activation, you can maintain a certain amount of control by specifying which plugins should be enabled on every blog that's created at your site.

If you previously chose to allow your users access to the plugin management screen, then any plugins that you activate across the network won't appear when members manage their plugins. This means that it won't be possible for a user to disable plugins that you wish to make a mandatory part of their blog. This is particularity useful when it comes to certain plugins such as those used to protect your community portal from spammers.

To activate a plugin on every blog in the network, you need to go about things a bit differently than usual. Typically, when you want to activate a plugin, you just click the **Activate** link. In this case, however, you instead need to click the alternate link for network activation. The following screenshot shows an example of what the network activation link will look like on your screen:

Plugin	Description
Akismet	Akismet checks your comments against the Akismet web service to see if they look like spam or not. You need a WordPress.com API key to use it. You can review the spam it catches under "Comments." To show off your Akismet stats just put `<?php akismet_counter(); ?>` in your template. See also: WP Stats plugin.
Activate | Network Activate | Edit | Delete	Version 2.2.7 | By Matt Mullenweg | Visit plugin site

With network activation, everything would seem to be perfectly configured so that you're able to dictate which plugins are mandatory. There is, however, a flaw in the system. Plugins that place a link to their configuration screen under another menu (such as the **Settings** menu) provide users with a way to circumvent your plugin management system.

While using network activation might restrict users from disabling certain plugins, they can still visit the plugin's settings screen and configure it as they see fit. This is the case whether you chose to allow your users to have access the plugin management screen or not. As a result, they could turn off all of the plugin's settings if they choose. So, while the plugin isn't technically disabled on their site, it can be rendered inoperable due to this loophole.

Battling bots and spam

It's unfortunate, but the sad fact of the matter is that your new community portal is probably going to become a magnet for spammers. If you don't take steps to protect your network, then it will most likely become overrun with spam blogs, which are known as **splogs**, as well as spam comments. It's best, therefore, to take as many precautionary measures as possible in order to provide your community portal (and your members) with the maximum amount of protection against these nuisances that plague the Internet.

Modifying .htaccess to stop splog registrations

The WordPress Codex website has some helpful information on various methods that can be used to battle comment spam. One of their techniques involves making a modification to the `.htaccess` file. The good news is that you can easily adapt this method to prevent spammers from filling your community portal with splogs.

To implement this spambot detection method, enter the following code at the bottom of the `.htaccess` file on your server. Next, change `example.com` to the URL for your domain. Be sure to enter this without the `http://www.` prefix.

```
RewriteCond %{REQUEST_METHOD} POST
RewriteCond %{REQUEST_URI} .wp-signup\.php*
RewriteCond %{HTTP_REFERER} !.*example.com.* [OR]
RewriteCond %{HTTP_USER_AGENT} ^$
RewriteRule (.*) http://%{REMOTE_ADDR}/$ [R=301,L]
```

What this addition to `.htaccess` does is verify whether a POST request for your registration page is coming from a legitimate user or a spambot. Requests that don't originate from your website—or that have an empty user agent string—are deemed to have been made by a spambot. If that determination is made, then the spambot is sent back where it came from and is prevented from creating a splog on your website.

Plugins aimed at spam prevention

Plugins are also important weapons in your arsenal as you work to protect your community portal from spam in various forms. For maximum protection, you should install each of the following plugins.

Introducing SI CAPTCHA Anti-Spam

This plugin, which can be found at `http://wordpress.org/extend/plugins/si-captcha-for-wordpress/`, adds CAPTCHA functionality to your community portal. Upon activation, the plugin can be configured to add a CAPTCHA to the registration form and login page. This measure goes a long way toward preventing spambots from attacking your site.

Setting up and configuring SI CAPTCHA Anti-Spam

After installing this plugin choose **Network Activation**. Then, click on **Plugins | SI Captcha Options**. The CAPTCHA difficulty level is currently set to **Medium**, which should be just fine. In the future, if you find that spam is still a problem, return to this screen and change the difficulty level to **High**.

You can choose to add a CAPTCHA on the login form, but this setting isn't recommended for two reasons. First, enabling this feature ruins the aesthetics of your website because a CAPTCHA will now appear under every login box. As you can see in the following screenshot, a CAPTCHA is even added to the login box on the frontend of your website. Secondly, enabling CAPTCHA on the login screen may give you the highest level of protection, but it will come at the cost of seriously annoying your members.

The default settings are configured so that a CAPTCHA appears on the registration page and comment forms by default. You should, however, remove this protection from the comment form. That's because there's a better plugin that you can use to protect the site's in your network from comment spammers.

Next, you can choose whether the CAPTCHA should remain hidden from some users and, if so, which users should be exempted. Tick the checkbox next to this setting to enable it. This setting is currently set to **All registered users**, which should provide a sufficient level of security.

Since a CAPTCHA isn't being added to the comment form, you can bypass the next two settings and move on to the **CAPTCHA Options** settings area. **Enable Audio for the CAPTCHA** is already activated by default so you can move on to the next setting. For ease of use, you should tick the checkbox next to **Enable Flash Audio for the CAPTCHA** because it makes it much easier for visitors to listen to the CAPTCHA if they're unable to see it. **Enable smaller size CAPTCHA image** is next and whether you choose to enable this setting will be up to you. **Disable CAPTCHA transparent text** should only be activated if CAPTCHA text is missing from the image. Otherwise, leave this setting disabled.

Enable aria-required tags for screen readers, which is the last setting found in the **Options** area of this screen, should be enabled so that your community portal is as accessible as possible.

After that, all that remains are the advanced options. Here you can customize the CSS and text labels associated with the CAPTCHA if you so desire. Once you've finished making changes, click **Update Options**.

Introducing Slide 2 Comment

Since you aren't using **SI CAPTCHA Anti-Spam** to protect the comment forms on your network from spam, you need to install another plugin to handle the job. That's where **Slide 2 Comment** comes in. This plugin, which can be found at `http://wordpress.org/extend/plugins/slide2comment/`, is designed to be a fun alternative to the anti-spam methods that are normally found on comment forms. Rather than displaying the typical CAPTCHA image or a challenge question, this plugin uses a slider that the commenter must use before they can add a comment to the site.

Setting up and configuring Slide 2 Comment

Install this plugin and then choose **Network Activate**. Spam protection will now be active on all of the comment forms across your network.

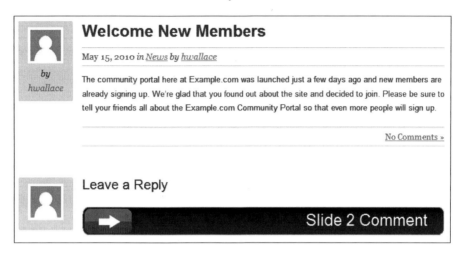

This plugin can be used as is or you can visit the settings screen if you would like to customize the slider's appearance. To visit the settings screen for this plugin, click on **Settings | Slide2Comment**.

In the **Edit Slider Appearance** area of the screen, you can make changes to the CSS used on the slider. Once you've finished making changes, click the **Submit** button found in this area.

Move Slider without clicking is the only other setting found on this screen, but it shouldn't be changed from **No** because the **Yes** setting isn't compatible with all themes.

Introducing Simple Trackback Validation

Spam comes in many forms and even trackbacks aren't immune. Luckily, the **Simple Trackback Validation** plugin, found at `http://wordpress.org/extend/plugins/ simple-trackback-validation/`, can protect even this aspect of your community portal from spam. This plugin takes two actions to prevent trackback spam. It first checks to see if the IP address of the trackback sender is identical to the IP address of the web server to which the trackback URL refers. After that, it then checks the web address used in the trackback and ensures that the page actually contains a link to your blog.

Setting up and configuring Simple Trackback Validation

Install this plugin and then choose **Network Activate**. Then, go to **Settings | Simple TB Validation**. This will take you to the **Simple Trackback Validation** settings screen.

In the first section, labeled **How to deal with spam trackbacks?**, choose the action that you would like to be taken when the plugin detects a spam trackback. **Add prefix** should remain enabled, so you can move on to the **Validation Phase 1: IP Address** section of the settings screen. **Validate IP Address** is the only setting found in this section and it's already enabled. This setting is ideal, so no changes need to be made.

The next set of settings that you need to configure are located in the **Validation Phase 2: URL** section of the screen. **Validate URL** is enabled by default, so turn your attention to the **Strictness** area of your screen. Here you need to choose the method that you would like the plugin to use when it checks to see if a link to your blog has been placed. Either method is acceptable, so the choice is up to you.

Depending upon your preferences, you may choose to leave the **Moderate in case of errors** option set at its default or you may choose to disable it. **Enable Log** is the last setting and, by default, it isn't activated. You may, however, enable this feature if you prefer.

With your configurations finished, click **Update Options** to save all changes.

Staying one step ahead of the spammers

Now, just because you've implemented these protective measures on your community portal, that doesn't mean that the war against spammers is won. You may have stopped the problem for now, but rest assured that spammers are continually updating their methods. That means what works today might not be so effective tomorrow, because these spammers could quite possibly discover an exploit in one of your plugins. To combat this problem, it's extremely important that you update your plugins each time a new version is released.

Preserving the privacy of BuddyPress member profiles

Some site members may wish to participate in your community but to also protect their information from viewing by the general public. The BuddyPress developers have yet to include privacy controls to protect profile data. Because of that, you will have to use a plugin to add this functionality to your site.

Introducing BuddyPress Profile Privacy

With the **BuddyPress Profile Privacy** plugin, found at http://wordpress.org/ extend/plugins/bp-profile-privacy/, you can either maintain control over your users' privacy by deciding which fields found on the profile page should be visible to everyone, friends, or users or you can, instead, give them complete control over the visibility of their personal information.

Putting your users in control will allow them to customize these settings to their liking in order to maintain the level of privacy that they're comfortable with. If they're given control over these settings, then they will need to visit the edit profile page to specify which pieces of information are visible and to whom.

Setting up and configuring BuddyPress Profile Privacy

After activating the plugin on the network, click on **BuddyPress | Profile Privacy Setup**. On this screen, you will need to configure the **Who Can See** setting associated with each field. The settings that you choose on this screen will depend upon your own preferences. Once you've finished performing these configurations, click **Save Changes**.

 If you add a new field to your site, you will need to return to this screen and then configure the **Who Can See** option for that field.

Giving your community portal a new look

The default BuddyPress theme is all well and good and it has served its purpose quite nicely up to this point, but using it out-of-the-box would be a bit like installing WordPress and never changing your theme to anything other than the default.

Before launch, you really should change the appearance of your community portal to make it unique. Here are some options for you to explore so that your theme will stand out from the crowd.

After installing and activating your new theme, in order for it to appear on the **Manage Themes** page, you will also need to activate it on the **Network Themes** screen. Doing this, however, will make it so that this theme is also available for use by all of the members of your site.

Customizing the BuddyPress Default

You could continue to use the BuddyPress Default theme, but, instead of leaving it as is, you could put your CSS skills to good use and customize it so that it looks slightly different.

If you really want to delve into theme development, then you could create a BuddyPress child theme of your very own. This option has the added benefit that your community portal would look like no other since its theme would be your own creation. If you decide to go with this option then read the *Building a BuddyPress Child Theme* article which can be found in the **Documentation** area of the BuddyPress site. This page, found at `http://codex.buddypress.org/how-to-guides/building-a-buddypress-child-theme/`, provides invaluable information on the entire process of creating a child theme for BuddyPress.

Installing a BuddyPress-compatible theme

If you don't want to edit BuddyPress Default or build a child theme, then the best option for theming your website is to install a BuddyPress-compatible design. BuddyPress themes aren't quite as abundant as WordPress themes, but there are a few of them out there to choose from. Here are a few places where you can begin your search for a new theme.

Free themes

You might not know this, but the theme management area in WordPress is actually a great source for free BuddyPress themes. Click on **Appearance | Themes**. At the top of the page, you will see two tabs. Click the one labeled **Install Themes**. Enter **BuddyPress** into the search box and then click **Search**. The results page that will be generated as a result of this search will contain a selection of BuddyPress-compatible themes for you to choose from. Once you find a theme that you like, install and activate it.

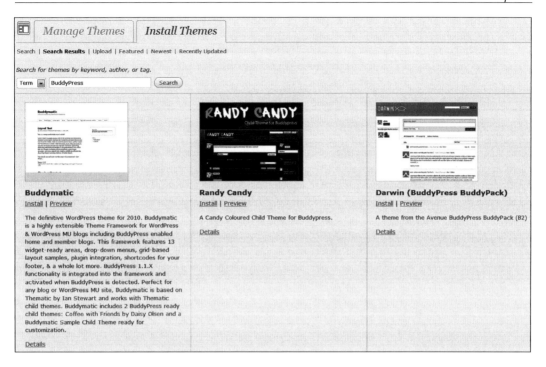

Premium themes

WPMU Dev Premium, which can be found at `http://premium.wpmudev.org/themes/`, offers a selection of premium BuddyPress themes to its members. The themes offered at this website are touted as being "immensely customisable through theme options", so you shouldn't have to make any edits to the CSS in order to get them looking exactly the way you want.

Adding BuddyPress support to an existing theme

If you don't care for any of the Buddypress-comptible themes that you've found, it's possible for you to use a standard WordPress theme on your site. For this to be possible, you will need to add BuddyPress support to your chosen theme. Doing this isn't as difficult as it sounds because you can use the **BuddyPress Template Pack** plugin, which is available at `http://wordpress.org/extend/plugins/bp-template-pack/`, to guide you through the process step by step.

Before you begin working with this plugin, however, you must first activate the WordPress theme that you're planning to use on your site. To do this, visit **Appearance | Themes** and then click the activation link for your theme.

Introducing BuddyPress Template Pack

With the help of this plugin, you will be able to edit a standard WordPress theme so that it's capable of managing and displaying all BuddyPress pages and content. Accomplishing this doesn't require you to make any edits to your template files and it's completely reversible.

Setting up and configuring BuddyPress Template Pack

Install the **BuddyPress Template Pack** plugin and then activate it on your site. BuddyPress requires extra template files that a standard WordPress theme doesn't include. The extra template files that you require are, however, provided with this plugin.

These templates are currently located in the `plugins/bp-template-pack` directory on your server and need to be moved to your theme's folder. It may be possible to move these files automatically, but, if that isn't possible, you will need to move them yourself.

Click on **Appearance | BP Compatibility** to be taken to the **Step One** screen. Once there, click **Move Template Files** so that the plugin will attempt to automatically transfer these templates to your theme's folder. If the transfer is successful, you will be taken to the **Step Two** screen where no actions need to be performed, so click **move on to step three** to proceed to the next screen.

If the transfer fails, the **Step Two** screen will alert you to that fact and provide you with detailed instruction that you can follow to manually move these templates. Basically, all you need to do is transfer the folders from the `plugins/bp-template-pack` directory to your theme's folder. Once the folders have been transferred, click the button labeled **I've finished moving template folders** to be taken to the next screen.

Now, open a new browser window and then visit your site. With those templates in place, your theme will now have a BuddyPress admin bar at the top of the page that you can use to navigate through various screens. If you find that certain elements aren't aligned correctly, you will need to take measures to correct this problem.

Detailed information for correcting alignment issues can be found on the **Step Three** screen under the heading of **Fixing Alignment**. Follow those instructions to correct any alignment issues that you might have.

Next, click **Finish**. After your screen refreshes, the **BuddyPress Theme Compatibility** screen will contain a couple settings, but they don't require any configuration. A **Reset** button is also provided for you to use if you ever want to run through the setup process again.

Removing the BuddyPress is ready message

As you can see, even through you've made your theme BuddyPress-compatible, the **BuddyPress is ready** message is still being displayed at the top of your screen. To make this message disappear, open your theme's `style.css` file. Then, look for the Tags line located in the stylesheet header. Now, add `buddypress` to this list of tags. Save `style.css` and then upload it to your theme's folder. Refresh your screen, and the **BuddyPress is ready** message will disappear.

Adding navigation links to your site

Since the theme that you're using wasn't originally designed to be compatible with BuddyPress, a few important navigation links are missing. You can, however, easily add these links to your site with the help of a widget.

As you can see, a complete list of the default set of links is provided on the **BuddyPress Theme Compatibility** screen. Copy this list of links to your text editor and then navigate to **Appearance | Widgets**. Now, add a **Text** widget to your site. In the **Title** textbox, enter **Navigation Links**. Format the first of these links so that it's clickable and then paste it into the text area for this widget. Repeat this process for each of the remaining links. Then, click **Save**.

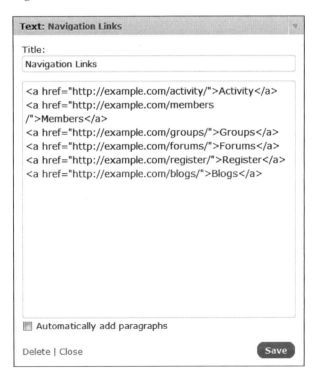

Going beyond the basic themes for users

As your community portal sits now, there are only a few themes that your users can activate on their blogs. Your users will, most likely, want a few more options and you can easy give them more choices by installing additional themes.

To do this, you will, once again, need to navigate to **Appearance | Themes** and then click on **Install Themes**. Now, perform another search for BuddyPress themes.

Once you find one that you like, install it. This time, when the screen appears to tell you that the theme has been installed, don't click the activation link. Instead, continue to install any additional themes that you would like to make available to your users.

When you've finished installing themes, click on **Super Admin | Themes** to visit the **Network Themes** page. On this screen, locate the themes that you just installed. When you locate them, tick the **Yes** option for each one. Then, click **Apply Changes**.

Now, when your visitors log in to their **Dashboard** and go to **Appearance | Themes**, they will have many more options to choose from.

Testing your installation of BuddyPress and bbPress

Even though you've conducted some tests, you still can't be certain that your users won't run in to any problems when using your community portal. That's where this next set of tests comes in. After these tests have been completed, you will have done everything that you can to put your community portal to the test and ensure that every feature is working as it should.

Creating a new account from the frontend

Visit the frontend of your site and then create a user account via your registration page. As you complete the form, be sure to tick the checkbox next to **Yes, I'd like to create a new blog**.

Adding a new group

Once your account has been created and verified, log in and then point your browser to `http://example.com/groups/`. You will, of course, need to replace `example.com` with the URL for your domain. On this screen, click **Create a Group**. Enter a name for this group into the **Group Name** textbox and then type a short description into the **Group Description** text area. Now, click **Create Group and Continue**. On this screen, the **Enable discussion forum** setting should remain enabled. In the **Privacy Options** area, chose any of the available settings. Then, click **Next Step**.

Now, click **Browse** to choose an image from your computer that you would like to use as the avatar for this group. After you've selected your image, click **Upload Image**. Then, click **Next Step**.

Since your site only has one member, you won't be able to test the invite feature that would normally be found on the **Invites** screen, so click **Finish** to create your group.

Managing your blog

Now, it's time to turn your attention to the blog that was created when you signed up for this account. So, visit the **Dashboard** associated with this blog. Once there, click on **Appearance | Themes** and then switch to a different theme.

If you previously chose to let your users have access to the plugin management screen, you will need to visit it now to make sure that everything functions properly. So, click on **Plugins | Installed**. Now, activate and deactivate a few plugins.

Performing additional tests

Once all of that's done, you will have tested the major components of your website. Now, return to the frontend of your community portal and test out a few of the miscellaneous features. Run some searches, add a few comments, and basically just click on anything and everything.

Concluding the testing process

After you've completed all of your tests, be sure to delete everything that was created during this evaluation process. With this process having been successfully completed, your community portal is now ready for launch.

Summary

There were many components required for this project, and each one built upon its predecessor to create the website that you see before you. You certainly have come a long way from the desire to create a community portal to the point where you find yourself now. With the technical aspect of this project complete, there's still one thing left for you to do. Just as a family makes a house a home, a social networking website requires members for it to become a community. So, in order to truly create a community portal, you must now concentrate on growing your membership base.

Put on your marketing hat and start recruiting members. Draw in the early adopters who will spread the word about your website. Then, continuously strive to increase your user base until news of your community portal spreads like wildfire throughout your target audience. Once that happens, you will have truly realized your goal of building a community portal.

In this chapter, you learned how to enable the network functionality in a standard installation of WordPress. From there, you were shown how to use BuddyPress and bbPress, along with a selection of other plugins, to transform a simple blog network into a full-fledged community portal.

In the next chapter, you will learn how to build an e-commerce website where you will be able to sell various products, manage your inventory, and integrate your site's shopping cart with many popular payment processors.

3

Project 3: Building an E-Commerce Website

When one thinks of ways in which to monetize a WordPress installation their mind typically turns to **Google Adsense**, CPM advertising, and sponsorships. That's because, when WordPress is involved, most people assume that it's being used solely for blogging. The wonderful thing about WordPress, however, is that it can be used for so much more.

As you consider the possibility of building an e-commerce website, you might think that you will need to sign-up to use a complicated CMS provided by some third-party. Going that route, however, would require learning a new system and paying costly monthly fees that would cut into your profits.

Such measures, however, aren't required, because WordPress can easily be made to function as an e-commerce website with all of the features offered by third-party vendors without any the hefty costs. Just install the appropriate plugin and your e-commerce website will be online in no time. To make this possible the free **WP e-Commerce plugin** is all that's required. Yes, you can add on a variety of paid upgrades that will enhance the functionality of your store, but they certainly aren't required in order to build a features-filled e-commerce store that's capable of selling thousands of products.

Using WordPress and the WP e-Commerce plugin for the backbone of your store has many benefits. Taking this route will save you money and allow you to use a CMS that you're familiar with (which will save you a considerable amount of time as well). With this extra money and time at your disposal, you can, instead, concentrate on important matters like promoting your products and increasing your profit margin.

In this chapter, you will learn how to:

- Categorize products for easy browsing
- Offer your customers product variations
- Use coupons, cross-selling, social networking, **Facebook**, and the **Google Merchant Center** to market your store
- Customize the presentation of your products
- Enable a variety of payment gateways on your store
- Use various upgrades to increase the functionality of your store
- Build the inventory for your store
- Feature products on your store's homepage

Once this project is complete, you will have succeeded in creating a site similar to the one shown in the following screenshot:

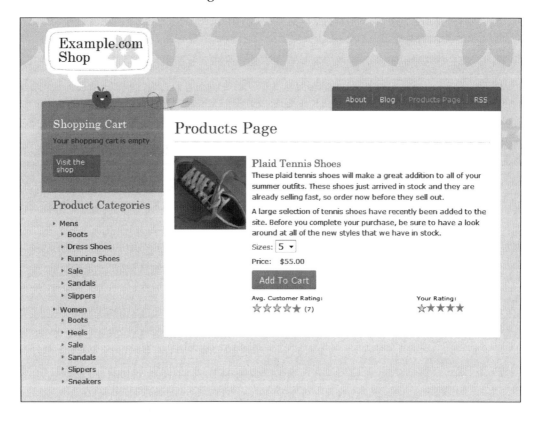

Introducing WP e-Commerce

The WP e-Commerce plugin dispels the myth that starting an e-commerce website requires a lot of time and money. In truth, all you need is a WordPress installation coupled with WP e-Commerce. This plugin, which can be found at `http://getshopped.org/`, offers a wealth of features at absolutely no cost and additional functionality for a fee, but those addons certainly aren't required in order to run a state-of-the-art e-commerce store. WP e-Commerce is easy to install and moderately easy to configure, which means that you can have a stable online store up-and-running in no time.

The free WP e-Commerce plugin offers many features to help your store become a success. For instance, when it comes to social networking, this plugin offers tools that make it possible for store owners to import products into the **Facebook Marketplace**. It also includes an integrated **ShareThis** feature that makes it easy for customers to share products with their friends.

If the payment process isn't easy, then shoppers will look to buy elsewhere. That's why the WP e-Commerce plugin makes it possible for merchants to offer their shoppers a wide range of payment options. The free version of the plugin integrates with **Google Checkout**, **PayPal**, **Authorize.net**, **Payment Express**, and many other payment processors. The Gold Cart upgrade also offers an additional selection of processors for those who require even more payment options.

Marketing is vital to the success of any online store and WP e-Commerce offers features to help store owners in that area as well. From the **Marketing** screen, this plugin allows store owners to create coupon codes as well as promote their entire inventory via cross-selling.

WP e-Commerce is also backed by an active forum where users can post questions and receive answers from both moderators and fellow users. This support system should prove useful should you encounter any problems as you use this plugin.

Setting up and configuring WP e-Commerce

Upon activation, you should notice that a new menu, labeled **Store**, has appeared on the right hand side of the **Dashboard**. This section houses the multi-page configuration area for the WP e-Commerce plugin. You will need to navigate through each of these screens as you work to get your online store ready for shoppers.

Sales

Begin your exploration and configuration of this plugin by clicking on **Store | Sales**. This will take you to the **Sales** screen which acts as a purchase log for your store. All transactions that occur in your store will be visible on this screen. From here, it will also be possible for you to download your sales logs as CSV files.

Since your store is new, and no purchases have been made, your purchase log will currently show zero sales. At this point, you should just take a look around and familiarize yourself with this screen since you're going to be using it quite a lot once your store is up and running.

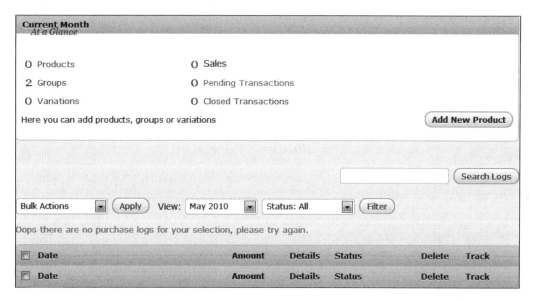

Categories

Rather than visiting the next settings screen, where you can manually add products, you should first create some groups that are specific to your store.

WP e-Commerce is similar to a standard WordPress blog in that it organizes content into easy to navigate sections. In WordPress, content is arraigned using only categories while WP e-Commerce uses categories and groups to organize products. The plugin has default groups included in the system. They are **Categories** and **Brands** and within those two groups are two categories named **Example category** and **Example Brand**. It's under the **Categories** and **Brands** groups that you will be placing each of your categories.

Before doing anything else, you should first delete the two default categories from your store. To delete **Example category**, select **Categories** from the **Select a Group to Manage** drop-down menu. Then, in the "**Categories**" **Group** area, click on the **Edit** link located next to **Example category**. Scroll down to the bottom of the page and then click **Delete**. Now, remove the **Example Brand** as well.

Rather than just haphazardly adding categories, you should form a plan as to how you would like things to be arranged in your shop. So, take some time to think about the organizational structure of your store. Once you have some idea as to how things should be organized, you might find it helpful to create an outline. This outline will give you a road map, of sorts, to follow as you create the various categories at your store. Suppose you're creating a shoe store. If that were the case, then your category outline might look something like this:

- Men
  - Boots
  - Dress Shoes
  - Sale
  - Slippers
  - Sandals
  - Tennis Shoes
- Women
  - Boots
  - Heels
  - Sale
  - Slippers
  - Sandals
  - Tennis Shoes
- Brands
  - Best Ever Boots
  - Splendorific Sandals
  - Super Soft Slippers
  - Terrific Tennis Shoes

Once you have a completed outline, you can move on to adding your first category. Click on **Store | Categories**. This will take you to the **Categories** configuration screen. To add your new category, leave the **Select a Group to Manage** drop-down menu at its default and, instead, click the link labeled **Add a new category to the "Categories" Group**. Doing this will reveal a configuration area where you will need to enter the information for this category.

In the textbox labeled **Name**, enter the title of your first category. Next, in the **Description** text area, enter a sentence or two to describe the items that shoppers might find in this section of your store. The category that you're currently adding should serve as a parent group, so don't select anything from the **Group Parent** drop-down menu. In the **Group Image** area, you may optionally upload an image that you would like to associate with this category, but doing this certainly isn't required.

Next is the **Target Market Restrictions** section which only contains the **Target Markets** setting. This setting lists countries around the world. If you plan on selling items in this category to select locations, then choose only those countries from the list.

Presentation Settings are next and can be left at their default. Now you will come to the **Checkout Settings** area. **This category requires additional checkout form fields** is the first setting located in this area. It, however, doesn't require any changes. Next is the **Products in this category use the billing address to calculate shipping** setting. If you would prefer for the billing address to be used when calculating shipping, tick the radio button next to **Yes**. Otherwise, leave this set to **No**. Click **Add Category** and this new parent category will be added to your store

Repeat this process for each of the parent categories that you would like to add to your store. Once you've added all of them, repeat the process once again for your sub-categories. This time, however, be sure to select the appropriate parent category from the **Group Parent** drop-down menu.

When you would like to begin entering brands, select **Brands** from the **Select a Group to Manage** drop-down menu. Next, click the link labeled **Add a new category to the "Brands" Group** and then repeat the same process that you previously used to add parent and sub-categories to your store.

Variations

If your products come in different sizes, colors, or have any other sort of variation, then you will need to stop by this next screen.

Suppose, once again, that you're working to create a shoe store. In that instance, you would have many variations since each shoe would be available in multiple sizes and, possibly, even colors.

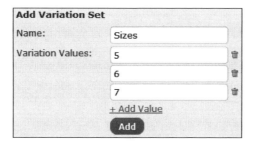

To add a variation, go to **Store | Variations**. There you will see the **Add Variation Set** area. In the textbox labeled **Name**, enter a descriptive title for this variation set. If you were creating a shoe store, then you would enter **Sizes**. Next, enter appropriate values into the **Variation Values** textboxes. In this example, you would enter **5**, **6**, **7**, and so on. If you need to add more values, click **+ Add Value** and an additional textbox will appear. When you've finished adding values, click **Add**.

Your newly created variation set will now appear on the left side of your screen along with a link that you can click to make edits as needed.

Marketing

In addition to the functionality needed to operate an online store, the developers of the WP e-Commerce plugin have also included a set of features designed to help you attract customers to your shop. These options can be found by visiting **Store | Marketing**.

On this screen, you will first encounter the **Coupons** area where you can create coupon codes for customers to use at your store. Suppose you want to create a 25% off holiday coupon. To do this, first click **Create Coupon**. This will reveal the hidden coupon creation fields. In the textbox labeled **Coupon Code**, enter either a word or random string of text. This will be the code that shoppers must enter during checkout in order to receive their special savings. Using the drop-down menu next to the **Discount** box, you can specify if the coupon should be for a fixed amount of dollars off, a percentage-based discount, or free shipping. If you selected the money off or percentage-based discount, you must now enter the amount of the discount into the **Discount** textbox. Next, in the textbox labeled **Start**, enter the date when the coupon can first be used. In the **Expiry** textbox, enter the date when the coupon will expire. The **Use Once** checkbox allows you to specify whether a coupon may be used more than once. If you would like customers to be able to use the coupon several times, leave this setting at its default. Otherwise, tick the checkbox to set the coupon to one-time-only use. Next, leave the **Active** setting at its default. If you want the coupon to be valid throughout your store, tick the checkbox next to **Apply On All Products**. If you want to restrict its usage to certain items, then leave this option at its default.

If you've opted to leave **Apply On All Products** disabled, then you must next configure the settings in the **Conditions** area. Here you can specify exactly which products the coupon may be applied to in order to receive the discount. For example, if you were to configure the settings so that item name is equal to a certain product, then customers would only be able to use this coupon code on that item. There are several additional settings in this area that you can use to specify just how the coupon can and can't be used in your store. Once you've finished configuring all of your coupon code settings, click **Add Coupon**.

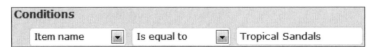

Next is the **Marketing Settings** section. If you like, you can enable the **Display Cross Sales** setting to have WP e-Commerce display a set of products that previous customers purchased along with the item that the current customer is presently viewing. Activating the **Show Share This** option will cause a ShareThis button to be displayed in your store, which will give your customers the ability to share various products via social bookmarking sites. If you would like to learn where your customers originated from and how they found your shop, then you should enable the **Display How Customer Found Us Survey** setting.

In the **RSS Address** section, you will find the product feed for your store. This feed can be used in conjunction with the **GetShopped!** Facebook application to promote your products via that social networking site. You can learn more about GetShopped! at `http://apps.facebook.com/getshopped`.

Lastly, you will find the area that provides information on how to go about importing your products into the Google Merchant Center, so that they will appear within Google Product Search results. To do this, open a new browser window and then visit `http://www.google.com/merchants/`. If you already have a Google account, log in. If you don't have an account with Google create one now.

Once you've logged in, you must first select a location. On the next screen, review the terms of services. Assuming that you've accepted the terms, you will next need to configure your account. Once that's done, you will be taken to the Google Merchant Account **Dashboard**.

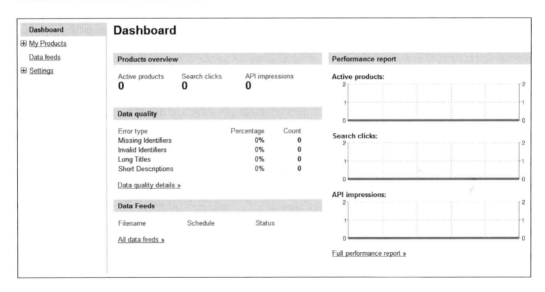

Now you need to register your data feed with Google, so click **Data feeds** and then, on the next screen, click the button labeled **New Data Feed**. Supply the required information and then click **Save changes**. On the **Data feeds** screen, in the **Upload schedule** area, click the **Create** link associated with this data feed. Configure the time-related settings and then paste the URL for your data feed into the **Url of file** textbox. The link to your data feed can be found in the **Google Merchant Centre / Google Product Search** section of the WP e-Commerce **Marketing** Screen. After these configurations have been completed, click **Schedule**.

Settings

Clicking on **Store | Settings** will take you to the **General Settings** configuration screen. This is the first of several settings screens accessible from this area. The first option that you will encounter is the **Base Country/Region** drop-down menu where you need to select your primary business location from the available options. Depending upon your selection, the screen may refresh to provide you with additional options for your state or province. If that happens, make the appropriate selection from the list.

Next, you need to provide information about the sales tax rate for your area. If your country has a nationwide sales tax rate, enter it into the textbox labeled **Tax Settings**. If different sales tax rates are used across your country, click on the link found in the **Tax Settings** area. Next, enter the sales tax rate for your location into the appropriate textbox and then click **Save Changes**.

GST/Tax Rate

Alabama:	0 %	Iowa:	0 %	New Hampshire:	0 %	Texas:	0 %
Alaska:	0 %	Kansas:	0 %	New Jersey:	0 %	Utah:	0 %
Arizona:	0 %	Kentucky:	0 %	New Mexico:	0 %	Vermont:	0 %
Arkansas:	0 %	Louisiana:	0 %	New York:	0 %	Virginia:	0 %
California:	0 %	Maine:	0 %	North Carolina:	0 %	Washington:	0 %
Colorado:	0 %	Maryland:	0 %	North Dakota:	0 %	Washington DC:	0 %
Connecticut:	0 %	Massachusetts:	0 %	Ohio:	0 %	West Virginia:	0 %
Delaware:	0 %	Michigan:	0 %	Oklahoma:	0 %	Wisconsin:	0 %
Florida:	0 %	Minnesota:	0 %	Oregon:	0 %	Wyoming:	0 %
Georgia:	0 %	Mississippi:	0 %	Pennsylvania:	0 %		
Hawaii:	0 %	Missouri:	0 %	Rhode Island:	0 %		
Idaho:	0 %	Montana:	0 %	South Carolina:	0 %		
Illinois:	0 %	Nebraska:	0 %	South Dakota:	0 %		
Indiana:	0 %	Nevada:	0 %	Tennessee:	0 %		

Save Changes

Now you need to configure the **Target Markets** setting for your store. By default, every country is selected. If you would like to sell to only a select number of countries, then click **None** and then tick the checkboxes next to the locations where you plan to sell.

In the **Currency Settings** area, use the **Currency type** drop-down menu to select your country's currency. Next, configure the **Currency sign location** option so that the currency symbol will be displayed in the correct location for your region. Click **Update** to save all of your changes. Then, click **Store | Settings | Presentation** to visit the **Presentation Settings** screen.

Presentation

The first thing that you will probably notice on this screen is the **Theme Customisation** message box. The purpose of this box is to alert you that your theme files aren't in a safe place and that automatic upgrades have been disabled until these themes are moved. You can easily remedy both of these problems by clicking the **Move your files** link. Doing this will relocate your theme files to a location that the plugin finds to be acceptable.

Theme Customisation

Your theme files have not been moved.
Until your theme files have been moved,
we have disabled automatic upgrades.

Click here to Move your files to a safe
place

Read Tutorials

The first set of options that you will see on this screen are in the **Button Settings** section. By default, your store's **Button Type** is set to **Add to Cart**. This setting allows customers to add multiple products to their cart prior to checkout. It should be noted that the **Buy Now** option is only compatible with PayPal and Google Checkout. With the **Buy Now** setting enabled, shoppers will be taken directly to the payment processor of your choosing when they click the button located next to any item. The setting that you choose for your store's button type will depend upon your circumstances and personal preferences. Also, in this area, you have the option of hiding your **Add to Cart** button. By default, this option is set to **No**, and it should retain that setting unless you feel the need to remove the selling capabilities from your store. If you were to set this option to **Yes**, then shoppers wouldn't be able to purchase any items until you once again return this setting to **No**. You will find that the **Yes** setting is ideal for those times when you need to perform maintenance on your store.

The **Product Settings** area is next and nearly all of the options in this section may be configured depending upon your preferences. The only option that you should be sure to set to **No** is the **Show Postage and Packaging** setting. Since nothing will be entered in the local and international shipping textboxes when creating your inventory, the **Postage and Packaging** section of your product description area will incorrectly display free shipping when the postage is, in fact, calculated using the settings entered in the **Shipping** area of the plugin. Setting this option to **No** will prevent this erroneous free shipping from being displayed on your store.

Now, move on to the **Product Page Settings** area. The **Catalog View** setting has three options, but, at this point, you can only select **Default View**. To use the other two options, you must purchase additional upgrades. Next is the **Theme** option. This is where things might get a bit confusing. In WordPress, when you think of a theme, you naturally think of the overall design of your website. Well, in this instance, the term "theme" doesn't refer to an overall design. These themes are only responsible for altering the appearance of the product area of your store. This means that you will still need a WordPress theme in order to change the style of your store. Now that that has been explained, select the theme that you would like to use to style your store's product area. Nearly all of the remaining settings on this screen can be configured to your preferences, so scroll through each of these options and make any changes that you like.

Once you reach the end of the page, you will find the **Comment Settings** section. Here you can choose to enable the **Use IntenseDebate Comments** feature, which you can learn more about at `http://intensedebate.com/`. If you choose to enable this setting, then you will need to enter your IntenseDebate account ID into the textbox and choose whether comments should be displayed for all products or per product. If you don't have an `IntenseDebate` account, then you will need to create one prior to enabling this feature.

After you've finished configuring all of these settings, click **Update** to save your changes. Now, it's time to visit the **Admin Settings** screen.

Admin

Navigate to **Store | Settings | Admin** to begin configuring the options in this area. If you're only planning on selling physical products, then disregard the first two options. However, if you will be selling digital goods, in the **Max downloads per file** textbox, enter the maximum number of times that a buyer will be permitted to download a purchased product. Digital sellers should leave **Lock downloads to IP address** as is because changing this setting could allow buyers to share their download link with others.

Check MIME types on file uploads should remain enabled, so turn your attention to the **Purchase Log Email** setting. In the textbox, type the email address (or addresses separated by commas) where you want sales notifications to be sent. Unfortunately, sales notifications are sent when shoppers are directed to your payment processor. That means that you may receive a payment notification even if a customer changes their mind before completing the sale.

In the **Purchase Receipt - Reply Address** textbox, enter the email address that you want buyers to see when they receive email from your store. Then, in the **Purchase Receipt - Reply Name** textbox, type the name of your store since this will be who messages to your customers will appear to be from.

Next is the **Terms and Conditions** text area. If you have special terms that you want your customers to agree to prior to purchase, enter them here. Otherwise, leave this section blank. It should be noted that this feature isn't compatible with Google Checkout, so customers using that payment method won't be given the option of reviewing your terms.

All of the remaining settings can be left at their defaults, so scroll to the bottom of the page and then click **Update**.

Shipping

To begin configuring the shipping options for your store, go to **Store | Settings | Shipping**. The **General Settings** area is up first. By default, **Use Shipping** is set to **Yes**. If you plan on selling digital products only, then this should be set to **No**. Otherwise, leave this option at its default. Next is the **Base Zipcode/Postcode** textbox where you must enter the appropriate postal code for your region. This is especially important for sellers in the U.S. because this information is required in order for the USPS and UPS shipping calculators to function properly. As you can see, the **ShipWire Settings** are set to **No**. This setting should only be changed if you use this order fulfillment company to manage your shipments. By default, **Enable Free Shipping Discount** is set to **No**. If you would like to offer your customers free shipping after a certain dollar amount is spent, you will need to enable this feature. If you set this to **Yes**, a textbox will appear where you will need to enter the dollar amount that must be spent in order for free shipping to be applied.

Next, you must decide which shipping calculation method you would like to use in your store. Each shipping calculator has it own set of options that must be configured, if selected. These configuration areas can be accessed by hovering over your desired shipping calculator and then clicking the **Edit** link that appears. The configuration process for each calculator is quite simple. Just enter the required information and then click the **Update** button located in that area. After you've finished configuring all of the options on this screen, click the **Update** button located in the **Shipping Modules** section of the screen.

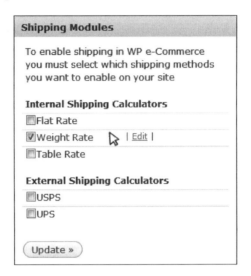

Payment Options

You won't have much of an online store if you're unable to accept payments. That's where the **Gateway Options** screen comes in. Click on **Store | Settings | Payment Options** to find all of the settings that you will need to configure in order to accept payments. By default, in the **General Settings** area, **Manual Payment/Test Gateway** is the only payment option enabled. You will, therefore, need to select each of the payment gateways that you would like to make available to your customers. After you've selected all of your desired payment gateways, click **Update**.

 A **Business** or **Premier** account is required in order for the **Paypal IPN** feature to function.

Next, you must configure each payment gateway separately. To do this, select a payment gateway from the drop-down menu on the right hand side of your screen. Enter the required information into this configuration section and then click the **Update** button located in that area to save your changes. Repeat this process for each payment gateway that you wish to offer in your store.

Checkout

For now, you can bypass the **Import** settings screen and, instead, proceed to the **Checkout Options** area, which is the final screen in the **Settings** section of this plugin. To access these options navigate to **Store | Settings | Checkout**. Once there, in the **Misc Checkout Options** area, you must first decide if you want to force shoppers to register prior to purchase. By default, this option is set to **No**. You may, however, change it to **Yes**. If you decide to enable this setting, then you will need to open a new browser window and then navigate to **Settings | General**. Once there, tick the checkbox next to **Anyone can register** and then click **Save Changes**. On the **Checkout Options** screen, configure the remaining **Misc Checkout Options** according to your preferences.

Next, in the **Form Fields** area, you can customize the forms that are displayed during checkout as well as decide which pieces of information should be included in the `purchase` log. You can even designate some fields as being mandatory or delete them entirely. All of these settings should be fine as they are, but you can certainly make any changes that you feel are required. You can also click **Add New Form Field** if you would like to have additional fields displayed to your customers. Once you're finished configuring the settings on this screen, click **Save Changes**.

Upgrades

The **Upgrades** screen contains descriptions of the various purchasable WP e-Commerce modules and plugins along with a link to `http://getshopped.org/extend/premium-upgrades/` where you can buy each one. Should you install an upgrade and then move to a new domain, you can also visit this page to reset your API key. This will allow you to install the upgrade at your new domain without issues.

Gold modules and plugins for additional features and specialized selling

With all of this talk about upgrades, it's time to turn your attention to the additional modules and plugins that can be installed to add even more features to a store using WP e-Commerce. The free version of this plugin is certainly filled with features, but there's still more that it can do with the installation of a few upgrades.

Gold Cart and Grid Module

While the free version of WP e-Commerce can do quite a lot, the Gold Cart allows you to do even more. With this module you can:

- Display your products differently
- Upload multiple images
- Provide a product search feature
- Accept payments using additional payment gateways

Even if you aren't interested in the features provided by the Gold Cart you may still need to purchase and install it. That's because nearly all of these upgrades require that the Gold Cart is installed in order to use them.

Once you've purchased the Gold Cart, you will need to install it using the instructions provided in the ZIP file. Now, from the **Dashboard**, navigate to **Store | Upgrades**. At the top of the screen you will see a **Gold Cart Activation** box. Enter your username and API key into the appropriate fields and then click **Submit**.

With that, all of the Gold Cart features will now be available to you. Unfortunately, these additional options are scattered throughout the various WP e-Commerce configuration screens. For example, if you would like to enable grid view, then you must return to **Store | Settings | Presentation** where this option will now be available to you. Take some time to explore the configuration screens and to investigate all of the additional options that are now available on your store.

DropShop

If you previously installed the Gold Cart, then you can also add on **DropShop**. What this upgrade does is add an AJAX driven drag-and-drop shopping cart to the footer area of your store.

Follow the instructions provided with this upgrade to install it on your store. To enable the DropShop feature, navigate to **Store | Settings | Presentation** and then scroll down to the **Shopping Cart Settings** configuration area. There you will find that the formerly grayed out DropShop option is now available. Ticking the radio button next to this setting will reveal some additional options. Now, you must decide whether you would prefer to have DropShop displayed on every page or only on product pages. Next, you may opt to leave **Use light Dropshop style** selected or, instead, choose either **Use dark Dropshop style** or **Crafty**. Once you've finished configuring these settings, click **Update**.

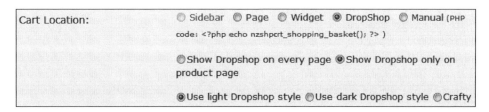

Even with all of that done, DropShop still won't appear on your store. That's because you now need to integrate it into your WordPress theme. To do this, you must add the following code immediately after the opening body tag:

```
<div id="page_container">
```

Next, open your footer template and look for the following line:

```
<?php wp_footer(); ?>
```

Once you locate that line of code, place a closing div tag just before it. With that, **DropShop** should now appear when customers visit your store.

MP3 Audio Player

The **MP3 Audio Player** is a handy addition for musicians and bands because it allows you to upload a preview of your music which customers can sample before buying. Once again, the Gold Cart is required to implement this feature.

After installation, visit the **Display Products** screen by clicking on **Store | Products**. Once there, scroll down to the **Product Download** area where you will find your newly available MP3 uploader. In the future, when adding audio products, you can use this uploader to submit previews.

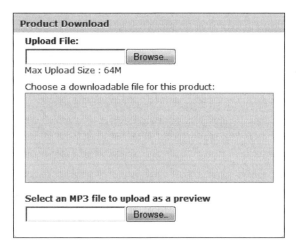

Members Only module

With a combination of the WP e-Commerce plugin, the Gold Cart module, and the **Members Only** module, it's possible to create a subscription site rather than just build a standard e-commerce store. Now, while it's possible to build a membership site using this combination of software, there's another plugin out there that's specifically designed for this purpose. Since it's dedicated to creating subscription sites, it would be best to use it should you ever wish to create a website of this type. This plugin is called **WishList Member** and it's the subject of *Chapter 9*.

That being said, if you're determined to use WP e-Commerce for your subscription site, then you must have the Gold Cart enabled and then install the **Members Only** module using the instructions found in the ZIP file. Next, click on **Store | Upgrades**. There you will find an API entry box where you must submit your username and API key for the **Members Only** module.

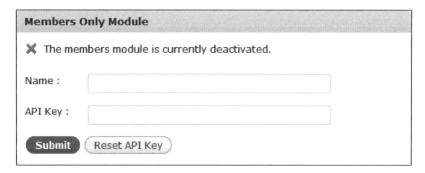

Once the **Members Only** module has been activated, you must then configure a few settings in order to offer subscription-based content from your website. First, navigate to **Settings | General**. On this screen you need to enable the **Anyone can register** setting, if you haven't already done so. This must be done because visitors need to be logged in to purchase a subscription and they certainly can't log in if they're unable to register in the first place. Next, click on **Store | Settings | Checkout**. If you haven't already enabled the **Users must register before checking out** option, do so now. Having done that, you can move on to creating a members only page or post.

To begin, create a new page or post that you want only subscribers to see. After creating the content of this page or post, scroll to the bottom of the screen and then tick the checkbox next to **Members Only**.

Next, navigate to **Store | Products**. Here you need to create a new product to serve as a subscription package. When you reach the **Categories and Tags** section, be sure to tick the checkbox for the category where you previously placed your subscription content. Once you reach the bottom of the screen, you will find the **Membership Control** settings. Tick the checkbox next to **Is this product a membership?** and then enter the number of days that the subscription will last. Lastly, click **Add New Product** to save your subscription.

NextGEN Gallery plugins

The **NextGEN Gallery Buy Now Buttons** upgrade is designed to work in conjunction with the **NextGEN Gallery** plugin. After installing both plugins, you will then be able to add either a Google Checkout button or a PayPal Buy Now button next to the images in your NextGEN gallery. This is ideal for photographers and painters who would like to sell their work online.

Since the NextGEN Gallery plugin is required in order to use this upgrade, begin by reading up on what NextGEN Gallery can do. After it's been installed, you will then need to create a gallery before beginning to work with the NextGEN Gallery Buy Now Buttons plugin.

Introducing NextGEN Gallery

The NextGEN Gallery plugin provides a way to include a fully-integrated image gallery on a website. It also offers the ability to create a Flash slideshow. The Flash slideshow, however, requires extra configuration. To implement the Flash option, you must visit the **Longtail Video** website at `http://www.longtailvideo.com/players/jw-image-rotator/`, download the JW Image Rotator, and then place the `imagerotator.swf` file into your WordPress `uploads` directory.

Setting up and configuring NextGEN Gallery

After installing and activating the NextGEN Gallery plugin you should notice a **Gallery** menu that has been added to the **Dashboard**. Click on **Gallery** to be taken to the **NextGEN Gallery Overview** screen. Once there, click **Upload pictures** to be taken to the **Add new gallery** screen. In the **New Gallery** textbox, type a name for your image gallery and then click **Add gallery**.

Now, click the **Upload Images** tab and then browse for images that you would like to add to your newly created gallery. Once you've finished browsing and selecting images, click **Upload Images**.

You can now add a gallery to any page or post by using one of two tags. If you would like to display your images as a gallery, then you should use the following tag. Be sure to replace x with the ID number of the gallery that you would like to display.

```
[nggallery id=x]
```

If you would prefer to display these images as a slideshow, then you should use the following tag instead. Once again, you must replace x with the appropriate ID number. In this instance, you must also replace width and height with numerical values.

```
[slideshow id=x w=width h=height]
```

With a gallery created and displaying on your store, you can now move on to installing and configuring the NextGEN Buy Now Buttons upgrade. It should be noted that the NextGEN Gallery plugin contains many, many additional configuration screens that you should explore if you plan to implement it and the NextGEN Buy Now Buttons plugin on your store. While the screens that you've visited are sufficient to get you started, you will find that the others allow you to manage every imaginable aspect of your image galleries.

Introducing NextGEN Gallery Buy Now Buttons

As previously mentioned, the NextGEN Gallery Buy Now Buttons plugin is meant to be used in conjunction with NextGEN Gallery. After this plugin has been installed new settings will be added to the NextGEN Gallery configuration area that you can use to sell images from your store.

Setting up and configuring NextGEN Gallery Buy Now Buttons

Since the installation instructions provided with NextGEN Gallery Buy Now Buttons are lacking, the steps that you need to follow are being provided here, so that you will be able to easily add this plugin to your site:

First, extract the contents of the ZIP file. Then, upload the `nextGen-BuyNow` folder to the `wp-content/plugins` directory. Now, move the `templates` folder from `nextGen-BuyNow` to the `nextgen-gallery/view` directory.

After the plugin has been activated, a new link will be added to the **Gallery** menu. You will need to access this link in order to configure this plugin, so click on **Gallery | Buy Now**. You will then be taken to the **Buy Now** settings screen. Once there, enter your information for either Google Checkout or PayPal and then click **Update**.

Now you must add prices to the images included within your gallery. To do this click **Gallery | Manage Gallery** and then click on the text link for your gallery. On this screen you will see a textbox, labeled **Price**, that appears next to every image. Enter a price into the textbox for each of the images that you want to sell and then click **Save Changes**.

Ideally, Buy Now buttons should now appear alongside the images in your gallery. For some, however, that may not be the case. In the WP e-Commerce support forum, some users have posted messages because the Buy Now buttons aren't visible after they completed all of the necessary steps. Unfortunately, there's no known fix at this time. If you discover that the Buy Now buttons aren't visible on your site, consult the forum as a solution may become available at any time.

Adding products to your store

At this point, you're now ready to begin adding products to your store. If you have a CVS file containing your products, then you can easily import them into your store. If you don't have a file of this type, then you will need to manually add each item.

Manually adding products

To begin, click on **Store | Products**. This will take you to the **Display Products** screen. It's here that you will be able to manually add new products and edit those that already exist. On the left hand side of your screen all of the products in inventory will be display. On the right, you will see a form where you can enter new products.

WP e-Commerce is capable of selling both physical and digital products. As you add the first item to your store, you're going to concentrate on the settings required for a physical product. Once you go through the process of adding a physical item it should be easy for you to apply what you've learned to the process of adding a digital product should you wish to do so.

When adding items, a product name, price, and category are all that's required. You can, however, add much more additional information as well.

To add your first product, enter a descriptive name for the item into the textbox labeled **Product Name**. If your product has an SKU, enter it in the **Stock Keeping Unit** textbox. Next, enter the retail price of your product into the **Price** textbox. For now, the textbox labeled **Sale Price** should be left empty because this field is only used if you would like to offer the product at a special discount.

Underneath those input fields you will see a text area where you can enter a description of the item. Next is the **Additional Description** text area. Text entered here will be placed into a collapsible area labeled **More Details**.

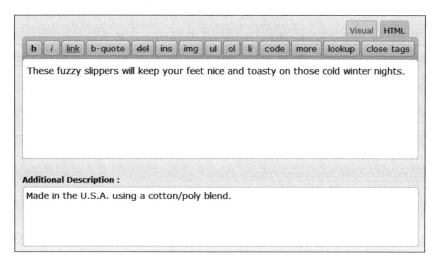

The next configuration area is labeled **Categories and Tags**. Here you should first assign your product to a category and a brand. Next, add a few tags that are applicable to this product. In order to display these tags, you will later need to add a **Products** widget to your store. Doing this will give shoppers an additional way to browse through your store's products.

Price and Stock Control is the next section that you will see. If the product that you're offering is non-taxable in your area, then tick the checkbox next to **Do not include tax**. Also, if you only have a few of this item in inventory, tick the checkbox next to **I have a limited number of this item in stock**. Then, enter the quantity that you have in stock into the **Stock Qty** textbox that appears. You may also want to tick the checkbox next to **If this product runs out of stock set status to Unpublished & email site owner**, but whether you choose to enable that setting will depend upon your own preferences.

All of the remaining settings found here can be very useful, but, for right now, they can be left at their default settings. Once you enter the actual management phase of your store, however, you should explore these options since they will allow you to offer volume discounts, specify a custom tax rate to be applied to certain products, and enable donation selling, which allows customers to set the product's price.

Now, move on to the **Shipping Details** section. First, enter the weight of your item and then select the appropriate unit of measurement from the drop-down menu. Next, enter your product's measurements into the **Height**, **Width**, and **Length** textboxes. Also, be sure to select the correct unit of measurement from the drop-down menus associated with each of these settings.

Since you already configured sitewide shipping settings, you don't need to enter anything in the local and international shipping textboxes. Underneath those settings you will notice an option labeled **Disregard Shipping for this product**. If you ever want to offer an item with free shipping and would prefer not to create a coupon code or, if you're selling a digital item, then this setting will certainly come in handy. For now, however, it should remain disabled.

Next is **Variation Control**. If this product includes variations, then select the appropriate variation set. If you previously ticked the checkbox next to **I have a limited number of this item in stock**, you can further specify just how many items you have in stock by entering the number of each variant that you have in your inventory into the **Stock** textbox next to each one. If you click the image located in the **More** column, you can also specify a weight for each variant if it happens to differ from the weight that you previously entered.

Now, it's time to move on to the **Advanced Options** section. In the **Custom Meta** area, add a name and description for this product into the appropriate fields. To make things simple, you could just copy and paste the text that you previously entered at the top of the **Products** screen. Providing meta details will help shoppers find your store in search results since the search engine spiders will be able to use these pieces of information to better index your store. Leave **Publish** set to **Yes** and then move on to **Personalization Options**.

If you would like to make it possible for shoppers to personalize this product, then enable either one or both of these settings. If not, leave them disabled. It's unlikely that your product is actually for sale on another website, so you should be able to ignore the **Off Site Product Link** area and, instead, move on to the **Product Images** section.

When selling online, an image can prove to be invaluable since it's the only way that shoppers can get a clear idea about an item's appearance. Click **Select Files**, locate a product image on your hard drive, and then upload it to your store. Various edits can now be performed using the collapsible **Thumbnail Settings** panel. To reveal this settings area, hover over the product image and then click on the **Edit** link that appears. From this area, you can perform several actions on the image. The default thumbnail setting should be fine, but you can perform edits or select a different setting, if you prefer.

The next section that you will see is the **Product Download** area. This section only applies to products sold as downloads. Since you're currently adding a physical item, you can ignore this section. If you previously added the Members Only module, then you will next see the **Membership Control** settings area. Since you're adding a physical product, these settings can also be ignored. So, click **Add New Product** to place this product into your store's inventory.

Importing products

Click **Store | Settings | Import** to visit the **Import Products CVS** screen. If you would like to import your products using a comma delimited text file, this is the place to do it.

The import feature built into WP e-Commerce is very basic and, unfortunately, it currently doesn't allow you to import any images and variations associated with your products. That means that you will have to manually add these images and variations to your products after importing them into your store.

Click **Browse** to locate and then select the file that you would like to import from your computer. Now, click **Import**. After the file has been imported, you aren't finished just yet. That's because you need to perform some additional configurations, so that the content found in each column is assigned to the correct field.

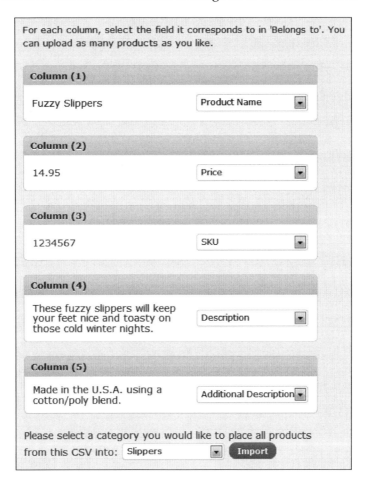

For example, if you were adding the **Fuzzy Slippers** to your store, you would need to select **Product Name** from the drop-down menu associated with the column that contains the name of this product. The column that holds the cost of this item needs to be assigned to the **Price** field, so **Price** must be selected from the drop-down menu found in that area. Continue this process until all of your imported columns have been assigned to the correct field.

With that finished, you must next select the category where you would like these products to be placed. To do that, just select the category from the drop-down menu and then click **Import**.

Customizing the appearance of your store

When it comes to the design of your store, you have a couple options. WP e-Commerce can be integrated into most WordPress themes, so you can search for and install a theme as normal. There are also a few WordPress themes built specifically to be used with this plugin. So, if you want a theme that comes already integrated with various WP e-commerce features, then that's the way to go.

Integrating WP e-Commerce into an existing theme

As previously mentioned, the WP e-Commerce plugin is compatible with most WordPress themes. Since most themes are built for blogging rather than e-commerce, you will probably find that this route requires some customization on your part. Luckily, this customization process shouldn't be too difficult since the developers of this plugin offer widgets, shortcodes, and PHP tags that can be used to enhance a site in order to create an e-commerce experience.

Widgets

As any WordPress user knows, widgets are a handy way to easily customize the content of your site. WP e-Commerce makes use of this feature inherent to WordPress by offering a set of widgets specific to the plugin. These widgets include the following:

- **Product Donations**
- **Latest Products**
- **Price Range**
- **Product Categories**
- **Product Tags**
- **Product Specials**
- **Shopping Cart**

With the use of these widgets you can do things like highlight products that are currently on sale or display a product tag cloud all with just a few clicks. Visit **Appearance | Widgets** to enable any of these widgets on your store.

Shortcodes and template tags

Shortcodes and template tags are another way that WP e-Commerce makes it possible to configure the look, feel, and functionality of your store. While they're useful, they aren't quite as simple to implement as widgets. To make use of these features you must either paste a shortcode into a post or page, or include the appropriate template tag in a template file. With these pieces of code you will be able to do things like display the shopping cart wherever you like or place a group of products on a page or post.

You can visit `http://getshopped.org/resources/docs/design-and-layout/shortcodes-and-tags/` where the developers of WP e-Commerce offer information about the shortcodes and template tags that are currently available for use. Should you ever wish to customize your store, just visit their website to see what you can accomplish with a few small pieces of code.

Adding shortcodes

Now that you know what shortcodes can do, you should walk through the process of adding one to a post so that you will be able to get an idea of how it's done. For this example, suppose that you want to feature a particular item in a post. To begin, click on **Store | Products**. On the left-hand side of the **Products** screen, click the name of the product that you would like to feature. Your screen will then refresh and the **Edit Product** area for this product will appear. To find all of the shortcodes associated with this item, click the circular blue information icon that's located next to the **Product Name** textbox. This will cause a window to appear that contains a variety of shortcodes and template tags. Copy the shortcode, located underneath **Display Product Shortcode**, to a text editor.

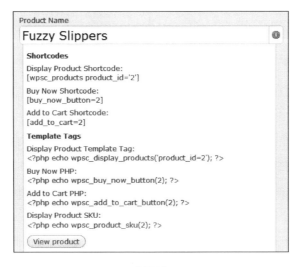

Now, click on **Posts | Add New**. Enter a title for this post and then, in the text area, paste the shortcode that you copied earlier, along with any other additional text that you would like to appear in this post. Categorize this post and add tags, if desired, then click **Publish**.

A post highlighting this one particular product will now appear on your store. As you can see, shortcodes are an excellent way to add various things to both the posts and pages that you publish to your site.

Adding template tags

Shortcodes and widgets are definitely the better way to go about adding various elements to your site, because template tags require you to make edits to your theme's files. If you really want to use template tags, however, here is how you go about it.

For the purposes of this example, suppose that you would like to add a link to the shopping cart in the header of your site. First, open `header.php`. Then, paste `<?php echo nzshpcrt_shopping_basket(); ?>` where you would like the link to the shopping cart to appear. Save `header.php` and then upload it to your server.

With that template tag in place, a link to your store's shopping cart will now be hardcoded into the header area of your site.

Starting fresh with a WP e-Commerce-friendly theme

If you want to install a theme that's specifically designed for selling, then a WP e-Commerce-friendly theme is the way to go. These themes have been designed to work with this plugin, which means that they make the most of the features that WP e-Commerce has to offer. When it comes to themes of this sort, you will find that your options are a bit limited, because very few developers have created themes with WP e-Commerce in mind. There are, however, two very good themes that are both freely available for download.

Free themes

The **Crafty Cart** theme, found at `http://www.billionstudio.com/news/free-crafty-cart-theme/`, is an e-commerce WordPress theme that was created by Billion Studios for the readers at King Cart. This theme was designed for selling t-shirts and handmade items, but it can easily be used for any other product that you plan on selling. The design is visually suited to a craft store, but those well-versed in CSS can easily customize the theme so that it's better suited to the products sold in their store.

SimpleCart(js), available at `http://www.chris-wallace.com/2009/07/17/simplecartjs-a-free-wp-e-commerce-thematic-child-theme/`, is a **Thematic Child Theme** that relies on the WP e-Commerce plugin for its e-commerce functionality. Features of this theme include AJAX cart functionality, a grid layout for products, and a flexible color scheme.

Putting products on the homepage

Since you're building an e-commerce website, you probably won't want blog posts scrolling across your front page. Instead, you will most likely want a selection of products to appear there. This can easily be accomplished by altering a few settings within WordPress.

First, navigate to **Settings | Reading**. Once there, in the **Front page displays** settings section, tick the radio button next to **A static page**. Then, for the **Front Page** setting, select **Products Page** from the drop-down menu. If you don't want to include a blog on your site, click **Save Changes**.

If you do want to include a blog on your store, open a new window and then navigate to **Pages | Add New**. Next, enter a name for this page, place it into a category, and then click **Publish**. Now, return to the **Reading Settings** screen. In the **Front page displays** section, look for the **Posts page** setting. From that drop-down menu, select the page that you just created. Then, click **Save Changes**.

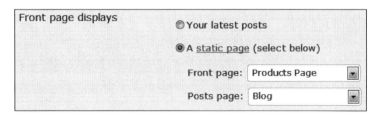

With these settings in place, the homepage of your website will contain products just like a standard e-commerce store. In addition, you will still be able to keep visitors up-to-date on the latest happenings at your store using the blog that you relocated to a different section of your site.

Making one or more purchases to test the system

With your store complete, there's just one more thing to do before it's ready to be unveiled. At this point, you need to make one or more test purchases to ensure that payments are being successfully processed. How many test purchases you make will depend upon the number of payment processors you plan to make available to your customers. To do this, you will need to make your purchase(s) using the sandbox provided by your payment processor(s).

If you don't currently have a sandbox account with the payment processor(s) of your choice, you will need to create one before you proceed. After your sandbox account has been created, perform any necessary configurations before clicking on **Store | Settings | Payment Options** to return to the **Gateway Options** screen.

Once you arrive at this screen, reconfigure the settings for your payment processor(s) if they require you to provide special information so that your sandbox account will be used when you make a test purchase. At the very least, you will need to tick the checkbox so that test mode is enabled.

After those configurations have been completed and saved, visit the frontend of your store and then make a purchase. If you're planning to use more than one payment processor on your store, then you will need to make a test purchase using each of the payment processors that are available on your site.

If this testing process is successful, you can reconfigure the payment gateway settings for your payment processor(s) if you previously changed them. Also, be sure to disable the test mode setting. Having done that, you will be ready to launch your store. If this testing process failed, read back through this chapter to ensure that all of the necessary steps were correctly followed. If you're still unable to successfully complete this test after confirming that your store is configured correctly, visit the WP e-Commerce Support Forums at `http://www.getshopped.org/forums/` for assistance.

Summary

With the components and functionality that you have at your disposal, it's now possible for you to begin selling online. With the right products, a lot of promotion, and a little bit of luck you should find that your online store is soon making sales.

Use the marketing methods provided with WP e-Commerce as a starting point and then implement several of your own. Spread the word of your store far and wide, so that everywhere online shoppers search, they can't help but stumble upon information about your shop.

Your online store certainly won't become the next **Amazon.com** overnight, but this plugin will undoubtedly give you a start toward becoming a presence in the online marketplace. Once that happens, anything is possible.

In this chapter, you learned how to use one very powerful free plugin to transform WordPress into an e-commerce destination. You were also shown how to use optional upgrades to add additional functionality to your store.

In the next chapter, you will learn how to create a classified ads website, centered around a particular locality, where users can register and then post ads to the site.

4
Project 4: Building a Local Classified Ads Website

Not too long ago an unlikely website took the Internet by storm. This website was, and still is, unassuming and quite simplistic and yet visitors flock to it in droves each and every day. This Internet sensation is **Craigslist** and its popularity doesn't show signs of fading any time soon. No one could've ever predicted the immense popularity that this simple classified ads website would enjoy and yet it's one of the Internet's most trafficked destinations.

While it would certainly be difficult to rival this powerhouse, it's not impossible to compete in the classified ads arena. The trick is to fill a need that Craigslist doesn't meet. While this site may allow visitors to localize their version of the site, it doesn't provide classified ads for all localities. As a matter of fact, it barely scratches the surface when it comes to providing a local option for most countries around the world.

This is a void just waiting to be filled. There are millions of web users out there who would love to discover a truly local option when it comes to a classified ads website and, with WordPress and **ClassiPress**, it's easy to fill this need.

With all of the localities out there, the possibilities are endless. Hundreds of thousands of these classified ads sites could be built for locations all over the world without ever competing with Craigslist. This means that you could draw in traffic and conquer these niches with little to no competition.

In this chapter, you will learn how to:

- Optimally configure WordPress for usage with ClassiPress
- Create ad packs that are priced at different rates
- Accept payments for ad listings using **PayPal** and **Google Checkout**
- Create custom fields to collect information from the people placing ads on your site

- Target your site toward a local market.

- Configure the various plugins included with ClassiPress

- Implement a private messaging system so that users can communicate via your website

- Handle problems caused by deleted ads and 404 errors

Once this project is complete, you will have succeeded in creating a site that's similar to the one shown in the following screenshot:

Introducing ClassiPress

Typically, when you want to add extra functionality to WordPress, you look for a plugin that can do the job. In this case, however, it isn't a particular plugin that's needed. Instead, what is required is a special theme by the name of ClassiPress which is available at `http://wpclassipress.com/`. The developers of ClassiPress have called this theme the "Craiglist of WordPress" which is handy since that's the type of website that you will be trying to emulate.

With WordPress and this theme absolutely anyone can build a classified ads website. ClassiPress is designed for use by both individuals and businesses, so it's the perfect solution for lone web developers or even large corporations. Users can choose to run a dedicated classified ads website or enable the blog feature to run a combination classified ads/blog site.

The features within this theme are numerous. So numerous, in fact, that there are too many to mention. Some of the more noteworthy features, however, should be highlighted to give you an idea of just what this theme can do.

- ClassiPress can be integrated with PayPal and Google Checkout so that you can charge a fee to post ads on your site. It also supports over 20 different currencies which means that users from around the globe should have no trouble localizing this theme to their region of the world

- Once again, ClassiPress makes it easy to build a classified ads website targeted toward a specific region because it comes with support for several different languages. In the **Resources** section, located at `http://wpclassipress.com/resources/`, the developers provide a collection of languages packs. If your language isn't available, then the developers have made it easy for you to change ClassiPress to your local language by simply following the instructions provided on their website at `http://wpclassipress.com/how-to-translate-a-wordpress-theme/`

- A classified ads site will soon falter without numerous visitors placing ads and responding to those that have already been placed. Luckily, ClassiPress was designed with search engine optimization in mind, which will certainly help you as you work to draw visitors in to your website

- The developers of ClassiPress have worked to make your classified ads site look as professional as possible. With features like a user dashboard and a themed login page, your website will look like you paid a developer thousands of dollars to design a features-rich classified ads site

Upon purchase, you will have the ability to receive all future updates to this theme at no additional cost. ClassiPress users can also take advantage of the support forum where the developers work hard to quickly supply an answer to any issues that users may encounter along the way. ClassiPress users also frequently help others troubleshoot their installations, so help should always be forthcoming if you need it.

Now that you've learned some of the things ClassiPress can do, it's time to get started building your classified ads website.

Before you can begin working with ClassiPress, however, you will first need to make some changes to your WordPress installation. Once that's done, you can move on to adding ClassiPress into the mix.

Configuring WordPress

In order to use ClassiPress on your site, a few changes need to be made to the settings found in WordPress. Now's a good time to perform these changes, so that WordPress will be ideally configured for usage with ClassiPress once it has been installed.

Enabling registrations

Once ClassiPress has been installed, it won't be possible for your visitors to post an ad until registrations are enabled in WordPress. To do this, simply click on **Settings | General**. On the **General Settings** screen, in the **Membership** settings area, tick the checkbox next to **Anyone can register**. The default user role should remain set to **Subscriber**, so scroll to the bottom of the page and then click **Save Changes**.

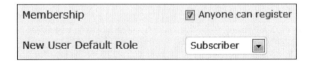

Creating Categories

Before you begin working with ClassiPress, it's important for you to first create the categories and sub-categories that you plan to include on your site. That's because some category-specific settings will be included later on during the configuration of ClassiPress. So, navigate to **Posts | Categories** and then begin adding categories and sub-categories to your site. In addition to adding new categories to your site, you must also rename the **Uncategorized** category. That's because, if this category isn't renamed, it will appear in the **Select a Category** drop-down menu that visitors must use when placing an ad on your site.

Changing your site's permalink structure

If this step isn't performed now, then, immediately after ClassiPress has been activated, a message will appear at the top of your screen to tell you that your site's permalink structure must contain at least /%postname%/ in order for ClassiPress to work properly. Making this necessary configuration now, before ClassiPress has even been installed, will ensure that everything operates smoothly later on.

Click on **Settings | Permalinks** and then, in the **Common Settings** area, tick the radio button next to either **Day and name**, **Month and name**, or **Custom Structure**. If you choose the **Custom Structure** option, then, in the textbox that accompanies this setting, enter **/%postname%/**. Then, click **Save Changes**.

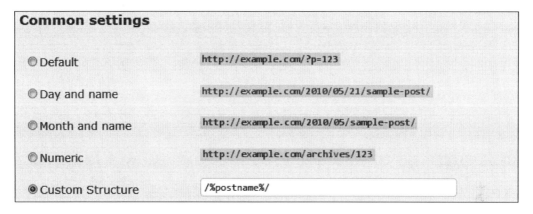

Now that your permalinks have been optimally configured to work with ClassiPress, it's time to move on to configuring the commenting options on your site.

Disabling comments

It's unlikely that you will want to give visitors the option of commenting on the classified ads found on your website. As your website stands now, however, that's exactly what they can do.

To remove this option, click on **Settings | Discussion**. At the top of the screen, in the **Default article settings** area, disable **Allow people to post comments on new articles**. Scroll to the bottom of the page and then click **Save Changes**.

Important information before installing ClassiPress

The process of installing ClassiPress is the same one used for any other WordPress theme. There are, however, a couple of things that you should know before you begin.

When you open the ZIP file, there will be a plugins folder and a `classipress.zip` file inside. The plugins folder should be ignored. Right now, you should install the ClassiPress theme by uploading `classipress.zip` via the **Install Themes** screen.

Setting up and configuring ClassiPress

After ClassiPress was activated, you should've noticed that a **ClassiPress** menu was added to your screen. This menu contains the multi-page configuration area for this theme. The settings located on these screens need to be configured prior to using your classified ads website, so you should work your way through these settings screens until the ClassiPress configuration process is complete.

Settings

There isn't any reason why you need to visit the ClassiPress **Dashboard**, so you can bypass it and, instead, click on **ClassiPress | Settings** to be taken to the **General Settings** screen for this theme. The **Site Configuration** area contains the first group of settings that you will need to configure. First are the **Home Page Layout** and **Color Scheme** settings which can both be configured according to your preferences.

By default, the **Enable Blog** setting is activated. If you want to run a blog on your classified ads site, then this setting should remain enabled. If, however, you would prefer not to blog from this site, then change this setting to **No**. If you decided to include a blog on your site, you will next need to ensure that the **Blog Category ID** setting is correctly configured. To learn the category ID that was assigned to the **Blog** category when it was automatically created by ClassiPress, open a new browser window and then navigate to **Posts | Categories**. On the right side of your screen, you will see the categories that can currently be found on your site. Hover over **Blogs** and then look at the URL that appears in your browser's status bar. You're looking for the number that appears right after `tag_ID=`. Make a note of this number and then look to see what the ID number is for the **Uncategorized** category since this additional piece of information will be important later on. Now, return to the ClassiPress **General Settings** screen. If the ID number that you found for the **Blog** category already appears in the **Blog Category ID** textbox, then no changes need to be made. If these numbers differ, then enter the correct value into the textbox.

Enable Logo is next and, if you have a logo, this setting should remain activated. If you don't have a logo, change this setting to **No**. That will cause your site's title and description to be displayed instead. Next, if **Enable Logo** is set to **Yes**, enter the URL where your website's logo image can be found into the **Web Site Logo** textbox.

The **Feedburner URL** setting is next. If you're planning to use Feedburner's service to host the RSS feed for your website, then this setting must be configured. If you've already added your site's default RSS feed to your **Feedburner** account, then you can simply type your RSS feed's Feedburner URL into the textbox. If you haven't added this site's RSS feed to Feedburner do so now by right-clicking on **Feedburner account** and then opening that link in a new browser window to visit `http://www.feedburner.com`. You will, of course, need a Feedburner account in order to have them host the feed for your site. Feedburner is owned by Google, so, if you already use one of Google's other services, you can use that log in information to access Feedburner. If you don't have an account with Google, you will need to create one now in order to use this service. Once you've logged into Feedburner, complete the necessary steps to burn your feed. When that process is complete, you can return to the ClassiPress **General Settings** screen and then enter the URL of your Feedburner RSS feed into the **Feedburner URL** textbox.

If you plan on incorporating **Twitter** into your site, then the **Twitter Username** setting will been to be configured. If you already have a Twitter account, enter your username into the textbox. If you would like to use this feature, but you don't have a Twitter account, right-click on **Twitter account** and then open that link in a new browser window to visit `http://www.twitter.com`. Once there, complete the sign up process. After your account has been created, return to the **General Settings** screen and then enter your Twitter username into the textbox.

Next is the **Google Maps Key** textbox, which is currently blank. If you don't want to include **Google Maps** as a part of your site, you don't need to do anything in this area and can, instead, move on to the next set of configurations. If you decide that you would like to add Google Maps to your site, then you will need to generate a Google Maps API key, if you don't already have one for this site. Once again, if you don't have a Google account, then you will need to set one up in order to use this feature. As previously mentioned, if you already use another Google service, you can use that account information to log in rather than creating a whole new account.

Either way, you need to right-click on **Google Maps API Key** and then open the link in a new window to be taken to the Google Maps API sign up screen found at `http://code.google.com/apis/maps/signup.html`. Once you're logged in to Google's site, review the information and terms and conditions before entering your URL into the **My website URL** textbox. After clicking **Generate API Key** you will be taken to a thank you screen where you will be provided with your newly acquired Google Maps API key. Copy the API key and then return to the **General Settings** screen. Now, enter the API key into the **Google Maps Key** textbox.

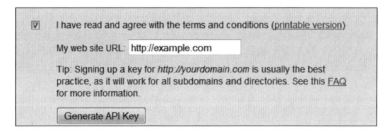

If you previously configured the **Google Maps Key** setting, you must now select your location from the **Google Maps Location** drop-down menu. If your country isn't included on the list, then you can enter it's **maps.google** URL into the **Google Maps Location Other** textbox. Once all of these configurations are complete, and visitors begin posting classified ads on your website, this is what the Google Maps area will look like.

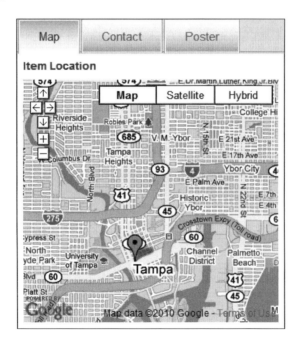

The **Exclude Pages** setting is next and what it does is prevent certain pages from appearing in your site's category links. ClassiPress automatically configures this setting so that certain pages are excluded by default. The category that was formerly known as **Uncategorized** is included in this list, but that will cause a problem. Since you can't delete this category, it will appear on the **Select a Category** drop-down menu when visitors place an ad. That's why you had to rename it earlier. It won't, however, appear among your site's category links since it's being excluded. To solve this problem, remove the ID number that you previously found to be associated with the **Uncategorized** category from the **Exclude Pages** textbox.

The remaining pages shouldn't be removed, but you can certainly add additional pages if you like. Once you start adding additional pages to your site, revisit this setting if you would like to add any of them to this list of excluded pages. For now, however, you can move on to the next setting.

For the **Tracking Code** setting, all you need to do is paste the tracking code for your chosen analytics service into the text area.

Now, you can move on to the **Security Settings** section which only contains one setting. **Back Office Access**, which allows you to specify which users will be able to access the WordPress admin area, is currently set to **All Access**. That, however, is much too lenient, so this setting should be changed to **Admins Only**.

Both of the options found in the **Search Settings** area can configured to your liking. Next is the **Ad Images Options** area. Here you will first encounter the **Allow Ad Images** setting. This is currently set to **Yes**, which is ideal. **Max Images Per Ad** is currently set to **3**, but you can raise or lower that number if you wish. It's best, however, if you don't increase the number by too much because you don't want to put a strain on your server by allowing your users to upload several images. **Max Size Per Image** can be left at it's default, while **Image Resize Type** can be configured according to your preferences.

The settings found in both the **Menu Category Options** and the **Home Page Category Options** areas can all be configured to your liking. Once those have been configured, you then need to begin work on the **Classified Ads Configuration** settings. **Allow Ad Editing, Ad Inquiry Form Requires Login, Allow HTML, Allow Ad Relisting**, and **New Ad Status** are all best left at their default settings, so scroll down until you see **Prune Ads**.

If you intend to charge for ad placements, then set **Prune Ads** to **Yes**. If, however, you will be allowing visitors to submit ads for free then you might prefer to leave them online for SEO purposes. If that's the case, then this option should be set to **No**. Now, in the **Ad Listing Period** textbox, enter the number of days that you would like ads to appear on your site.

Form Validation Language is next. This setting allows you to specify the language that will be used for your submission form error messages. If you want them to be displayed in English, leave the textbox blank. If you would prefer for another language to be used, enter your region's two letter country code into the textbox.

 Translations aren't available for all languages. To see if a translation is available for your language, look in the `/classipress/includes/js/validate/localization` directory or visit `http://wpclassipress.com/resources/`.

The **Email Notifications** and **Advanced Options** sections are next, but no configurations need to be made to the settings found in either area since all of them are already ideally configured. So, proceed to the **Classified Ads Messages** portion of your screen. In the **Home Page Message** text area, edit the welcome message that will appear in the sidebar area of your site's home page. In the **New Ad Message** text area, you can either completely rewrite this message, which will appear at the top of your site's classified ads listing page, or just remove the **Lorem Ipsum** text while leaving the first paragraph in place. Now you will come to the **Terms of Use** text area. You can either use the pre-written terms that are provided with ClassiPress or rewrite them to your liking.

Next is the **Header Ad (468x60)** section. At present your website isn't displaying a 468x60 ad in the header. If you would like to enable this ad placement, choose **Yes** from the **Enable Ad** drop-down menu. Assuming that you've elected to display this ad placement, you will need to provide ad information. If you're using ad code provided by a third-party, such as **Google Adsense**, enter it into the **Ad Code** text area. As an alternative, you can instead enter the URL to an ad image into the **Ad Image URL** textbox and then place the destination link for this ad into the **Ad Destination** textbox.

Now, it's time to configure the **Single Ad (336x280)** settings area. If you would like a 336x280 ad to display underneath each of the classified ads on your website, select **Yes** from the **Enable Ad** drop-down menu. If you plan on displaying this ad spot on your website, then you will need to follow the same steps previously provided for configuring the 468x60 header ad. Once you've completed your configurations, click **Save changes**.

Pricing

Click **ClassiPress | Pricing** to be taken to the next settings screen. On this page, you will first encounter the **Pricing Options** area. Here you must begin by deciding whether you would like to charge for classified ad placements on your website or allow visitors to submit ads for free. If you want to offer free ad placements, leave **Charge for Listing Ads** at it's default. If you want to charge a fee for placing an ad on your site, then select **Yes** from the drop-down menu.

The **Show Featured Ads Slider** is enabled by default and shouldn't be disabled since featured ads purchased by your visitors will appear in this area. **Featured Ads Title Length** also doesn't require any changes.

Featured Ad Price is next. Take a moment to think about how much you would like to charge visitors for a featured ad placement on your website. Once you've arrived at a number, enter it into the textbox. Then, enter the currency symbol for your area of the world into the **Currency Symbol** textbox. Now, from the **Symbol Position** drop-down menu, choose the location where the currency symbol should be positioned. Finally, select your country's currency from the **Collect Payments in** drop-down menu.

The **Pricing Structure** settings area follows and it's here that you will need to use the drop-down menu to choose the method that will be used when charging for classified ad placements. If you decide to go with the **Fixed Price Per Ad** option then you will need to setup at least one ad pack on the next configuration screen. If you chose the **% of Sellers Ad Price** option, then the percentage that you enter into the **% of Sellers Ad Price** textbox, along with the amount that your visitor is selling their item for, will be used to calculate the fee that visitors are charged for their ad placement. For example, suppose that you enter **10** into the **% of Sellers Ad Price** textbox. That means that, if someone were to place an ad in which they're selling an item for $10.00, they would be charged a listing fee of $1.00.

If you select the **Price Per Category** option, you can specify the amount that you would like to charge for ads based upon the category where they will appear. In that case, fees for each of your site's categories need to be entered in the **Price Per Category** area. With this setting, it's possible to charge for ad placements in some categories while offering them for free in others. To offer free ad placements in a particular category, just enter **0** into the textbox associated with that category. Once you've finished configuring these settings, click **Save Changes**.

Price Per Category:					
	For Sale:	0.00	USD	Jobs: 7.00	USD
	Real Estate:	10.00	USD	Vehicles: 4.00	USD

Ad Packs

If you previously selected the **Fixed Price Per Ad** option when configuring the **Pricing Structure**, then you will need to visit this next settings screen to perform additional configurations. If you chose either of the other two options, then you can bypass this screen since ad packs can only be offered with the **Fixed Price Per Ad** pricing model.

To visit this screen, click on **ClassiPress | Ad Packs**. As you can see, ClassiPress includes a default ad pack. You can begin by editing that ad pack and then move on to creating a few of your own. So, in the **Actions** section of the screen, click on the edit icon. That will take you to the **Edit Ad Package** screen where you can make changes to the information found in the **Ad Pack Information** area. Suppose that you would like to offer an ad pack that includes 15 days for $15. In the **Name** textbox enter **15 days for only $15**. Now, enter some descriptive text into the **Description** text area. In the **Price Per Listing** textbox, type **15**. Then enter **15** into the **Number of Days** textbox. **Package Status** should be left set to **active**, so click **Save changes**.

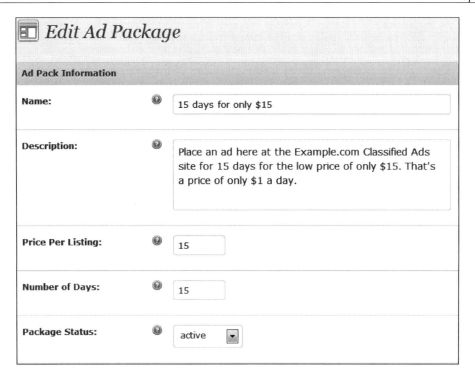

The default ClassiPress ad pack will now have been customized to your liking, which means that you can concentrate on adding a completely new ad pack to your site. At the top of the **Ad Packs** screen, click **Add New** to be taken to the **New Ad Pack** screen. Once again, you will see the **Ad Pack Information** area, but this time it won't contain any content since you're working on adding a brand new ad pack. The process for entering this information is, however, exactly the same as when you previously edited the default ad pack. So, create an ad pack that's to your liking and then, once you've finished, click **Create New Ad Package**.

Continue this process of creating new ad packs until you've added all of the ones that you would like to offer on your site. Once you're finished, click on **ClassiPress | Gateways** to visit the **Payment Gateways** screen.

Gateways

If you aren't planning on charging for ad listings on your site, then there's no reason for you to visit this screen. If, however, you will be charging a listing fee, then you must configure these settings so that payments can be processed on your site.

The PayPal settings area comes first and **Enable PayPal** is currently set to **Yes**. If you would like to offer PayPal as a payment method, then don't make any changes. If you don't want to allow payments to be made by PayPal, then change this setting to **No**. Keep in mind that you must have a PayPal account in order to use this feature. If you don't have a PayPal account, right-click on **PayPal** and then open the link in a new browser window. That will allow you to visit the PayPal website at `http://www.paypal.com/` where you can sign up for an account.

If you left **Enable PayPal** set to **Yes**, then you will need to configure the remaining PayPal-related settings. First, enter the email address associated with your PayPal account into the **PayPal Email** textbox. The **Sandbox Mode** setting is next. Normally, this setting should remain disabled. If you're charging for ad placements, however, then you will need to enable this setting when placing a test ad on your site. Keep in mind that you must have a **PayPal Sandbox** account set up in order to use **Sandbox Mode**. A PayPal Sandbox account can be created at `http://developer.paypal.com/`.

The next section of this screen is devoted to settings related to Google Checkout. If you don't want to offer Google Checkout as a payment option on your site, change the **Enable Google Checkout** setting to **No**. Otherwise, this setting should remain set to **Yes**.

If you choose to include Google Checkout on your site, you will need to provide information from your Google Checkout merchant account in the **Merchant ID** and the **Merchant Key** textboxes. Once again, if you use one of Google's other services, you can use that account information to log in to the Google Checkout site for merchants. Otherwise, you will need to create a new account. Either way, you need to visit the Google Checkout site, so open a new browser window and then navigate to `http://checkout.google.com/sell/`.

Once you've signed in, if you haven't already done so, set up a Google Checkout Merchant account. Once that's finished, click the **Settings** tab and then click the **Integration** link. On this screen, under **Account Information**, you will find your merchant ID and key. Return to the ClassiPress **Gateway** screen and then enter those two pieces of information into the appropriate textboxes.

Sandbox Mode is the last setting found in this area, but no changes need to be made to it at this time. Now that your site's payment gateway settings have been completely configured, click **Save changes**. **Form Layouts** is the next settings screen, but it's best if you don't visit it just yet, so click on **ClassiPress | Custom Fields** instead.

Custom Fields

The fields included on your ad submission form are already numerous. It's quite likely, however, that there might be a field or two that you would like to see included on your website that ClassiPress doesn't include among it's default selection of fields. If that's the case, then you can easily add additional fields on this screen. For example, suppose that you're building a classified ads site that includes a real estate section for realtors in your area to post listings. If that were the case, then you would need to add a field so that these realtors could select how many rooms there are in the property that they're trying to sell.

To add this field, first click on **Add New** to be taken to the **New Custom Field** screen. In the **Field Name** textbox, enter the name that you would like to assign to this field. Following this example, you would enter **Number of Rooms**. Now, in the **Field Description** text area, enter some descriptive text. From the **Field Type** drop-down menu, choose what type of entry method should be used for your new field. In this case, it would be best to select drop-down menu. Making that selection will cause the **Field Values** textbox to appear. In this textbox, enter a comma-separated list of the values that you would like to include in your drop-down menu. In this case, that would be a list of numbers for the realtors to choose from. Once you've finished entering values, click **Create New Field**.

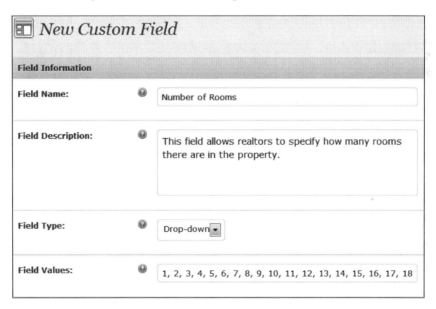

The custom field that you just created will then be added to the list of fields available for usage on your site's ad submission form. This field, however, doesn't currently appear anywhere else on your website. That's because the custom fields that you create must be added to a form layout in order for them to be visible on your website. Before that process is addressed, however, you must first make some changes on the **Custom Fields** screen to begin localizing your website.

	Name	Type	Description	Modified	Actions
1.	**Number of Rooms**	drop-down	This field allows realtors to specify how many rooms there are in the property.	May 24, 2010 2:50 pm by hwallace	

Creating a localized Custom Field

Even if you're quite happy with the selection of fields supplied by default, you must still perform a few actions on this screen so that your classified ads site will be targeted toward a particular region. In this instance, you don't need to create a new field, instead, you need to edit some of the ones that already exist. If you look at the list of available fields you will see that some are location-specific. They are **Region**, **City**, **State**, **Country** and **Zip/Postal Code**.

As you can see, when you look at the description for some of these listings, they state that they're "Needed on your forms for Google maps to work best". That means that you must include at least one of these fields in order for Google Maps to be displayed along with your classified ad listings.

There are several ways that you could go about editing these location-based fields, so that your site becomes localized. How you approach the process will depend upon the location that you're targeting as well as the fact that certain fields must be included on your ad submission form in order for Google Maps to appear. Here's an example of one possible way to go about localizing your site.

Imagine that you're targeting your site toward the residents of west central Florida. First, click on the edit icon associated with the **Region** field. Then, when you get to the **Edit Custom Field** screen, replace all of the text in the **Field Values** textbox with localities specific to that region. So, for this example, you would need to enter **Citrus County**, **Hernando County**, **Pasco County**, **Pinellas County**, and so on into the textbox. Once you've finished performing these edits, click **Save changes**.

Now, click the edit icon associated with the **State** field. On the **Edit Custom Field** screen, remove every state except for **Florida** and then click **Save changes**.

Now it's time to return to the **Forms Layouts** screen that you previously skipped, so click on **ClassiPress | Form Layouts**.

Form Layouts

The **Form Layouts** screen is quite useful, because it allows you to make several customizations to your site. From here, you can do all of the following:

- Create a customized ad submission form that's used sitewide
- Create a collection of category-specific ad submission forms
- Add the custom form fields that you previously created to your site's ad submission form(s)
- Complete the final step that must be performed in order to localize your site

The actions that you choose to perform on this screen will partially depend upon your own preferences and the design of your classified ads site.

Currently, your website is setup so that one form is being used to process all of the ad submissions on your site. If your site doesn't contain any categories that require information that's unique to them, then using one ad submission form is fine. If, however, you have categories that require specific information to be provided, then it would be better if you created additional ad submission forms. Either way, you will need to perform configurations on this screen in order to localize your site. Also if you previously create any custom fields then you will need to add those to your ad submission form(s).

Creating a Sitewide Ad Submission Form

To implement a **Sitewide Ad Submission Form** on your site, click **Add New.** On the **New Form Layout** page enter **Sitewide Ad Submission Form** into the **Form Name** textbox. Next, enter a description for this form into the **Form Description** text area. In the **Available Categories** area, select every category except for **Blog**. Now, click **Save changes**.

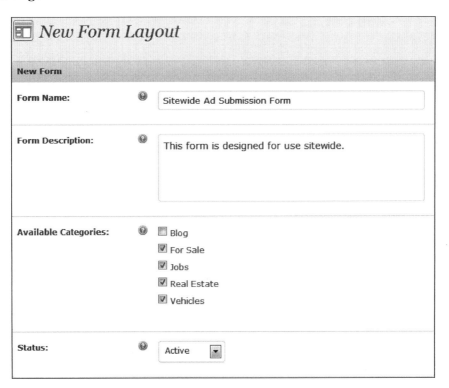

Creating category-specific Ad Submission Forms

Rather than using one ad submission form on your website, you may find it beneficial to have a collection of them instead if some, or all, of your categories require unique information to be collected. The **Real Estate** category that was previously mentioned is a perfect example of a category that would require it's own ad submission form. That's because this category requires fields to collect pieces of information that aren't needed by any other category.

To create an ad submission form for this category, click on **Add New**. On the **New Form Layout** screen, you need to follow the same process used when creating a **Sitewide Ad Submission Form** with one exception. In this instance, when you're configuring the **Available Categories** area, only the **Real Estate** category should be selected.

Repeat this process for all of the categories on your site that require unique information to be collected. Once you've finished creating your category-specific ad submission forms, you may find that a few categories remain that would be better suited to a sitewide form. If that's the case, then just create another form to be used with these categories. Then, when you reach the **Available Categories** settings area, assign these remaining categories to this form.

Localizing the Ad Submission Form(s)

How you go about performing the final configurations to localize your site will depend upon whether you previously created a collection of category-specific ad submission forms or if you, instead, will be using one form to process all of the ad submissions on your site.

If you created a sitewide form, click on its edit form layout icon. If you created several category-specific forms, click the edit form layout icon associated with the first form on your screen. Once you arrive at the **ClassiPress Form Builder** page, tick the checkbox next to the **Region** field that you previously localized and then click **Add Fields to Form Layout**. Next, in the **Form Preview** area, tick the checkbox next to this field to designate it as being required.

Available Fields		
Field Name	**Type**	
☑ Region	drop-down	
☐ Size	drop-down	
☐ Feedback	text area	
☐ Number of Rooms	drop-down	
Add Fields to Form Layout		

Now it's time to remove the **Country** field from the ad submission form. So, click the remove from layout icon associated with that field.

There's just one more step that you must complete before your configurations on this screen are complete. In the **Order** column, use the drop-down menu to assign a number to each field. This number will determine the order in which each of these fields appears on your ad submission form. Once that's done, click **Save Changes**.

If you created more than one ad submission form, then you will need to repeat this process until all of your forms have been localized.

Adding Custom Fields to your form(s)

Adding the custom fields that you previously created to your form(s) is quite easy. Just click on the edit form layout icon associated with the form that you would like to edit. On the **ClassiPress Form Builder** screen, in the **Available Fields** area, tick the checkbox next to the field that you would like to add and then click **Add Fields to Form Layout**. Now, use the drop-down menus located in the **Order** column to arrange these fields to your liking. Then, click **Save Changes**. If you have multiple forms on your site, and would like to add custom fields to them as well, then just repeat this process for each form.

Transactions

Depending upon which version of ClassiPress you're using, the features provided on the **Order Transactions** screen may or may not be available to you. Even if you're using a version of ClassiPress that includes access to this screen, there really isn't any reason to visit it at this time since it currently doesn't contain any information. Once visitors begin posting ads on your site, however, you can then visit this area to view information related to your site's ad listings transactions.

Placing an ad or two to test the system

Once the configuration of ClassiPress is complete, you should then test the system to ensure that every thing is working as it should be. If you will be charging for ad listings on your website, navigate to **ClassiPress | Gateways** and then enable **Sandbox Mode** for the payment processor(s) that you're planning to use on your site.

Simply ticking those checkboxes isn't all that's required to begin using the sandbox. Before you can begin testing, you must first visit PayPal at `http://developer.paypal.com/` and/or Google Checkout at `http://checkout.google.com/sell/` to perform additional configurations. If you will be accepting payments via PayPal, then you can learn more about their sandbox feature and how to use them by reading the guide, entitled *Getting Started with PayPal Sandbox*, that can be found at `https://cms.paypal.com/us/cgi-bin/?&cmd=_render-content&content_ID=developer/howto_testing_sandbox_get_started`. In addition, if you will be using Google Checkout on your site, read the *Using Sandbox for Testing* web page found at `http://code.google.com/apis/checkout/developer/Google_Checkout_Basic_HTML_Sandbox.html` to learn how to use this testing environment.

Also, be sure to reconfigure your settings if the payment processor(s) that you've chosen to use require(s) special information to be provided, so that your sandbox account will be used when placing a test ad.

Once you've set up your sandbox account(s) and performed the necessary configurations on the **Gateways** screen, log out of WordPress and then visit the frontend of your website. Once there, click the **Post an Ad** button. Next, provide all of the information required to place your ad. As you do this, be sure to upload an image. If you're charging a fee for ad placements, choose an option from the **Payment Method** drop-down menu. Now, complete the ad placement process.

Once you've completed the steps required to place an ad on your site, log in to WordPress and then navigate to the **Dashboard**. Now, click on **Posts | Edit**. As you can see, your newly placed ad is listed as **Pending**. Click on the title for your ad. Then, on the **Edit Post** page, click **Publish** to make this ad active on your site.

If all goes well, then a classified ad should now appear on your website. If you're planning to accept payments using both PayPal and Google Checkout, then you will need to repeat this test using the payment processor that's as yet untested.

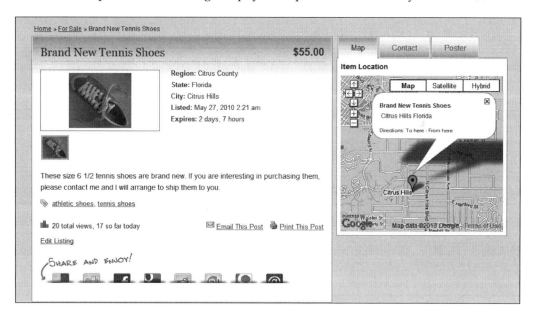

Before your website goes live, you must be sure to delete the user account that was created during the course of this test as well as the ad that now appears on your website. In addition, you must disable **Sandbox Mode** and then reconfigure the payment gateway settings (if you previously changed them).

Activating and configuring the ClassiPress-provided plugins

The plugins included with ClassiPress aren't in ZIP files, which means that to install them on your site, you will have to upload each of theme either via FTP or the file manager provided by your web host. Rather than going about things that way, you should, instead, just search for the plugins by name on the **Install Plugins** screen and then add them to your site from there. Not only is using this method easier, it also allows you to ensure that you're adding the latest version of each of these plugins to your site.

Introducing New User Email Setup

With this plugin, found at `http://wordpress.org/extend/plugins/new-user-email-set-up/`, you will be able to customize both the email that new users will receive upon registration and the message that you will be sent alerting you to the fact that someone has joined your site.

While this plugin may have been included with ClassiPress, it's installation is purely optional. If you're happy with the default text that ClassiPress includes in these messages, then you shouldn't bother with this plugin. If, however, you would like to make changes to either of those messages, then proceed with the installation and configuration of this plugin.

Setting up and configuring New User Email Setup

Install and activate **New User Email Setup**. Then, click on **Settings | New User Email** to be taken to the settings screen for this plugin.

The **User Email Settings** are the first thing that you need to configure on this screen. As you can see, this configuration area is currently collapsed. To expand this settings area, hover over the right hand corner of the gray bar and then click the arrow that appears.

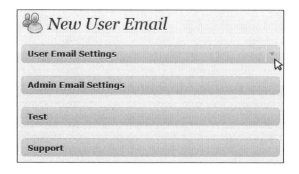

Allow HTML in Email Content is the first setting and it's currently configured to **Yes**. That's fine, so move on to **Registration Email Subject**, which you can either edit or leave as is. Next, in the **Registration Email Text** area, you can perform edits to the message that will be sent to users upon registration.

> When performing edits to the email subjects and messages included on this screen, be sure to use the variables that have been provided so that variable information can included in both.

In the **From Address** textbox, enter the email address that you want these messages to appear to have been sent from. Next, in the **From Name** textbox, enter the name of your site. Click **Save** and then you can begin editing the **Admin Email Settings**.

Access the **Admin Email Settings** by, once again, clicking the arrow to reveal this area. The first setting found in this section is **Send Notification Email to Admin on New Registration?** and it should be left set to **Yes**. If you would like to have these notifications sent to a email address different from the one that you previously entered in the **From Address** textbox, then set the **Send Notification Email to a Different Address than From Address?** option to **Yes**. Otherwise, no changes need to be made to this setting. If you changed that setting to **Yes**, then you next need to enter the email address where you would like to receive these notifications into the **Administration Notification Email Address** textbox. Now, just edit the **Administration Notification Email Subject** and the **Administration Notification Email Text** to your liking before clicking **Save**.

Introducing SexyBookmarks

With this plugin installed, you will be able to add a wide range of social bookmarking links to every classified ad listing included on your site. This highly customizable plugin, which is available at `http://wordpress.org/extend/plugins/sexybookmarks/`, makes it possible for you to choose exactly which social bookmarking sites should be made available to your users.

Setting up and configuring SexyBookmarks

Now that **SexyBookmarks** has been installed and activated, navigate to
Settings | SexyBookmarks. The **Enable Networks** area is first and it's here that you
can choose which social networking sites you would like to include on your site. By
default, all of the available networks are currently selected, which would result in
far too many of them being included on your site. For that reason, you should click
None to deselect all of them. Then, choose only those networks that you would really
like to make a part of your site.

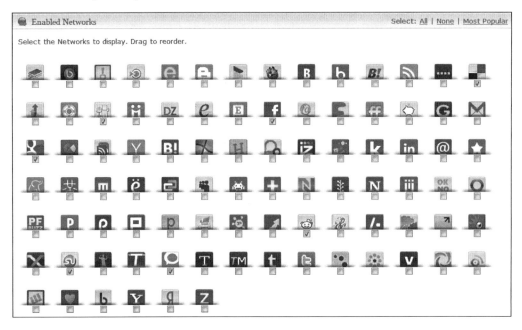

The **Functionality Settings** area is next. If you previously chose to include **Twitter,
Yahoo! Buzz**, and/or **Twitterly** on your site, then you will need to perform several
configurations in this area. If you didn't choose to include any of those sites, then you
will only need to concern yourself with the **General Functionality Options** section
of this settings area.

Assuming that you opted to include each of those three sites, you will first need to
configure the **Twitter Options**. In the **Configure Tweet** text area, use the provided
strings to customize the output of your tweet. Next, make the selection of your
choice from the **Which URL Shortener?** drop-down menu. Now, in the **Yahoo!
Buzz Defaults** area, first choose an appropriate category from the **Default Content
Category** drop-down menu. Since you're operating a classified ads site, the **Default
Media Type** will be fine with its setting of **Text**, so proceed to the **Twittley Defaults**
settings area. Choose a category from the **Primary Content Category** and then enter
some keywords that are related to your site into the **Default Tags** textbox.

Now, in the **General Functionality Options** area, configure both of the options found here to your liking.

Next is the **Plugin Aesthetics** settings section. The first setting, which is **Override Styles With Custom Mods Instead?**, should remain disabled. All of the settings found in the **jQuery Related Options** area should also be fine as is, so proceed to the **Background Image Options** section. If you want to include one of the available images on your site, leave **Use a background image?** enabled and then choose the image that you prefer. If you would rather not display one of these images on your site, then remove the checkmark from **Use a background image?** to disable this option.

Menu Placement is the last settings area that you will encounter. In this section, **Menu Location (in relation to content)** is the first setting that you will see. ClassiPress was designed so that the SexyBookmarks menu is manually integrated into the theme. That means that you should select **Manual Mode**. Failure to choose this setting will result in the SexyBookmarks menu being displayed twice on your page.

The **Posts, pages, or the whole shebang?** setting is currently set to **Post**, which means that the SexyBookmarks menu will only appear on post pages. If you like, you can choose a different option so that this social bookmarking menu is included on additional areas of your site. The last two settings, which are **Show in RSS feed?** and **Hide menu from mobile browsers?**, can both be configured according to your preferences. Once you've completed your configurations, click **Save Changes**.

If a bullet list appears on your website instead of the SexyBookmarks menu, then navigate to the `wp-content/plugins/sexybookmarks` directory. Once there, CHMOD the `spritegen` directory to 777. Now, click on **Settings | SexyBookmarks** where you will, once again, need to click **Save Changes**. Having done that, you should find that the SexyBookmarks menu now appears on your website.

Introducing User Photo

Once the **User Photo** plugin from `http://wordpress.org/extend/plugins/user-photo/` has been installed people who post ads on your site will be able to add an image to their profile page. As the admin, you will be able to specify the size and compression of these images via the plugin's settings screen.

Setting up and configuring User Photo

Once you've installed and activated this plugin, click on **Settings | User Photo**. Doing that will take you to the **User Photo Options** screen. The first two settings, which both dictate the size of your user's image, should be fine with their default settings, but you can make changes to either of them if you wish.

Serve Avatar as Fallback, which should be enabled, causes an avatar to display when a user doesn't upload a custom image. Since **Serve Avatar as Fallback** is enabled, **Override Avatar with User Photo** should be activated as well. This will ensure that a user's uploaded image will always be shown if one is available.

The **JPEG compression** setting is next and it's currently set to **90%**. This means that the images that your users upload will be subjected to quite a bit of compression so they certainly won't look their best. Try 90% for now, but if you discover that the quality of your users' profile images suffer too much, then lower this number slightly so that quality will improve. Just be sure not to lower this setting too much because you don't want to put a strain on your server.

Notify this administrator by email when user photo needs approval is currently disabled. That means that images that your users upload won't require any approval on your part. It's unlikely that you will want to take the time required to moderate each and every image uploaded by your users, so this is probably the best configuration for this setting. **Require user photo moderation for all users at or below this level** is the last setting found on this screen. Since you don't want to require moderation for any of the users on your site, change this setting to **(none)**. Then, click **Update options**.

Introducing WP-Email

The **WP-Email** plugin, which can be found at `http://wordpress.org/extend/plugins/wp-email/`, was created to add only one additional feature to your site. The plugin places an **Email This Post** link on each and every one of the classified ads that are published to your site.

You can already incorporate an email to a friend link into your site using the SexyBookmarks plugin, so whether you choose to use WP-Email will be up to your own preferences. If you do decide to use this plugin on your site, then use the instructions that follow in order to configure it.

Setting up and configuring WP-Email

After this plugin has been installed and activated, a new multi-page menu, titled **E-Mail**, will be added to the WordPress admin area. Click on **E-Mail | Options** to navigate to the only screen that you will need to visit in order to configure this plugin.

If your server uses SMTP then you will need to provide the required information in the **SMTP Settings** area. Otherwise, bypass this section and proceed to the **E-Mail Styles** settings area. While all of the settings found here are fine as is, you can certainly make changes to any of them if you wish.

The **E-Mail Settings** portion of the screen follows. By default, all of the options found in the **E-Mail Fields** area are selected, which is fine. If, however, you would like to exclude any of this information, just remove the checkmark next to the item that you would like to exclude. **E-Mail Content Type** is currently set to **HTML**, but it should be changed to **Plain Text**. The **Method Used To Send E-Mail** setting is currently set to **PHP**, which should be fine unless your server uses SMTP. If that's the case, then you will need to choose **SMTP** from the drop-down menu. All of the remaining settings found in this area are already ideally configured, so scroll down until you reach the **E-Mail Page Templates** area.

No changes are required in either this section or the **After Sending E-Mail Templates** area that follows, but, if you would like to edit the email templates used in connection with this plugin, then this is where you will need to do it. If you choose to perform edits, then be sure to incorporate the variables found in the **Template Variables** section of your screen. Once all of your configurations are complete, click **Save Changes**.

Introducing WP-Print

The **WP-Print** plugin, located at `http://wordpress.org/extend/plugins/wp-print/`, is designed to do one simple, but very useful thing. After this plugin has been activated on your site, a **Print This Post** link will be added to each of your classified ad listings.

Setting up and configuring WP-Print

After the installation and activation of this plugin is complete, there really isn't anything more that you need to do. If you wish, you can navigate to **Settings | Print** to visit the **Print Options** screen, but this really isn't necessary since all of these options are fine at their default settings.

Implementing a private messaging system

At present, the only way users of your site have to contact each other is via the email contact form included with ClassiPress. It's possible, however, to provide your visitors with a way to send and receive private messages through your site with the **WP Private Messages** plugin, which is available at `http://wordpress.org/extend/plugins/wp-private-messages/installation/`.

If, after activating **WP Private Messages**, you see an alert box at the top of your screen informing you that you have a new message, then you will know that the plugin is functioning properly. To send or receive private messages users need only navigate to **Users | Private Messages**.

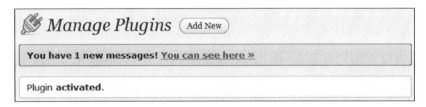

Dealing with deleted ads and 404 errors

With **Ad Pruning** set to **Yes**, old content won't appear on your site. Links to those listings will, however, still appear in the search engines until they update their indexes. That means that visitors may click on links for ads that have since been deleted. Instead of arriving at the page that they hoped to find they will, instead, be presented with a 404 error page.

There's a simple solution to this problem that will be very effective for keeping these visitors on your website. All you need to do is edit the `404.php` template supplied with the ClassiPress theme so that visitors will be automatically redirected from this error page to your website's home page.

Open the `404.php` file included with the ClassiPress theme and then replace all of the text in this template with the following lines of code. When performing this edit, be sure to enter the URL for your site in place of `http://example.com`. After saving these changes, the redirect will now be in place.

```php
<?php
header("Status: 301 Moved Permanently");
header("Location: http://example.com");
?>
```

Summary

When you first decided to build a local classified ads website you might have been wary because you thought that it would require a lot of time and effort. Having reached the end of this project, however, you can see that it really wasn't any trouble at all. With ClassiPress and a collection of plugins, creating a classified ads website couldn't be simpler.

With the technical side of your local classified ads website complete, you can begin to work on the next phase of this project. Now you will need to draw in web traffic and generate a constant stream of ad placements to keep visitors coming back. There are many ways that you could go about successfully launching your classified ads website. For example, you could begin by leveraging the contacts that you have in the area, because you might be able to encourage a few of them to place ads on your site. However you decide to approach this portion of the project you can rest assured that ClassiPress will be able to handle the job once visitors start coming in.

In this chapter, you learned how to use the ClassiPress theme to build a local classified ads website. From there you learned how to use various plugins to improve your classified ads site, so that visitors can do things like share listings, easily print ads, and include images on their profile pages.

In the next chapter, you will learn how to build a consumer review website where visitors can post their ratings and opinions about various products and/or services.

5
Project 5: Building a Consumer Review Website

When it comes time for consumers to purchase a product or service, nothing holds quite as much power over their buying decision as the opinions of others. Advertisements and articles can be viewed as being biased, but shoppers consider consumer reviews to be impartial opinions that they can trust. Building a consumer review website makes it possible to earn a nice profit since your site will act as a conduit between shoppers and sellers.

Building a consumer review website will allow you to supply consumers with the information that they seek and then, once they've decided to make a purchase, your site can direct them to a source for the product or service. This process can ultimately allow you to earn some nice commission checks because it's only logical that you would affiliate yourself with a number of the sites to which you will be directing consumers.

The great thing about using the **WP Review Site** plugin to build your consumer review website is that you can provide people with an unbiased source of public opinions on any product or service that you can imagine. You will never have to resort to the hard sell in order to drive traffic to the companies that you've affiliated yourself with. Instead, consumers can research the reviews posted on your website and, ultimately, make a purchase feeling confident that they're making the right decision.

In this chapter, you will learn how to:

- Present reviews in the most convenient way possible for visitors browsing your site
- Specify the ratings criteria that site visitors will use when reviewing the products or services included on your website
- Display informational comparison tables on your site's index and category pages

- Provide visitors with the location of local businesses using **Google Maps**
- Perform the additional steps required when writing a post now that the WP Review Site plugin has been introduced into the process
- Perform either automatic and manual integration so that you can use a theme of your own rather than either of the ones provided with this plugin

Once this project is complete, you will have succeeded in creating a site that's similar to the one shown in the following screenshot:

Introducing WP Review Site

With the WP Review Site plugin you will be able to build a consumer review site where visitors can share their opinions about the products or services of your choosing. The plugin, which can be found at `http://www.wpreviewsite.com/`, can be used to build a dedicated review site or, if you would like consumer reviews to make up only a subsection of your website, then you can specify certain categories where they should appear. This plugin gives you complete control over where ratings appear and where they don't since you can choose to include or exclude them on any category, page, or post.

The WP Review Site plugin seamlessly integrates with WordPress by, among other things, altering the normal appearance and functionality of the comments submission form. This plugin provides visitors with a way to write a review and assign stars to the ratings categories that you previously defined. They can also write a review and opt to provide no stars without harming the overall rating presented on your site, since no stars is interpreted as though no rating was given.

WP Review Site plugin makes it easy for you to present your visitors with concise information. Using the features available with this plugin, you can build comparison tables based upon your posts and user reviews. In order to accomplish this, you will need to configure a few settings and then the plugin will take care of the rest.

Typically, WordPress displays posts in chronological order, but that doesn't make much sense on a consumer review site where visitors want to view posts based upon other factors such as the number of positive reviews that a particular product or service has received. The developer behind WP Site Review took that into consideration and has included two alternative sorting methods for your site's posts. The developer has even included a **Bayesian weighting** feature so that reviews are ordered in the most logical way possible.

Right about now, you're probably wondering what Bayesian weighting is and how it works. What it does is provide a way to mathematically calculate the rating of products and/or services based upon the credibility of the votes that have been cast. If an item receives only a few votes, then it can't be said with any certainty that that's how the general public feels. If an item receives several votes, then it can be safely assumed that many others hold the same opinion. So, with Bayesian weighting, a product that has received only one five star review won't outrank another that has received fifteen four star reviews. As the product that received one five star review garners more ratings, its reviews will grow in credibility and, if it continues to receive high ratings, it will eventually become credible enough to outrank the other reviews.

If you're planning to create a website where visitors can come and review local businesses, then you might consider this plugins ability to automatically embed Google Maps quite handy. After configuring the settings on the plugin's **Google Maps** screen you will be able to type the address for a business into a custom field when writing a post and then the plugin will take care of the rest.

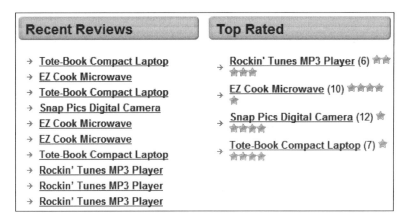

The WP Review Site plugin also includes two sidebar widgets that can used with any widget-ready theme. These widgets will allow you to display a list of top rated items and a list of recent reviews.

> **Tote-Book Compact Laptop**: So small that you can that you can take it... ☆
> ★★★★★ Review by Example.com on May 27, 2010
> PCs, the **Tote-Book**, and other laptops are discussed in this ... I heard great things about the **Tote-Book** and I was pleasantly surprised to learn that all of the hype was true...
> www.example.com/computers/.../tote-book/ - 21 hours ago - Cached - Similar

Lastly, the themes provided with this plugin include built-in support for the hReview microformat. This means that Google will easily be able to extract and highlight reviews from your website. That feature will prove to be very beneficial for driving search engine traffic to your site.

Installing WP Review Site

Once you've installed WordPress you can then concentrate on the installation of the WP Review Site plugin and its accompanying themes. First, extract the `wpreviewsite.zip` archive. Inside you will find a plugins folder and a themes folder. Within the plugins folder is another folder named `review-site`. Since none of these folders are zipped, you will need to upload them using either an FTP program or the file manager provided by your web host. So, upload the `review-site` folder to the `wp-content/plugins` directory on your server. If you plan to use one of the themes provided with this plugin, then you will next need to upload the contents of the `themes` folder to the `wp-content/themes` directory.

Setting up and configuring WP Review Site

With the installation process complete, you will now need to activate the WP Review Site plugin. Once that's finished, a **Review Site** menu will appear on the left side of your screen. This menu contains links to the settings screens for this plugin.

Before you delve into the configuration process you must first activate the theme that you plan to use on your consumer review website. Using one of the provided themes is a bit easier. That's because using any other theme will mean that you must integrate the functionality of WP Review Site into it. Now that you know the benefits offered by the themes that are bundled with this plugin, click on **Appearance | Themes**. Once there, activate either **Award Winning Hosts**, **Bonus Black**, or a theme of your choice.

General Settings

Navigate to **Review Site | General Settings** to be taken to the first of the WP Review Site settings screens. On this screen, **Sort Posts By** is the first setting that you will encounter. Rather than displaying reviews in the normal chronological order used by WordPress you should, instead, select either the **Average User Rating (Weighted)** or the **Number of Reviews/Comments** option. Either of these settings will provide a much more user-friendly experience for your visitors.

If you want to make it impossible for site visitors to submit a comment without also choosing a rating, tick the checkbox next to **Require Ratings with All Comments**. If you don't want to make this a requirement, then you can leave this setting as is.

This setting will, of course, only apply to posts that you would like your visitors to rate. On normal posts, that don't include rating stars in the comment form area, it will still be possible for your visitors to submit a comment.

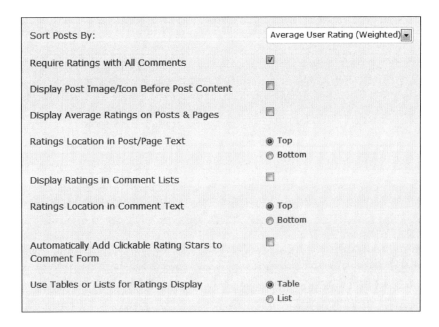

When using one of the themes provided with the plugin, none of the other settings on this screen need to be configured. If you would like to integrate this plugin into a different theme, then, depending upon the method that you choose, you may need to revisit this screen later on. No matter how you're handling the theme issue, you can, for now, just click **Save Settings** before proceeding to the next screen.

Rating Categories

To access the next settings screen, click on **Review Site | Rating Categories**. Here you can add categories for people to rate when submitting reviews. These categories shouldn't be confused with the categories used in WordPress for organizational purposes. These WP Review Site categories are more like ratings criteria. By default, WP Review Site includes a category called **Overall Rating**, but you can click the remove link to delete it if you like. To add your first rating category, simply enter its title into the **Add a Category** textbox and then click **Save Settings**.

The screen will then refresh and your newly created rating category will now appear under the **Edit Rating Categories** section of the screen. To add additional rating categories, simply repeat the process that you previously completed.

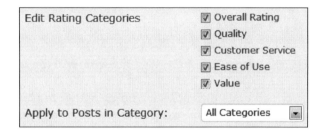

Once you've finished adding rating categories, you will next need to turn your attention to the **Bulk Apply Rating Categories** section of the screen. In the **Edit Rating Categories** area you will see all of the rating categories that you just finished adding to your site.

If you want to simplify matters, and apply these rating categories to all of the posts on your site, tick the checkbox next to each of the available rating categories. Then, from the **Apply to Posts in Category** drop-down menu, select **All Categories**. This is most likely the configuration that you will use if you're building a website entirely dedicated to providing consumer reviews. Once you've finished, click **Save Settings**.

If you, instead, want your newly added rating categories to only appear on certain categories, then bypass the **Edit Rating Categories** area for now and first look to the **Apply to Posts in Category** settings area. Currently this will only show **All Categories** and **Uncategorized**. The lack of categories in this menu is being caused by two things. First, you haven't added any WordPress categories to your site yet. Secondly, categories won't be included in this menu until they contain at least one post.

To solve part of this problem, open a new browser window and then, navigate to **Posts | Categories**. Then, add the categories that you would like to include on your website. Now, click on **Posts | Edit** to visit the **Edit Posts** screen. At the moment, the **Hello world!** post is the only one published on your site and you can use it to force your site's categories to appear in the **Apply to Posts in Category** drop-down menu. So, hover over the title of this post and then, from the now visible set of links, click **Quick Edit**. In the **Categories** section of the **Quick Edit** configuration area, tick the checkbox next to each of the categories found on your site. Then, click **Update Post**.

After content has been added to each of your site's categories, you can delete the **Hello world!** post, since you will no longer need to use it to force the categories to appear in the **Apply to Posts in Category** drop-down menu.

Now, return to the **Rating Categories** screen and then select the first category that you want to configure from the **Apply to Posts in Category** drop-down menu. With that selected, in the **Edit Rating Categories** area, tick the checkbox next to each rating category that you want to appear within that WordPress category. Then, click **Save Settings**. Repeat this process for each of the WordPress categories to which you would like rating categories to be added.

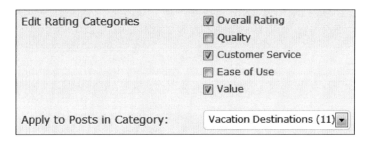

Comparison Tables

If you wish, you can add a comparison table to either the home page or the category pages on your site. To do this, you need to visit the **Comparison Tables** screen, so click on **Review Site | Comparison Tables**. If you want to display a comparison table on your home page, then tick the checkbox next to **Display a Comparison Table on Home Page**. If you would like to include all of your site's categories in the comparison table that will be displayed on the home page, then leave the **Categories To Display On Home Page** textbox as is. However, if you would prefer to include only certain categories, then enter their category IDs, separated by commas, into the textbox instead.

You can learn the ID numbers that have been assigned to each of your site's categories by opening a new browser window and then navigating to **Posts | Categories**. Once there, hover over the title of each of the categories found on the right hand side of your screen. As you do, look at the URL that appears in your browser's status bar and make a note of the number that appears directly after `tag_ID=`. That's the number that you will need to enter in the **Comparison Table** screen.

Display a Comparison Table on Home Page	☑
Categories To Display On Home Page	-1
	(Separate category IDs with commas, -1 for all)
Display a Comparison Table on Category Page(s)	☑
Categories To Display Comparison Table On	4,7,11
	(Separate category IDs with commas, -1 for all)

If you want to display a comparison table in one or more categories, then tick the checkbox next to **Display a Comparison Table on Category Page(s)**. Now, return to the **Comparison Table** screen. If you want a comparison table to be displayed on each of your category pages, leave the **Categories To Display Comparison Table On** textbox at its default. Otherwise, enter a list of comma separated category IDs into the textbox for the categories where you want to display comparison tables.

The **Number of Posts in the Table** setting is currently set to **5**, but you can enter another value if you would like a different number of posts to be included in each comparison table. When writing posts, you might use custom fields to include additional information. If you would like that information to be displayed in your comparison tables you will need to enter the names of those fields, separated by commas, into the **Custom Fields to Display** textbox. Lastly, you can change the text that appears in the **Text for the Visit Site link in the Table** if you wish or you may leave it at its default. With these configurations complete, click **Save Settings**.

In this screenshot, you can see what a populated comparison table will look like on your website:

Google Maps

If you plan on featuring reviews centered around local businesses, then you might want to consider adding Google Maps to your site. This will make it easy for visitors to see exactly where each business is located.

You can access this settings screen by clicking on **Review Site | Google Maps**. To activate this feature, tick the checkbox next to **Display a Google Map on Posts/Pages with mapaddress Custom Field**. Next, you need to use the **Map Position** setting to specify where these Google Maps will appear in relation to the content. You can choose to use either the **Top of Post** or **Bottom of Post** position.

> You need a Google Maps API Key for each domain you want to display maps on. You can get one here.

The **Your Google Maps API Key** textbox is next. Here you will need to enter a Google Maps API key. If you don't have a Google Maps API key for this domain, then you will need to visit Google to generate one. To do this, right-click on the link provided on the **Google Maps** screen and then open that link in a new browser window. You will then be taken to the Google Maps API sign up screen, which can be found at `http://code.google.com/apis/maps/signup.html`. If you've ever signed up to use any of Google's services, then you can use that username and password to log in. If you don't have an account with Google, create one now.

Take a moment to read the information and terms presented on the Google Maps API sign up page. After you've finished reviewing this text, if it's acceptable to you, enter the URL for your website into the **My web site URL** textbox and then click **Generate API Key**. You will then be taken to a thank you screen where your API key will be displayed. Copy the API key and then return to the **Google Maps** screen on your website. Once there, paste your API key into the textbox for **Your Google Maps API Key**.

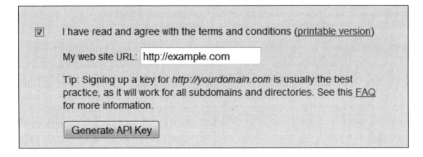

The **Map Width** and **Map Height** settings are next. By default, these are configured to **400px** and **300px**. If you would prefer that the maps be displayed at a different size, then enter new values into each of these textboxes. The last setting is **Map Zoom Level (1-5)**, which is currently set to **3**. This setting should be fine, but you may change it if you wish. Finally, click **Save Settings**.

When you publish a post that includes the **mappadress** custom field, this is what the Google Map will look like on your site.

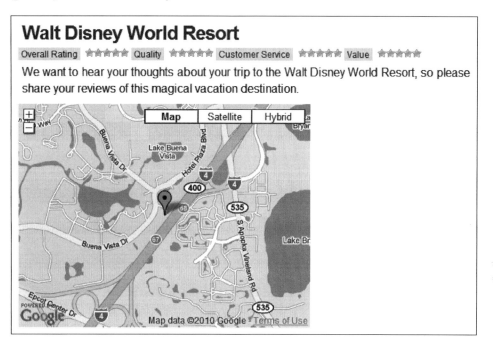

Adding your first post

Adding a post to WordPress is usually a pretty straightforward process. When using the WP Review Site plugin, however, the process of writing a post becomes a bit different. To give you an idea of the differences involved, a walk through has been provided to guide you through the creation of your first post.

Navigate to the **Add New Post** screen by clicking on **Posts | Add New**. Once there, things will start out as usual since your first task will be to enter your post title and description. Next, select a category and then add tags, if desired.

Now is the part where things become a bit different. As you can see, there's a **Rating Categories** area that contains all of the rating categories that you created earlier. All of these rating categories are currently deselected. This means that if this post were published right now, there wouldn't be any criteria that your visitors could use to rate this product or service. You must, therefore, tick the checkbox next to each of the rating categories that you want to appear along with this post.

Next, in the **Post Image** textbox, enter the URL for an image related to this post. Use the **"Visit Site" Link** textbox to enter the URL where you want visitors to be taken if they would like to receive more information about this product or service. This can be a direct link or, if you're engaging in affiliate marketing, it can be an affiliate link. If you do place an affiliate link in this field it won't be masked so visitors will know that they're not clicking on a typical URL.

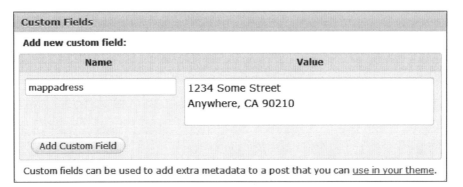

If you previously enabled the setting to add Google Maps to your posts, you will now need to scroll down until you reach the **Custom Fields** portion of the screen. In the **Name** textbox enter **mappadress**. Then, in the **Value** text area, type the address where this business is located. Finally, click **Add Custom Field**.

You may also want to include additional information such as price, size, color variations, and so on. If that's the case, then you can use custom fields for that as well. The process for doing this will depend upon whether you've already used a custom field on your site. If you haven't, begin by entering the name that you would like to give this custom field into the **Name** textbox. For example, you might enter **Price**.

If you've already created a custom field, then the **Name** textbox will have been replaced with a drop-down menu that contains the names of all of the custom fields that you've created prior to this. In this instance, you need to click the **Enter new** link located under the drop-down menu. Once clicked, the **Name** textbox will reappear and you will then be able to enter the name that you would like to give this field.

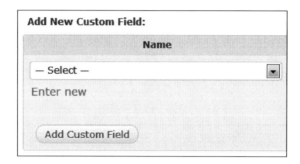

Now, you need to type information relevant to this custom field into the **Value** text area. Once again, as an example, if you're creating a price-related custom field, you would need to enter the amount of this item. Finally, click **Add Custom Field** before scrolling to the top of your screen where you must then click **Publish**.

Integrating WP Review Site into an existing theme

As you know, the WP Review Site plugin comes with two themes. You might, however, wish to set your consumer review website apart from all the others using this plugin, by using a different theme. If that's the case, then you need to integrate the functionality of the WP Review Site plugin into the theme that you've chosen. There are two ways that this can be done. One is automatic while the other requires you to add various functions to your theme's template files. Both options will now be examined so that you can choose the method that's right for you.

Integrating WP Review Site automatically

Automatically integrating the WP Review Site plugin into your own theme is, by far, the easiest way to approach things. The only downside to this method is the fact that you will have absolutely no control over where the various features of the plugin are placed on your site.

 Because of the way that some themes are designed, they aren't compatible with the automatic integration method. If you discover that the rating stars that accompany the comments form appear underneath the **Submit** button, then you will either need to manually integrate WP Review Site into your theme or select a different theme that's compatible with automatic integration.

To begin you will need to return to the **General Settings** screen, so click on **Review Site | General Settings**. Once there, you first need to decide if you're going to enable the **Display Post Image/Icon Before Post Content** option since it's optional. The **Display Average Ratings on Posts & Pages** setting is next. This option should be enabled, so that visitors can see the overall rating given by reviewers to your website. The **Ratings Location in Post/Page Text** option is next. By default, this is set to **Top**, but you may change this setting to **Bottom** if you prefer. The checkbox for the **Display Ratings in Comment Lists** option should also be ticked, so that your visitors' star ratings will appear along with their comments. **Ratings Location in Comment Text** is set to **Top**, but may be changed to **Bottom** depending upon your preferences. Next, **Automatically Add Clickable Rating Stars to Comment Form** must be enabled in order for your visitors to be able to submit ratings. Use **Tables or Lists for Ratings Display** is the last setting. If you want the ratings to be displayed vertically, then leave this set to **Table**. If you would prefer that they appear horizontally, then select **List** instead.

To finalize these configurations, click **Save Settings**. The features and functionality of WP Review Site will now be automatically integrated into your site.

Integrating WP Review Site manually

Manually integrating the WP Review Site plugin into your theme will, of course, require more effort than using the automatic method. You may find, however, that automatic integration just doesn't cut it. Various elements might not integrate properly using that method which will leave you with no other alternative than to integrate this plugin manually. To do this, you need to use the functions provided by the plugin's developer to integrate its various features into your theme's templates.

A plugin function reference guide, along with examples, can be found on the WP Review Site website at `http://www.wpreviewsite.com/documentation#install_3`.

Displaying the average ratings

You should begin by adding either an average ratings table or list to your posts, so open your theme's `single.php` template. Next, look for the beginning of The Loop. You will need to place one of the following lines inside The Loop, wherever you want the average ratings information to appear.

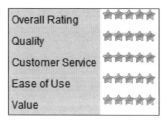

If you would like the average ratings to be displayed in table format, then place the following line of code within The Loop:

```php
<?php if (function_exists('ratings_table')) ratings_table(); ?>
```

If you would prefer to display the average ratings information for each post as an unordered list, then enter this line inside The Loop instead:

```php
<?php if (function_exists('ratings_list')) ratings_list(); ?>
```

Now, open the `index.php` template and, once again, locate the beginning of The Loop. Determine where you would like the average ratings information to appear within The Loop on this page and then enter either of the previously shown functions into this template as well.

Displaying a Visit This Site link

Currently, visitors to your consumer review website will be unable to visit the link that you provide with each post. That's because a function doesn't exist within any of your template files to retrieve and display that information onscreen. To have that information printed onscreen, you need to add the appropriate function to your `single.php` and `index.php` templates. Once again, you must place this function with The Loop found in each of these templates in the location where you would like this link to appear:

```php
<?php visit_site_link('Visit This Site'); ?>
```

Displaying user submitted ratings

When WordPress 2.7 was released the comment system used by WordPress was completely changed. From that version forward, the `<?php wp_list_comments();` `?>` template tag was used to display the comments that have been submitted to your site. As a result, it became more difficult to edit the area of your website that contains the user submitted comments. This is important because the way that you go about displaying the ratings submitted by your visitors will depend upon which WordPress commenting system your theme was designed to use.

 It should be noted that the user submitted ratings function won't display properly if your theme doesn't use the `$comment` variable. If you find that your theme lacks this variable, then you can try the automatic method to integrate this function. If that doesn't work either, then you will have to choose a new theme that uses the `$comment` variable.

Adding user submitted ratings to a theme that uses the old WordPress commenting system

In order to display the ratings submitted by each of your visitors, along with their comments, you will need to add a function to the `comments.php` template.

Once again, you can choose to either display these ratings as a table or an unordered list. The option that you choose will depend upon your personal preferences, and the overall design of your theme.

Open the `comments.php` template and then look for the section of code that's responsible for displaying comments on your site. This is known as the comments loop. If you would like the user submitted ratings to be displayed as a table, then enter the following line inside the comments loop where you would like them to appear:

```
<?php if (function_exists('comment_ratings_table')) comment_ratings_
table(); ?>
```

If you would prefer to display the user submitted ratings as an unordered list, then enter this line inside the comments loop instead:

```
<?php if (function_exists('comment_ratings_list')) comment_ratings_
list(); ?>
```

Adding user submitted ratings to a theme that uses the WordPress 2.7+ commenting system

If your theme was designed to be compatible with the new commenting system introduced with the release of WordPress 2.7, then you will find that manually integrating this function is a bit more difficult.

The `comments.php` file included with themes that have been built to be compatible with WordPress 2.7+ isn't quite the same as the one included with themes built prior to the release of this version of WordPress. It differs in that it includes the `<?php wp_list_comments(); ?>` template tag which is responsible for generating the section of your site where submitted comments appear. That means that it's impossible for you to add the user submitted ratings function to this file, since all of the code that's used to display the submitted comments section is contained within a different file.

Now, here is where things get a bit tricky. If the `<?php wp_list_comments(); ?>` template tag contains a **callback**, then you will be able to proceed with manual integration of this function.

If it doesn't include a callback, then the manual integration process would become so involved that it wouldn't be worth all of the trouble that would be required. In that instance, you would really just be better off automatically integrating this function into your site.

> A callback is a custom function that's used to customize the display of each comment. When a callback is included in this template tag, the internal WordPress functionality that would normally be used is overridden.

So, how, you might wonder, do you know if your theme's `<?php wp_list_comments(); ?>` template tag contains a callback? Well, the best way to determine this is by looking at an example from the **Twenty Ten** theme.

```
<?php wp_list_comments( array( 'callback' => 'twentyten_comment' ) );
?>
```

As you can see, this template tag includes a callback to `twentyten_comment`. If the `<?php wp_list_comments(); ?>` template tag included in your theme's `comments.php` template looks similar to this, then you can proceed with the manual integration process.

If you've discovered that the template tag includes a callback, then the next step is to determine where that callback function can be found. The most likely place that you will find it is in the `functions.php` file. If it isn't located in that file, then investigate all of the other files included with your theme until you find it. Once you've located the callback function, add either of the following pieces of code somewhere within that callback.

If you want to include the user submitted ratings as a table, insert the following:

```php
<?php if (function_exists('comment_ratings_table')) comment_ratings_
table(); ?>
```

To have the user submitted ratings displayed as an unordered list, enter this line instead:

```php
<?php if (function_exists('comment_ratings_list')) comment_ratings_
list(); ?>
```

Collecting ratings from visitors

If you performed the edit to `comments.php` detailed in the previous section, you must now enter the function responsible for displaying each of the criteria that you want reviewers to use when rating the products and/or services found on your site. If you didn't perform that edit, then go ahead and skip to the next section.

As was previously the case, this function can either display the output as a table or a list. For table formatting, enter the following line between the `<form>` and `</form>` tags.

```php
<?php if (function_exists('ratings_input_table')) ratings_input_
table(); ?>
```

This line of code can be used to format the output as an unordered list. To be used on your site, this function must also be placed between the `<form>` and `</form>` tags

```php
<?php if (function_exists('ratings_input_list')) ratings_input_list();
?>
```

Displaying a comparison table

If you would like a comparison table to be included on a particular page of your site, then you will have to add the function that generates the table into the appropriate theme template. The comparison table includes three parameters that will allow you to specify how many posts should appear in the table, what link text should be used, and which categories should be included.

To add a comparison table to the home page, open the `index.php` template and then locate an area outside of The Loop where you would like the table to appear. Now, paste the following function into your theme's template file:

```
<?php rs_comparison_table(5, 'Visit This Site'); ?>
```

That will add a comparison table that displays the top five rated posts from all of the categories on your site. You can, of course, change the number 5 to anything you like so that a different number of posts appear in the table.

In addition, if you only want to display the top posts from a particular category, you can accomplish that by adding a category parameter to the function. The specific category ID that you add to this parameter will, of course, depend upon the construction of your site. For example, if you wanted to display only the top rated posts from the category with the ID 7, then this is the function that you would need to use.

```
<?php rs_comparison_table(5, 'Visit This Site', 7); ?>
```

If you're using custom fields on your site and you would like them to be included in this table, then you will need to click on **Review Site | Comparision Table** to visit the **Comparison Tables** screen. Once there, simply enter the names of the custom fields that you would to include in the table into the **Custom Fields to Display** textbox.

Displaying positive and negative reviews

The functions that you've added to the various template files of your theme are the ones that it's of the utmost importance to have in order to manually integrate the features of the WP Review Site plugin into your website. There are, however, two more functions that you can also place within your template files if you so desire. While these functions aren't required, they do add a nice informational element to your reviews. With these functions in place, the total number of positive and negative reviews that a product or service has received will be displayed onscreen.

You can add the following line of code, within The Loop, to the `single.php` template to display the number of positive reviews received.

```
<?php if (function_exists('positive_reviews')) echo positive_
reviews(); ?> Positive Reviews
```

To display the total number of negative reviews received, enter the following line of code inside The Loop found in `single.php`:

```
<?php if (function_exists('negative_reviews')) echo negative_
reviews(); ?> Negative Reviews
```

 Don't forget to save your files after you've finished performing all of the edits detailed in the preceding sections.

Blending WP Review Site's functions into your theme's design

These functions may technically be integrated into your theme, but you will undoubtedly find that some of them haven't exactly meshed visually with the design of your website. If that's the case, then you will need to edit the CSS that's being applied to these functions in order for them to blend in seamlessly.

Open `review-site.css`, which can be found in the `/plugins/review-site` folder. Edit the styles that are contained within this file and then save your changes. Once that's finished, you should find that the output of this plugin has now been integrated both technically and visually into your website.

Summary

Your website is now online and just waiting to be filed with reviews. Luckily, generating content of this type couldn't be easier, since everyone has an opinion that they're more than happy to share. The biggest obstacle that you will face is the fact that very few people are going to want to be the first one to post their opinion. This problem can easily be overcome, however, with the help of your family and friends. Simply ask them to visit your website and then submit honest reviews of the products and/or services that they've used.

Since you can't rely on your family and friends to write all of the content on your website, you're going to need to draw in visitors so that content is being continually generated. One way that you can do this is by performing keyword optimization on those first few posts. This can be done by providing your family and friends with a few keywords that you would like them to weave into the reviews that they will be submitting to your site.

Once you've got some keyword-rich reviews in place, visitors should begin finding your consumer review website via the search engines. Once these visitors arrive at your website, and see that it's populated with content, they shouldn't have any hesitation about adding reviews of their own.

In this chapter, you learned how to use the WP Review Site plugin to build a site were visitors can share their reviews on products and/or services. You were also shown how to either build your site using one of the two themes provided with this plugin or, instead, integrate the functionality of WP Review Site into the theme of your choosing.

In the next chapter, you will learn how to build a job board site where employers can post listings for prospective employees to browse.

6
Project 6: Building a Job Board Website

No matter how good or bad the economy might be at any given time there will always be job seekers. Every day people search online to find employment in a variety of industries. Searching the bigger job boards can be overwhelming and time-consuming because job seekers must sort though the myriad of job listings in an attempt to locate positions that match their unique skill sets. What would greatly benefit these job seekers is a fine-tuned job board that concentrates on a smaller segment of the overall job market. That's where **JobPress** comes in.

With this WordPress theme, you can easily create a niche job board to serve a particular segment of job seekers. With so many types of jobs out there, the possibilities for niche job boards are almost endless. Drawing in traffic shouldn't prove to be too difficult either because, after being populated with niche-specific job listings, your job board will be filled with a wide variety of targeted keywords. Once these job seekers arrive at your niche job board they should transition into repeat traffic since they will be able to easily peruse job listings that are appropriate to the skills that they posses. That will remove much of the hassle that job seekers suffer as they seek employment.

FoxNews and **Smashing Magazine** are two users of the JobPress theme who have zeroed in on a niche for their job boards. FoxNews only covers positions available within their own company while Smashing Magazine provides job listings primarily targeted toward those seeking design and programming-related jobs.

So, as you can see, opting to focus on a niche will put you and your job board in good company.

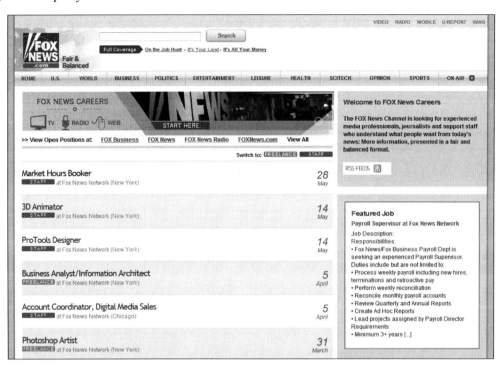

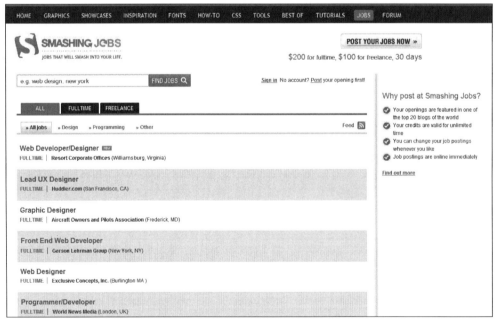

The previous screenshots of the FoxNews and Smashing Magazine job boards will give you some idea of just what you can do with this theme. As you can see, JobPress can be integrated into the design of an existing website so that the two blend together nicely.

In this chapter, you will learn how to:

- Build a dedicated job board website
- Make the JobPress sidebar widget-ready
- Run JobPress alongside an existing web site

Once this project is complete, you will have succeeded in creating a site that's similar to the one shown in the following screenshot:

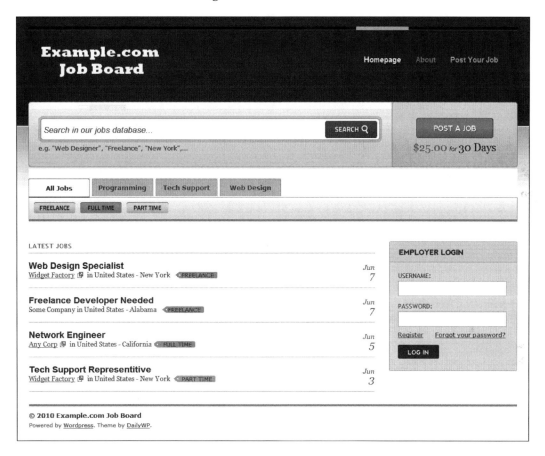

Introducing JobPress

JobPress, which can be found at `http://www.dailywp.com/jobpress-wordpress-theme/`, took the inspiration for its features from several of the job boards already in existence on the Internet. As you would expect, the theme offers those building a job board site the ability to edit and customize various features using a theme-related settings screen. This one screen houses all of the settings specific to this theme, so the customization of JobPress and its features can be completed in record time.

If you're looking to earn a profit from your job board, then you have two options. You can either include advertisements in their various forms or you can charge a fee in order to post a job listing. If you would like to go with the latter option, then you can simply enter your **PayPal** information into the appropriate settings area and JobPress and PayPal will take care of the rest. JobPress also includes a feature whereby payment is verified between PayPal and JobPress, so that you can always be sure that the job listings that appear on your website have, in fact, been paid for.

JobPress makes the job hunt easier for your visitors by allowing them to use the **FREELANCE, FULL TIME**, and **PART TIME** tags to sort listings. These sort options are available on both the front page and within categories to make locating a suitable job as easy as possible. If job seekers want to search for a specific job, instead of browsing, then they can do that too by using the search box provided by JobPress.

JobPress also includes a feature that will alert job seekers when a listing has been online for more than 30 days. That way they will be able to see which listings are fresh and which ones are likely to have already been filled by another applicant.

Running a job board isn't just about pleasing the job seekers who come to your site looking for listings. It's also about catering to the desires of those who will be placing ads. After all, without them your job board won't contain any job listings which means that there will be nothing there to draw in visitors. The developer behind JobPress took that into consideration when designing this theme by making the job listing submission process virtually hassle-free.

Setting up and configuring JobPress

After uploading and activating the JobPress theme, a new **JobPress Settings** link will appear. From this screen, all of your JobPress settings can be configured. So, to begin customizing JobPress to your liking, click on **JobPress Settings**.

The **Publishing & Payment Settings** area is the first section that you will need to concentrate on during this configuration process. The **Auto Publish?** setting allows you to publish job listings automatically or manually. This setting is currently set to **On**, but you may switch it to **Off** if you prefer to have more control over the ads that appear on your website. The **Paid Submission?** setting is currently enabled. If you would like to charge a fee for placing a job listing, then this setting shouldn't be changed. Otherwise, change it to **Disable** to offer job listing placements for free.

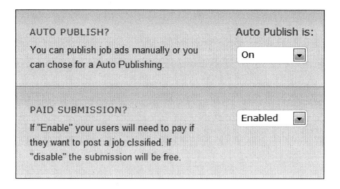

If you've decided to offer job listing placements for free, then proceed to the **Custom Information** settings area. If, you've instead opted to charge for the placement of job listings, then you will need to configure the remaining settings found in the **Publishing & Payment Settings** area. First, enter the email address associated with your PayPal account into the **PayPal Mail** textbox. In the **Submission Price** textbox, enter the amount that you would like to charge for standard ad placements. The last setting in this area is the **Currency** drop-down menu. Here you need to choose the currency associated with your area of the world.

PAYPAL MAIL
Enter your Paypal mail address. You need to be registered at PayPal to ask for a Submission Price

hwallace@example.com

SUBMISSION PRICE
How much a job submission costs.

25.00

Must be numeric!

CURRENCY
You are able to choose from 18 currencies.

U.S. Dolars

The **Custom Information** section of this settings screen is next and **Renew Jobs** is the first option that you will see. This feature is currently set to **Enabled** which means that job posters will be able to renew their listings if they would like to do so. This setting can be left at its default or you can, instead, set it to **Disable** if you would rather not provide a renewal option. It's best, however, for ease of use, if this setting remains enabled.

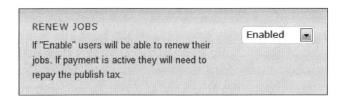

The **Apply Online** option is also set to **Enabled** and it's probably best if this is left as is so that your job board offers the highest level of convenience to job seekers. With this setting in place visitors to your job board will be able to apply online for the jobs that they're interested in.

The **Sociable** setting is also currently enabled, which is ideal since this will provide your visitors with a way to share a job listing that they see on your site with someone who might be interested in applying.

Featured Job is next and, like all of the proceeding settings, it's also enabled. If you want to provide job posters with the option of upgrading from a standard listing to one that's featured, then this setting should remain enabled. If, however, you would rather not offer featured job listings on your website, then change this setting to **Disable**. If you opted to leave this setting enabled, then enter the price that you plan to charge for featured job listings into the **Submission Featured Job Price** textbox.

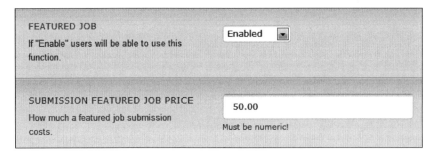

Now, in the **Items Per Page** textbox, enter the number of job listings that you would like to appear on a single page.

In the **Success Message** text area you will find a pre-written message that's displayed on the confirmation page when a job listing is submitted. It's best if you rewrite this message to correct grammar issues and to add any additional information that you would like to provide.

Success Mail is next and this setting contains a few different options that must be addressed. First, you must choose whether you would like to leave this feature set to **Enabled** or, instead, set it to **Disable**.

> If you would like to use this feature, then you will first need to heed the advice included below the drop-down menu which advises you to contact your web host before enabling this setting. When you contact your web host you will need to ask them to if the mail() function is activated because the **Success Mail** feature won't work if that function isn't enabled. If the mail() function isn't enabled, then you should next ask your web host to activate it on your account. If they're unable to do so, then you will have no choice other than to set **Success Mail** to **Disable**.

If it was possible for your web host to enable the mail() function, and you set **Success Mail** to **Enabled**, you must next deal with the **Subject** textbox. The default text provided in this textbox is certainly sufficient, but you might want to add the name of your job board to the subject line. That way recipients will be able to easily identify that the message that they're receiving isn't spam. The message within the **Content** text area is fine as is, but you may certainly rewrite it if you like. If you do decide to create your own message, then be sure to include the tags provided by JobPress for usage in this area so that this unique information can be populated before the message is sent. The **From** textbox that follows should be left at its default. Now, click **Save** to finalize your changes.

Companies submitting job listings to your site will have the ability to include their company logo along with their submission. This feature won't function properly, unless you change the permissions on the upload folder, which can be found inside the wp-content directory. So, navigate to the upload folder and then CHMOD it to 777.

Making the sidebar widget-ready

Unfortunately, JobPress doesn't have a widget-ready sidebar. You can, however, easily make a few edits to two of the JobPress theme files in order to correct this issue. First, open up the sidebar.php file included with this theme. Once it's open, scroll to the bottom of the file and then add the following lines of code right above the final </div> tag.

```
<?php if ( !function_exists('dynamic_sidebar')
        || !dynamic_sidebar() ) : ?>
<?php endif; ?>
```

With this code placed in that area any widgets that you add will appear just below the employer login box located at the top of your sidebar. Before you can start adding widgets via the **Dashboard** you need to first edit the functions.php file. Open that file and then enter the following code just below the opening <php> tag.

```
if ( function_exists('register_sidebar') )
    register_sidebar();
```

After saving and uploading both files, widgets will be usable on your JobPress-themed site.

If you ever update your JobPress theme to a new version, then it's likely that you will need to perform these edits again as these files will, most likely, be overwritten. Also, since widgets previously were not a factor, you may find that the styles being applied to this area aren't to your liking. If that's the case, then you will need to perform some edits to both sidebar.php and style.css in order to add widget-specific styling.

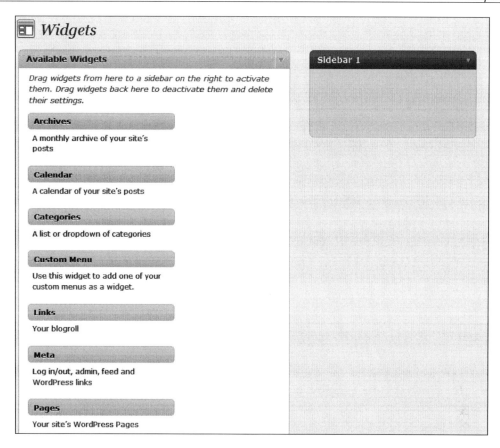

Unfortunately, widgetizing the JobPress sidebar does have a downside. That's because the `add_action('admin_head', 'jobpress_style');` function, found in `functions.php`, conflicts with the code that you just added to that file as part of this process. As a result, the **Widgets** page located in the administration area, won't display properly. Instead of the various elements being aligned in a collection of rows they will, instead, appear in one long line. There isn't a known fix for this problem. It is, however, merely an inconvenience and won't hinder the usage of widgets on your site.

Adding a job listing to test the system

Before launching your job board, it's important for you to ensure that people will actually be able to post job listings and, if you're charging a fee, that they will be able to complete the payment process. To do this, you will need to post an ad yourself.

If you decided to require payment for the placement of job listings, then you will need to temporarily lower the price of a standard ad placement in order to conduct this test. In addition, if you're planning on selling featured job listings, then you will need to lower the price of that as well. That's because JobPress doesn't provide a way for you to switch over into a test mode so that you can perform this test using the **PayPal Sandbox**.

So, click on **JobPress Settings** to visit this settings screen. Once there, replace the number found in the **Submission Price** textbox, with a nominal fee. If **Featured Job** is enabled, then replace the fee found in the **Submission Featured Job Price** textbox with a lower amount. Now, click **Save**.

Navigate to the frontend of your website and then click on either the **Post Your Job** link or the **Post a Job** button. Then, work your way through the multi-page job listing submission process. When you reach the **Create Account** screen, be sure to create a new account, rather than logging in to your administrator account. If you're charging a fee for submitting job listings, you will be directed to PayPal where you will need to complete the payment process.

 When making this payment at PayPal, you must use a funding source and an email address that isn't attached to your PayPal account.

Now, visit your job board's home page and then click on the title for the listing that you just placed. If all went well, then your fictional job listing should look similar to the one shown in the following screenshot:

If anything went wrong during the testing process, then read over this chapter once again to ensure that all of the configurations were performed properly. If you find that your site is correctly configured, but the issue persists, then, depending upon the problem that you're experiencing, you will need to contact either JobPress or PayPal support.

Once you've finished performing this test, if you previously lowered either of the fees associated with posting a job listing on your website, you will need to return to the **JobPress Settings** screen and then return those fees to their original amount. Then, click **Save**. Next, delete the job listing that you submitted during this test. Finally, delete the user account that was created as a result of this test.

Replacing the JobPress logo with your own

To add your website's logo to your JobPress-powered site, open the `style.css` file located in the JobPress theme folder and look for the following lines:

```
.header { background: url(images/headerBg.jpg) no-repeat top left;
height:150px; }
.header h1 a { background: url(images/logo.gif) no-repeat top left; }
```

Once you've located that portion of code you will then need to replace it with the following code designed to point to the location of your website's logo. You will, of course, need to replace `logo.gif` with the filename of your website's logo. Once that's done, be sure to upload your website's logo to the image folder found within the JobPress theme directory.

```
.header { height:150px; }
.header h1 a { background: url(images/logo.gif) no-repeat top left;}
```

 To fit perfectly in this space, the height of your logo must not exceed 65px.

Having saved and uploaded this edited file, your job board will now be branded with your logo.

Running JobPress alongside an existing website

It may be the case that you don't want to set up a dedicated job board but would prefer to add one to a website that you already have online. If that's the case, you will need to run JobPress alongside your existing website since it's powered by a unique theme rather than a plugin. This means that you will need separate installations of WordPress for your main website and your JobPress-powered job board.

Your first WordPress installation will need to be placed at the location where you want visitors to access your main website. This will, most likely, be at the root of your domain. After you've finished building the main website to your liking, you can then focus on the installation and configuration of JobPress. You can choose to either place this second WordPress installation in a sub-directory or you can, instead, place it on a sub-domain. The choice is yours. With these two separate websites set up you now need to make it appear as though they flow together seamlessly. The first thing that you need to do is work on editing JobPress so that your two sites are similar in appearance. As things stand, your JobPress site will look very different from your main site since it's appearance is being dictated by an entirely different theme. The easiest way to make these websites similar in appearance is to make a few edits to the JobPress theme.

Customizing the appearance of JobPress to match your main site

Open both the JobPress stylesheet and the stylesheet being used by your main site. Then, find the section of your main site's stylesheet that dictates how the background should look. Once you've located that section, copy it and then return to the JobPress stylesheet where you need to look for the following line:

```
body { background: url(images/bg.jpg) repeat-x center top; }
```

This section should be completely overwritten by the line of code that you just copied. If you're using a background image and it's being referenced using a relative path, then you will need to copy that background image into the images folder within the JobPress theme directory in order for it to display properly.

This procedure for replacing the background on your JobPress site with one of your own will only work under ideal conditions. That's because, if the CSS used on the background image that appears on your main site includes `repeat-y` or if the image is too tall, the content area will be obscured. If you find that you're unable to use this method to edit the background image of your JobPress site, then more in-depth changes will need to be made to the stylesheet for the JobPress theme. In that case, it would be impossible to predict the exact changes that you would need to make since there are just too many variables involved.

The last visual elements that you will need to concern yourself with are the colors used for various elements such as links. The colors used in the JobPress stylesheet will need to be changed until they match nicely with your main website. Once that's done, the visual aspects of your main website and your JobPress site should blend together nicely.

Adding seamless navigation between your websites

As things stand, visitors who arrive at your main website have no way to get to your job board while those who land on your job board will find it impossible to click through to your main website. This scenario is less than ideal, so you must now work to link these two websites together in such a way that it appears as though they're both part of one big website.

The easiest way to provide visitors to your main website with access to your job board is to place a widget somewhere on your main website that links over to your job board. As an alternative, if your main website has a navigation menu, you could also hard code a link to your job board either before or after the template tag that's responsible for creating your site's navigation menu. Depending upon the design of your theme this will either be the `wp_list_categories()` or the `wp_nav_menu()` template tag. If you do perform this edit to one of your main site's template files, then be sure to save and upload the edited template. Getting back to your main website from your job board, however, is still impossible. Your visitors are also likely to become confused because the JobPress navigation menu includes a link named **Homepage**, but it directs them to the front page of the JobPress site rather than the home page of your main site.

Correcting both problems is a simple matter of editing that link to the home page so that, when clicked, it will direct your visitors to your main site. Open the `header.php` file associated with the JobPress theme. Then, look for the following section of code.

```
<li class="page_item<?php if(is_home() && $_GET['poststeps']=="")
{ ?> current_page_item<?php } ?>"><a href="<?php bloginfo('url');
?>">Homepage</a></li>
```

To create a link to the home page of your main site, the following piece of code must be replaced:

```
<a href="<?php bloginfo('url'); ?>">
```

So, select the proceeding portion of code and replace it will the following. You will, of course, need to enter the web address of your main site in place of `example.com`.

```
<a href="http://example.com">
```

Having made that change, visitors will now be able to navigate from your job board to your main site. They won't, however, be able to reach any of the other sections found on your primary website. To make that possible, you need to once again edit the JobPress navigation links so that the various sections of your main site are represented as well.

In the JobPress `header.php` file look for the following line:

```
<?php $setPageExclude = get_option('setPageExclude'); wp_list_pages
("title_li=&depth=1&sort_order=DESC&exclude=$setPageExclude"); ?>
```

Now, suppose that you would like to add a link to the Contact Us page found on your main site. If that were the case, then you would need to add the following list item directly after the line of code shown above. Once again, the `example.com` URL should be replaced with a link to a page found on your primary website.

```
<li><a href="http://example.com/contact-us/">Contact Us</a></li>
```

Continue adding list items until all of the sections found on your main site have been included on the JobPress menu. Once all of these changes have been made, save and then upload `header.php`, so that your newly updated navigation menu will be available to your visitors.

Summary

As you can see, the installation and configuration of JobPress isn't that difficult. This project is so easy to complete that there really isn't any good reason why you shouldn't either build a dedicated job board or add one to your pre-existing website. Either way, you will be providing web users with a valuable service with very little effort on your part.

Even content generation will be practically effortless since you don't have to toil away writing material, as is the case with some websites. Instead, your content will be generated by businesses looking to hire employees.

A job board really does prove to be beneficial for everyone involved. For you, there are two obvious benefits associated with running a job board. You might use your job board to drive traffic to your main website or you could use it to generate revenue from job listing fees. Job seekers will benefit by being able to save time since your job board will provide them with job listings specifically targeted to their industry. Lastly, businesses will benefit since the job seekers visiting your website will be particularly qualified to perform the jobs that these businesses are looking to fill.

In this chapter, you learned how to build a job board as either a stand-alone website or as an additional element to another website. You were also shown how to improve the JobPress theme by making the sidebar widget-ready.

In the next chapter, you will learn how to build a microblog that's ideal for usage by families, friends, groups, or companies who would like a quick and easy way to stay in touch.

7
Project 7: Building a Microblogging Website

Technology has revolutionized the way we live in so many ways. Today, updating people about events in our day-to-day lives is as simple as sending an email or posting a short Tweet. Yes, **Twitter** offers a great way to post quick updates that are viewable by anyone following your account and, while Twitter may allow you to easily keep others informed, it isn't exactly ideal for colleagues, family, or friends looking to carry on private conversations.

Now, if you aren't familiar with Twitter, then you may be wondering what all the fuss is about. If that's the case, then take a moment to visit the Twitter website at `http://twitter.com` to see just what it is all about.

The features offered by Twitter are the inspiration for this project which will allow you to create a microblog of your own. This microblog will differ from Twitter, however, in that it's specifically designed so that a small group of users can confine their conversation to a central, private location. In order to accomplish this task the **P2** theme, along with a few plugins, will be required.

This theme was released by **Automattic**, who are the same people behind WordPress, and it makes it possible for absolutely anyone to set up their own microblog. This is perfect for organizations because, with P2, employees can quickly keep each other informed about work-related topics and projects. A microblog is also ideal for families and friends who would like an easy way to keep in touch.

So, Twitter may be great for keeping everyone up-to-date about everything, but when you want a private, smaller scale site dedicated to just your group's conversation, then P2 is the way to go. It's for this reason that you will be building a Twitter-like website with a few twists for this project.

In this chapter, you will learn how to:

- Customize the background of your microblog website
- Add a login box to the sidebar
- Create a members' page that includes individual RSS feeds for each user
- Make your microblog private so that log in is required to view the site
- Hide your microblog from search engine crawlers
- Moderate sign ups in order to prevent unwanted users from joining your group
- Mark particular posts as favorites so that following certain conversations is easy

Once this project is complete, you will have succeeded in creating a site that's similar to the one shown in the following screenshot:

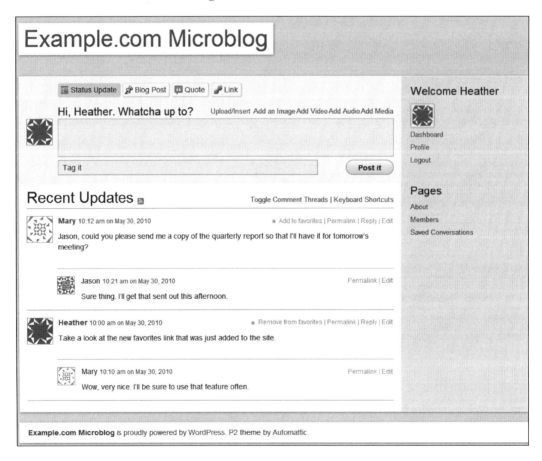

Introducing P2

The team over at Automattic drew their inspiration for this group blog theme from Twitter. While they liked what Twitter had to offer, they found themselves wanting more. Specifically, they wanted a way to send internal updates about what they were doing or working on as well as a way to post private messages that would only be visible to certain groups. It was for those reasons that they developed the **Prologue** theme.

After undergoing updates and improvements, Prologue evolved into P2. Today, this theme is jam-packed with many features that make microblogging as easy as can be. Here is just a sampling of what P2 has to offer:

- Front page posting
- Dynamic page updates
- Threaded comments on the front page
- In-line editing of both posts and comments
- Live tag suggestion
- Show or hide comments
- Keyboard shortcuts
- Real-time notifications

P2, which can be found at `http://p2theme.com/`, offers ease of use by providing access to many features right on the front page.

 Unfortunately, P2 version 1.1.3 isn't compatible for usage with either Internet Explorer 7 or 8.

Setting up and configuring P2

After installing and activating the P2 theme, you can access the **P2 Options** screen by clicking on **Appearance | P2 Options**. The **Functionality Options** section of this settings screen appears first. It contains the **Posting Access** setting which is currently disabled. To activate this setting, tick the checkbox next to **Allow any registered member to post**, so that users of all roles will be able to join in the conversation. Next is the **Hide Threads** setting, which should be left unchecked so that this setting will remain disabled.

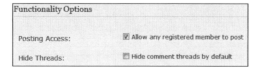

Having configured the **Functionality Options** it's now time to move on to the **Design Options** section. You will first encounter the **Custom Background Color** setting. It allows you to easily choose a color for your site's background. You can select a color for your website's background in one of two ways. You can either click the **Pick a Color** button to reveal a color wheel and a color palette or, if you know the hex number of the color that you would like to use, you can instead enter that number into the textbox located next to the **Pick a Color** button.

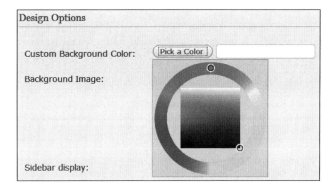

If you would prefer for your website to have a background image rather than a solid background color, then you can select from a few predefined images provided in the **Background Image** section. If, however, you prefer to stick with a solid color rather than using any of these images, you can leave this set to **None** and just move on to the **Sidebar display** setting.

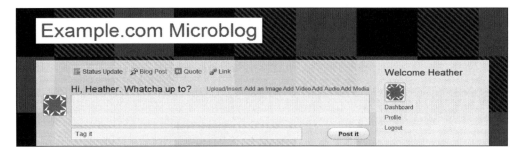

Currently, the sidebar is being included on your website which is ideal since you will need to add content to this section of your website later on. **Post prompt** is the next setting to be configured. What this setting does is allow you to customize the text that appears right above the post area on the frontend of your website. If you would like to display a custom prompt, enter it into the textbox. If nothing is entered here, then the default **Whatcha up to?** text will continue to be displayed. **Post Titles**, which is the last setting on this screen, should be left enabled, so click **Update Options** to save your changes.

Adding a login form to the sidebar

Out of the box, the P2 theme doesn't provide a handy way for users to log in and begin posting right away. Instead, those looking to use the site will need to navigate to the standard WordPress login page which, after log in, will redirect them to the **Dashboard**. This means that users will need to navigate from the **Dashboard** back to the front page of the website in order to add their posts.

As you can see, this situation is quite a nuisance for users. All of this hassle can easy be avoided just by adding a login box to the frontend of your microblog and, with the addition of the **Sidebar Login** plugin, which can be found at `http://wordpress.org/extend/plugins/sidebar-login`, you can easily implement this functionality.

Introducing Sidebar Login

With the Sidebar Login plugin installed, users will be able to log in from the frontend of your microblog and begin posting right away. Once they've logged in, users will be redirected right back to the page that they started at rather than ever being taken to the **Dashboard**. The Sidebar Login plugin also makes it easy to integrate the login box into your site using either a widget or a template tag.

Setting up and configuring Sidebar Login

After installing and activating the plugin, click on **Appearance | Sidebar Login**. This will take you to the **Sidebar Login** settings screen. The first setting that you will see is **Login redirect URL**. If there's a specific page that you want visitors to be taken to after logging in, enter it here. If this textbox is left empty then, after logging in, visitors will be redirected back to the page where they began, which is probably best since taking them to a different page will most likely cause confusion.

The **Logout redirect URL** setting is similar to **Login redirect URL** in that you can specify a web address where you would like visitors to be taken after they log out. Once again, if left blank, visitors will be returned to their current page upon log out, which is ideal. Both **Show Register Link** and **Show Lost Password Link** should be left set to **Yes**. The **Logged in links** setting should be left as is, so click **Save Changes**.

Implementing the Sidebar Login box

With all of the Sidebar Login settings configured, you now need to make the Sidebar **Login** box available to visitors. While you can place the sidebar login box using the `<?php sidebarlogin(); ?>` template tag, it's far easier to use the widget provided with this plugin instead.

To activate this widget, click on **Appearance | Widgets**. As you can see, there's only one widgetized area available with this theme named **Sidebar 1**. To make the login box available on your website, simply drag the **Sidebar Login** widget to **Sidebar 1**. With that done, visitors will now be able to log in from any page of your microblog by using the newly available sidebar login box.

Enabling registrations

With your current settings, it's impossible for users to join your microblog. That's because registrations are currently disabled. This issue can be dealt with easily by clicking on **Settings | General**. Once there, tick the checkbox next to **Anyone can register**. After enabling that setting, scroll down to the bottom of the screen and then click **Save Changes**.

Listing members with a follow-like feature

Currently, it's possible to follow certain members by clicking on their name and then subscribing to the RSS feed found on their individual author page. This process, however, makes it a bit of a chore to subscribe to individual group members, since their RSS feeds aren't listed in one central location. There is, however, a way to make the process of subscribing to certain authors much easier. All that's required is a page that includes the RSS feeds for each of your group members. From this page users can easily subscribe to the feeds of absolutely any other member.

To accomplish this objective the creation of both a template and a page will be required. To begin, open your text editor and then enter the following text.

```php
<?php
/*
Template Name: Members
*/
?>
<?php get_header() ?>

<div class="sleeve_main">

  <div id="main">
    <h2><?php the_title(); ?></h2>
    <?php wp_list_authors('show_fullname=0&optioncount=0&feed_image=/
wp-content/themes/p2/i/feed.png'); ?>
  </div> <!-- main -->

</div> <!-- sleeve -->

<?php get_footer() ?>
```

Save this template file as `members.php` and then upload it to the P2 theme folder. With that, you now have a template that can be used to create a members' page.

Publishing the Members' page

Having created this template you can now complete the second part of the process which is to publish the members' page. To do this, click on **Pages | Add New**. First, give the page a title. In this case, **Members** seems like the ideal title. Then, in the **Template** configuration area, select this template from the drop-down menu. Finally, click **Publish**. With that, all of your members, as well as their RSS feeds, will be conveniently displayed on one page.

While the members' page is all set up and ready to go, it still isn't accessible to site visitors because of the way that the P2 theme was designed. At present, P2 doesn't include links to any published pages. Luckily, you can easily make a link to this page available with the help of the **Pages** widget. To activate this widget, navigate to **Appearance | Widgets**. One there, drag the **Pages** widget into **Sidebar 1**. With that, visitors can now click over to the members' page via the link that now appears in your website's sidebar.

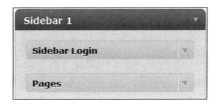

Making your microblog private

After you finish building your microblog, it's unlikely that you will want your site to be seen by everyone with an Internet connection. It doesn't matter whether you're building the site to be used in connection with your job or for usage by your family and friends. Either way, you and your users will most likely want to conduct your conversations in private. This means that you will need to block casual visitors as well as search engine crawlers from accessing your microblog. Luckily, in the case of the former, there's a way to make your microblog completely private with the help of the **Absolute Privacy** plugin found at `http://wordpress.org/extend/plugins/absolute-privacy/`. When it comes to the latter, the settings included with WordPress will be sufficient to keep the crawlers out.

Introducing Absolute Privacy

With the Absolute Privacy plugin installed, your microblog will become completely hidden from outside visitors. Even RSS feeds will be inaccessible to non-members. When someone navigates to your website the content that they would normally expect to see on any given page will, instead, be replaced by the WordPress login screen along with a message informing them that they must log in to view your site.

Once it's been activated, the plugin also alters the standard WordPress registration page so that it includes fields for first name, last name, and a password in addition to the username and email fields typically found there. The new registration page also informs users that their account must be approved before they will be able to take part in the site. That's because, with this plugin installed, the admin is given complete control over who may or may not gain access to the site.

After registration, the Absolute Privacy plugin sends two messages. One is sent to the user to tell them that their account is under review and that they will be unable to log in until their account has been approved.

The other is forwarded to the admin, which would be you, to alert you that a new registration has occurred. Upon receiving this notification, you must log in to the WordPress administration area and then either approve or delete the new registrant. After the user's account has been approved, they will receive another message telling them that they can now log in to the site.

Setting up and configuring Absolute Privacy

Once you've installed and activated the plugin, click on **Settings | Absolute Privacy**. The **General Settings** section is first. As you can see, the **Lockdown Website** setting is currently enabled. That's exactly what you want since it's this setting that will prevent random visitors from being able to access your website.

No changes need to be made to either the **Redirect Non-logged in Users To** or the **Allowed Pages** settings. The **Block Admin Access** setting is currently disabled. If this setting is enabled, subscribers will be unable to access any administrative pages, such as their profile page or the **Dashboard**. Depending upon your preferences, you may leave this feature disabled or you may enable it if you wish.

If you choose to enable the **Block Admin Access** feature, then, once you've finished configuring the Absolute Privacy plugin, you will need to return to the settings screen for the Sidebar Login plugin to perform some additional configurations. Once there, look for the **Logged in links** section. After both the **Dashboard** and **Profile** URLs you will now need to add `|true`. This will prevent either of those links from being displayed to anyone other than an admin level user.

RSS Disabled is currently selected in the **RSS Control** settings area. Once again, that's ideal since that option will make it so that only logged in users can access your microblog's RSS feeds.

General Settings		Setting Description:
Lockdown Website:	☑ Yes	If checked users must be logged in to view your blog. They will be redirected to the page they were looking for after they login.
Redirect Non-logged in Users To:		By default, non-logged in users will be redirected to the login form. Alternatively, you can enter a page ID here that you want non-logged in users to be redirected to instead.
Allowed Pages:		List page IDs separated by a comma (eg: 2,19,12). These pages will be accessible to non-logged in users.
Block Admin Access:	☐ Yes	This blocks subscribers from viewing any administrative pages, such as their profile page or the dashboard. If they try to access an administrative page they will be redirected to the homepage.
RSS Control:	◉ RSS Disabled ○ RSS On ○ Limited to headlines ○ Limited to [ ] Characters	Viewing your website's RSS feed does not require the user to login. Thus your RSS feed is publicly accessible if it is enabled. You may disable or limit the RSS feed above.

Next is the **Message Settings** area. This section contains the **Pending Welcome Message**, **Account Approval Message**, and **Admin Notification Message**. No changes are required in this section, but, if you would like to edit the text contained in these messages, then you can certainly do so. If you perform edits, just be sure to include the variables that already appear within these messages. That way those variable pieces of information will be fed into the text of each of these messages when they're generated.

Methods for moderating users

Once someone registers at the website you will have to either approve or delete their account. With the Absolute Privacy plugin, you can either moderate your users in bulk or one at a time.

Moderating users in bulk

To moderate your users in bulk, click on **Users | Moderate Users**. On this screen, you will see a list of the users who have signed up and are awaiting moderation. Tick the checkbox next to each of the users that you would like to approve and then click the **Approve Selected Users** button. Next, tick the checkboxes next to the users that you would like to delete and then click the **Delete Selected Users** button.

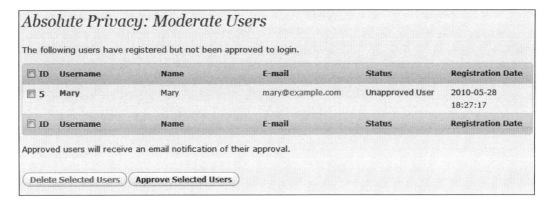

Moderating users one at a time

If you click the link found in the email that you receive when a new member joins your microblog, you won't be directed to the **Moderate Users** screen. Instead, you will be taken to the **User Waiting Approval** screen where you can approve or delete a pending user. On this screen you will only be able to moderate the account associated with the email that you received. This is done by clicking either the **Delete User** or the **Approve User** button.

Preventing your microblog from being indexed

Now that you've put measures in place to prevent unauthorized users from accessing your microblog, it's time to deal with the search engine crawlers. To block the crawlers from indexing your website you need to access the **Privacy Settings** screen by clicking on **Settings | Privacy**.

On this screen, in the **Privacy Settings** area, you will most likely find that the option to make your blog visible to everyone, including search engines, is enabled. If that's the case, then you need to select the option to allow normal visitors, but block search engines. That way your website will be protected. With that change made, click **Save Changes**.

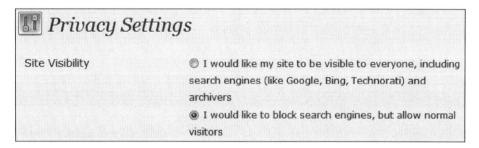

Following a particular conversation

A microblog is basically designed to provide users with a way to carry on discussions and post updates via their browsers. It can, however, become a bit difficult to follow each topic if the site becomes overrun with conversations. Providing users with a way to mark certain conversations as favorites can do a lot to alleviate this problem. Once a user marks a topic as a favorite, they will easily be able to keep up with and take part in that conversation. To add a feature such as this a plugin is, of course, required.

Introducing WP Favorite Posts

With the **WP Favorite Posts** plugin, found at `http://wordpress.org/extend/plugins/wp-favorite-posts/`, users can mark certain posts as favorites, which will make it easy for them to keep track of the conversations that they want to follow. With this plugin, favorites are saved in two ways. For users who aren't logged in, favorites are saved using cookies. Since users of your website will always be logged in when using this plugin, this method of saving favorites will never be used. Instead, the second method, which is to save favorites to the database, will be used.

Setting up and configuring WP Favorite Posts

Once this plugin has been activated, navigate to **Settings | Favorite Posts** to begin configuring its settings. In the **Options** area, you will first see the **Only registered users can favorite** setting, which should remain enabled. Next, you will see the **Before Link Image** setting. Currently, the larger star image is selected, but you may choose any of the available images that you like. You may also specify the URL for a custom image or opt not to show an image at all. **Most favorited posts statics** is the last setting that you will see in this area. This setting can be left set to **Enabled** or changed to **Disabled** if you prefer.

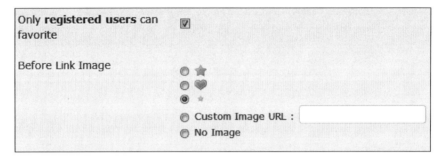

As you look at the settings found in the **Label Settings** area, you will see that they're mainly designed to let you specify the various lines of text used in connection with this plugin. If you wish, you may edit any of this text. In this area, you will also see the **Show remove link** and **Show add link** settings. Both are currently disabled, so tick the checkbox next to each of these settings to enable them.

Since that's the only edit that needs to be performed in this section of the screen, click **Update options** to save your settings.

Implementing the functionality of the WP Favorite Posts plugin

Even though the WP Favorite Posts plugin is installed and configured, it's currently impossible for anyone to use its features. That's because, until you place the WP Favorite Posts template tag into one of the appropriate P2 theme files, the **Add to favorites** link won't appear. In addition to making that change, you must also create a special page that will be used to house all of the favorite conversations saved by your users.

Begin by opening the `entry.php` file, which is found in your theme's folder, so that you can put the features of this plugin into action. Once you have that file open, look for `<span class="actions">`. Once you locate that, place `<?php wpfp_link(); ?> |` directly after it. That section of your `entry.php` file should now look like this.

```
<span class="actions">
<?php wpfp_link(); ?> |
<?php if ( !is_single() ) : ?>
<a href="<?php the_permalink() ?>" class="thepermalink"><?php _e(
'Permalink', 'p2' ) ?></a>
```

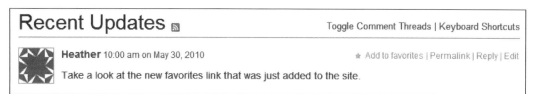

Now, when you visit your website, you will see the **Add to favorites** link is visible, which means that visitors can now save conversations as favorites. Until you create the favorites page required by this plugin, however, they will have no way to access those saved conversations.

Creating this page is easy and requires that you first click on **Pages | Add New**. Next, give your page an appropriate name. For example, you might want to call it Favorites or, perhaps, **Saved Conversations**. After naming your page, paste **[wp-favorite-posts]** into the text area. Now, all that's left to do is click **Publish**.

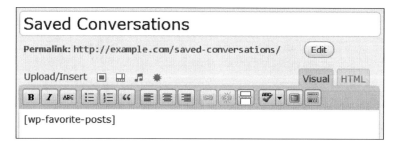

To see this page in action, visit your website and then click the **Add to favorites** link next to any conversation. Next, visit the page that you just created and, as you can see, your newly favorited conversation is shown there. You will also find a **remove** link next to the saved conversation so that, when the conversation has run its course, you can delete it from your list of favorites. If you like, you may also click the **Clear favorites** link to delete all of the conversations that you've saved.

Saved Conversations

- Take a look at the new favorites link th... remove

* Clear favorites

Changing the Discussion Settings

Your site is almost complete, but there are still two more settings that must be configured before your microblog is finished. To take care of these last two settings, click on **Settings | Discussion** to reach the **Discussion Settings** screen.

Disabling comment notifications

With the way WordPress is currently configured, your inbox will quickly become flooded with messages. That's because you will receive an alert every time a user adds a comment to your microblog. Since that's certainly not ideal, this feature will have to be disabled.

Look for the **E-mail me whenever** settings area. In this section, you need to remove the checkmark next to **Anyone posts a comment** to disable this setting. Once that's done, your users will be able to conduct conversations without inconveniencing you.

Removing commenting restrictions

As things stand now, if new users submit comments in an attempt to reply to a conversation, their responses won't appear right away. That's because the settings in WordPress currently require that users must have had one comment previously approved by the administrator before they can start posting comments that don't require any approval. This will certainly cause confusion for your users since they will be unsure why their comment isn't being published to the site. It will also create a considerable amount of unnecessary work for you because you will have to approve comment after comment.

To disable this feature, remove the checkmark from the setting labeled **Comment author must have a previously approved comment**. Now, all of the comments that your users submit will immediately be published on your microblog. With these changes made, you can now scroll to the bottom of the screen and then click **Save Changes**.

Summary

Having reached the end of this project, you will now have a microblog set up where you and your colleagues, family, or friends can talk privately amongst yourselves. With the privacy features that you've enabled, you and your users can rest assured that your microblog is completely private. That means that random strangers will never be able to access your website and view your conversations. The ability to mark certain posts as favorites will also make it easy for the members of your site to follow the conversations that they're actively participating in so that they never miss a thing.

In this chapter, you learned how to use the P2 theme, the Absolute Privacy plugin, and the **Site Visibility** settings in WordPress to build a private microblog. From there, you were shown how to make it easy for your users to follow messages posted by certain members as well as mark conversations as favorites.

In the next chapter, you will learn how to build a local business directory where potential clients can browse member profiles submitted by businesses in that particular area.

8
Project 8: Building a Local Business Directory

All over the world people are looking for local businesses to hire while local businesses are searching for clients to serve. Just imagine how grateful both would be if you managed to bring the two together. It's by building a WordPress-powered local business directory that you can do just that.

Unlike some of the other projects detailed in this book, this one requires no premium plugins or premium themes. Instead, it can be completed using only free resources. With the combination of plugins, custom pages, and the right configurations and edits you will be able to build a directory where businesses in a particular area can showcase themselves.

Sure, a local business directory is beneficial to both businesses and potential clients, but what about you? What do you get out of building this site besides the satisfaction that comes with knowing that you're helping to bring businesses and clients together? The answer is ad revenue. The great thing about sites of this type is that they're ideally suited to selling advertising. Rather than going the **Adsense** route you can, instead, solicit advertising from local businesses. If your site is well-designed, filled with member listings, and well-trafficked, then you shouldn't have any trouble securing advertisements. Given how unpredictable CPC advertising can be, this alternative revenue source could actually prove to be much more stable.

With all of the localities out there you could quite easily build several of these sites to serve multiple locations. You could then build them up, drive traffic to them, and watch your earnings multiply with every new site that you add to your portfolio.

In this chapter, you will learn how to:

- Brand the registration and login pages
- Protect your site from spam registrations

- Add additional fields to your website's registration page
- Let users add a photo to their profile page
- Create a custom template, so that the information provided by your users will be included on their profile pages
- Build another custom template and use it to create a static home page
- Create a template that will be used to build a page that contains a searchable, sortable listing of your members

Once this project is complete, you will have succeeded in creating a site that's similar to the one shown in the following screenshot:

Introducing Register Plus

The **Register Plus** plugin, found at `http://wordpress.org/extend/plugins/` `register-plus/`, will play an integral part in the creation of your local business directory. The main feature that makes it so important to this project is the fact that it allows you to add additional fields to both the WordPress sign up screen and the **Profile** page found in the **Dashboard**. This is important because you can use those new fields to request relevant information from the business people signing up at your site since it's this information that will be used to build their profile pages. In addition to that feature, this plugin can also do quite a lot more. Here are just some of the other things that you will be able to do once this plugin has been installed.

- Brand your local business directory by replacing the WordPress logo with your own custom image
- Bypass the usual auto-generated passwords provided to new users and, instead, allow registrants to choose a password during registration
- Protect yourself legally by displaying a disclaimer, license agreement, or privacy policy during registration
- Safeguard your directory from spam registrations by using either the Simple CAPTCHA or the reCAPTCHA feature to verify that each sign up is genuine
- Ensure that the email address provided by each registrant is real by requiring users to click the validation link that's included in their registration email

Setting up and configuring Register Plus

After installing and activating this plugin, a **Register Plus** link will be added to the **Settings** menu. Click on that link to be taken to this plugin's configuration screen.

Password is the first setting that you will see and it contains two options. They are **Allow New Registrations to set their own Password** and **Enable Password Strength Meter**. Both of these can be configured to your liking.

 Unfortunately, even if the **Allow New Registrations to set their own Password** setting is enabled, registrants who log in to the **Dashboard** will still be shown a notice that tells them that they're using the auto-generated password for their account. It will also ask them if they would like to change it.

If you tick the checkbox next to **Enable Password Strength Meter**, four textboxes will appear. These textboxes contain the prompts that will be shown if a user enters a password that's too short, bad, good, or strong. These prompts are fine at their defaults, so there's no need to edit them. Instead, move on to the next settings area which will allow you to upload a custom logo.

Click the **Browse** button in the **Custom Logo** settings area to locate the image on your computer that you would like to use as the logo on your local business directory's login page. Once you locate the image, select it, and then click **Open**.

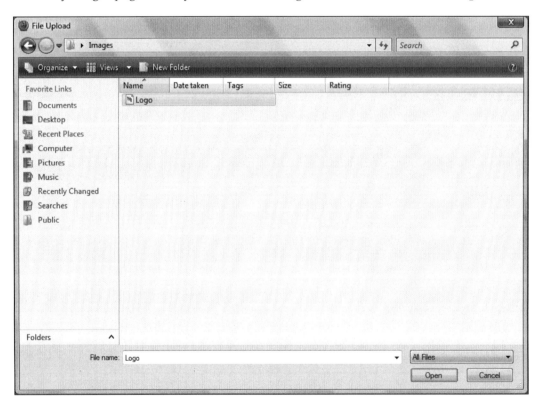

The **Email Verification** setting is currently disabled and, if you plan on enabling **Admin Verification**, it must remain that way. If you don't want to moderate your users, tick the checkbox next to **Prevent fake email address registrations** to activate the **Email Verification** feature. With this setting enabled, new registrants will need to click a link in their notification email to verify their email address and enable their account. Once this setting has been activated, additional settings will become available that will let you specify the length of the grace period that registrants will be given to click the verification link before their account is deleted. This is currently set to **7** days. You can either leave that number as is of change it to a different length of time.

If you chose to activate **Email Verification**, then skip **Admin Verification** and move on to the next setting. If, however, you opted to leave **Email Verification** disabled, so that you could moderate user registrations, then activate the **Admin Verification** feature by ticking the checkbox next to **Moderate all user registrations to require admin approval**.

It doesn't really make sense for you to enable the **Invitation Code** setting since it would prevent local businesses who stumble upon your site from signing up, so skip this setting and move on to **CAPTCHA**. With this setting, you have three options. You can either set it to **None**, **Simple CAPTCHA**, or **reCAPTCHA**. You should make every effort to safeguard your site against spammers and spoof sign ups, so it's best to enable one of these CAPTCHA features. **reCAPTCHA** is well-known, widely used, and supports a good cause, so it seems like the best choice. So, tick the radio button next to **reCAPTCHA** to select it as the spam prevention measure that you will use on your site.

After **reCAPTCHA** has been selected, two textboxes will appear where you need to enter your public and private keys. If you've already signed up to use this service, and added this site to your account, then enter those keys into the appropriate boxes. If you don't have keys for this site, then you need to get them, so right-click the **Sign up** link and then open it in a new browser window to visit the reCAPTCHA website at http://recaptcha.net.

Once you reach this website, click on **My Account**. Since reCAPTCHA is owned by Google, if you already have an account to use one of their other services, you can use that username and password to log in now. If you don't have an account with Google, then you need to click on **Create an account now** in order to use this service.

Now that you have access to the site, click **My Account | Add a New Site**. On this page, enter the URL of your local business directory into the textbox. **Enable this key on all domains (global key)** should remain disabled, so click **Create Key**. Having done that, you will now be taken to a page that contains the public and private keys that have been assigned to your domain. Now that they've been generated, copy and paste them into the appropriate textboxes on your website.

The **Disclaimer**, **License Agreement**, and **Privacy Policy** settings are next and, to protect yourself legally, you should enable both the **Disclaimer** and **Privacy Policy** settings. It's unlikely, given the nature of your site, that you will have any need for the **License Agreement** setting, so this can, most likely, remain disabled. After enabling these settings, text areas will appear where you can enter the text of your disclaimer and privacy policy. If you wish, you can also edit the text found in the **Agreement Text** fields. This text is displayed along with each of these agreements.

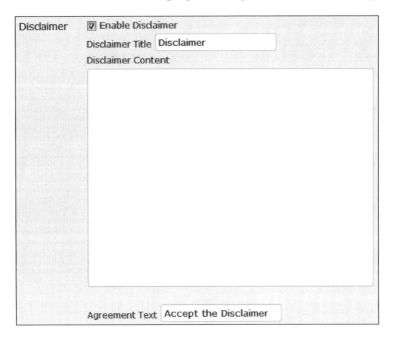

The **Allow Existing Email** setting is next and what this does is allow more than one person to sign up at your website using the same email address. Unfortunately, this feature doesn't exactly function properly. Yes, registrants sharing the same email address could sign up if this feature were to be enabled. If they visit their **Profile** page and attempt to make any edits, however, they will receive the following error message. For that reason, this setting shouldn't be enabled.

> **ERROR:** This email is already registered, please choose another one.

The next group of settings that you will need to configure is located in the **Additional Profile Fields** section of this configuration screen.

First, select which fields you would like to add to your website's registration screen. Next, in the **Required Profile Fields** area, choose which fields you would like to designate as being required.

The last configurable setting that you will find in this area is **Required Field Style Rules**. Here you can edit the CSS that governs the appearance of the required fields. While no changes need to be made to this setting, you may make any edits that you like if you would prefer for these required fields to be styled in a particular way.

Additional Profile Fields

Check the fields you would like to appear on the Registration Page.

Name	☑ First Name ☑ Last Name
Contact Info	☑ Website ☑ AIM ☑ Yahoo IM ☑ Jabber / Google Talk
About Yourself	☐ About Yourself
Required Profile Fields	☐ First Name ☐ Last Name ☑ Website ☐ AIM ☐ Yahoo IM ☐ Jabber / Google Talk ☐ About Yourself
Required Field Style Rules	border:solid 1px #E6DB55;background-color:#FFFFF

The **User Defined Fields** area is next. In the **Custom Field** section, you can create additional fields that you would like to include on both the registration screen and the **Profile** page located in the **Dashboard**. In the **Additional Profile Fields** section, there was no option for adding a company name field, so you should add that now.

Since you require nothing more than a simple textbox, **Extra Options** can be left blank. To name this field, enter **Company Name** into the unlabeled textbox. Leave the drop-down menu set to **Text Field** and then tick the checkboxes next to **Add Registration Field**, **Add Profile Field**, and **Required**.

Click the green plus sign image to add another blank **Custom Field**. Then, repeat this process to create two more custom fields called **Phone** and **Street Address**. In this instance, however, don't tick the checkbox to make either of these a required field.

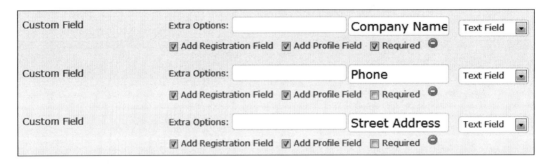

Since this is supposed to be a local business directory you need to configure it so that only businesses in your area can join. To do that you can create a drop-down menu that only contains locations in the area that your website targets. For this example, suppose that you're building a website targeted to Los Angeles county. If that were the case, then you would need to create a menu that only contains cities located within that area.

To do that, begin by clicking the green plus sign image to add a new **Custom Field**. In the **Extra Options** textbox enter the cities that you would like to allow your users to choose from. Next, enter **City** into the unlabeled textbox. Then, from the drop-down menu, choose **Select Field**. Finally, tick the checkboxes next to **Add Registration Field**, **Add Profile Field**, and **Required**. With the creation of this drop-down menu your website will now be set up so that businesses outside of your chosen area will be unable to select their location and, therefore, unable to sign up.

There's still one more custom field that you need to add, so click the green plus sign image once again. In the **Additional Profile Fields** section it was possible to add an **About Yourself** field. The title of this field, however, would only confused registrants since it's not themselves, but their businesses, that you want them to share information about. For that reason, it's better to create a custom field where they can enter this information. Nothing needs to be entered in the **Extra Options** textbox, so move on to the unlabeled textbox where you will need to enter **Company Profile**. Next, from the drop-down menu, select **Text Area**. Finally, place checkmarks next to **Add Registration Field**, **Add Profile Field**, and **Required**.

In addition to adding textboxes, select fields, and text areas, you can also create date fields, checkboxes, radio boxes, and hidden fields. Once again, any additional fields that you decide to create will be dictated by your preferences and the specific type of businesses that you plan to feature on your site.

Since it's unlikely that the registration page would require a date field, you can bypass the **Date Field Settings** area. You can also scroll past the **Auto-Complete Queries** section and, instead, concentrate on the **Customize User Notification Email** area.

Customize User Notification Email

Custom User Email Notification	☑ Enable
From Email	hwallace@example.com
From Name	Local Business Directory
Subject	[Local Business Directory] Your username and passw
User Message	

Replacement Keys: %user_login% %user_pass% %user_email% %blogname% %siteurl% %firstname% %lastname% %website% %aim% %yahoo% %jabber% %about% %company_name% %user_ip% %user_ref% %user_host% %user_agent%

```
%blogname% Registration
---------------------------

Here are your credentials:
Username: %user_login%
Password: %user_pass%
Confirm Registration: %siteurl%

Thank you for registering with %blogname%!
```

☐ Send as HTML   ☐ Convert new lines to <br/> tags (HTML only)

Login Redirect URL   http://example.com   This will redirect the users login after registration.

The default text sent to users upon registration is a bit sparse, so it would be best to rewrite this message so that it includes more information. To do this, tick the checkbox next to the **Custom User Email Notification** setting. Once this feature is enabled, a configurations area will appear. Here you can can edit **From Email**, **From Name**, **Subject**, and **User Message**.

As you rewrite your message, be sure to make use of the **Replacement Keys**, which are used to insert variable information into the message, such as the registrant's login name and password. If you would like to include HTML within your message, then be sure to tick the checkboxes for **Send as HTML** and **Convert new lines to <br/> tags (HTML only)**.

The **Login Redirect URL** setting is next and is already pre-populated with the root domain for your site. If you would prefer for users to be redirected to a different page after log in, then enter that URL in the textbox instead.

Next, you will come to the **Customize Admin Notification Email** settings area. Currently, the **Admin Email Notification** setting is enabled, which means that you will receive an email every time someone registers at your site. It's best to leave this setting enabled, because these notifications will allow you to monitor the registrations at your site, so that you can be sure that no spammers have slipped through. Next is the **Custom Admin Email Notification** setting. If this setting were to be activated, you would be able to make edits to the admin notification email. This feature, however, is disabled and there's really no point in activating it, because the default text is perfectly fine.

In the **Custom CSS for Register & Login Pages** area you can enter custom CSS that will override the styles currently being applied to the registration and login pages. If you would like to style either of these pages to your liking, then do so now. Otherwise, click **Save Changes**.

Inspecting the changes made to the login and registration pages

Once you've finished configuring the Register Plus plugin, your registration and login pages will look very different from the ones typically used by WordPress. Their exact appearance will, of course, depend upon the CSS changes that you made during the configuration of Register Plus.

Your login page will differ from the standard WordPress login screen, because it will now display the logo that you uploaded during the configuration of Register Plus.

When you visit your site's registration page you will see that it has undergone the most drastic change. First, the logo that you previously uploaded has also been added to this screen. The custom fields that you created during the configuration of Register Plus are also being included here. Lastly, the reCAPTCHA box is being displayed to deter spam registrations.

Allowing members to include a profile photo

There are many reasons why a business might want to include a photo along with their profile. They might want to display a picture of their business, a photo of one of their products, or simply add a company logo. With your present setup, it's impossible for users to add an image to their profile, but, with the addition of the **User Photo** plugin, which can be found at `http://wordpress.org/extend/plugins/user-photo/`, they will be able to do just that.

Introducing User Photo

The User Photo plugin provides the members of your site with a way to associate a profile photo with their account while also allowing the admin to maintain a great deal of control over the image uploaded by each user. For example, the admin can control image size and image compression, and even moderate submitted photos.

Unfortunately, the image upload box used by this plugin won't be added to the registration page, so registrants won't be able to submit their photo at sign up. Instead, the image upload box is added to the **Additional Information** section of the **Profile** page. That means, after registration, the user will need to log in and visit their **Profile** page in order to add a profile photo.

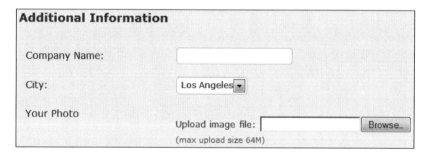

Setting up and configuring User Photo

Once this plugin has been installed and activated, a link, entitled **User Photo**, will be added to the **Settings** menu. Click on that link to be taken to the **User Photo Options** screen.

The first two settings deal with image size. Both should be fine with their current settings, but you may change them, if you like.

The **Serve Avatar as Fallback** setting is next and, since some people won't upload images, it's a good idea to enable this setting. You want to make sure that the image that a user uploads is always shown instead of their avatar so **Override Avatar with User Photo** should also be enabled.

The **JPEG compression** setting is currently compressing uploaded images by 90%. At this percentage, the images that your users upload certainly won't be displayed at their highest quality. You should, however, probably leave this at 90% to ensure that your server isn't put under a strain caused by serving these images. If you find that the quality of these user-submitted images is too poor at 90%, then you could try slightly lowering this number until quality improves. Just be sure not to reduce compression too much as it's better to sacrifice image quality, rather than put too much of a burden on your server's resources.

The **Notify this administrator by email when user photo needs approval** setting is currently set to **(none)** which means that the images uploaded by your users won't be moderated. This is fine, because it's unlikely that you will want to undertake the time-consuming task of moderating the images submitted by your users. Next you will see **Require user photo moderation for all users at or below this level**. This is currently set to **Author**, but it should be changed to **(none)**, so that moderation isn't required for users of any level.

Adding the company name to the title bar

On a typical author page the username is included in the title bar, but, given the nature of this site, it has no place being there. Instead, it would be more appropriate to display the company name entered by the user. To accomplish this, edits will need to be made to your theme's `header.php` file.

In a text editor, open your theme's `header.php` template file and then enter the following lines of code just above the opening `<title>` tag:

```php
<?php
  if(isset($_GET['author_name'])) :
    $curauth = get_userdatabylogin($author_name);
  else :
    $curauth = get_userdata(intval($author));
  endif;?>
```

What this piece of PHP does is retrieve all of the information that's specific to the author whose page is currently being viewed. This information can then be included by echoing `$curauth->field_name;` with `field_name`, of course, being replaced by the name of the field that you want to display.

With `header.php` still open, you next need to replace the code currently being used to display the title on your site with a new, conditional title. This new code will check to see if the page being displayed is an author page and, if it is, the company name for that member will be included in the title. So, replace the opening `<title>` tag and the closing `</title>` tag, along with everything found in between them, with the following code. Then, save your changes.

```
<title>
<?php if (is_author () ) {
    single_cat_title(); echo $curauth->company_name, ' &laquo; ' ;
bloginfo('name');
} else { wp_title('&laquo;', true, 'right'); bloginfo('name');
} ?>
</title>
```

Later on you will be able to see this new title in action. For now, however, you should move on to building the page that will be used to display all of the information provided by your users.

Building a customized profile page

With the help of the Register Plus plugin, your registration page is now configured in such a way that it collects quite a lot of information from your users. Most of that additional information is, however, currently useless because, without a customized `author.php` file, much of it won't even appear on your users' profile pages.

In order to display this information, you will need to create a custom `author.php` file that's specifically designed to retrieve the information entered into those additional fields. To create this file, you can build off of the page template included with your theme.

In your text editor, open the `page.php` file that's included with your theme. As you take a look at the file, you will see that the header is called at the top of the page and that the footer is, most likely, called at the bottom. Depending upon the design of your theme, you may also see a call to the sidebar. To build your custom page, nearly all of the content must be deleted from this file. The only things that should remain are `<?php get_header(); ?>`, `<?php get_footer(); ?>`, and, if your file includes a call to the sidebar, `<?php get_sidebar(); ?>`.

You will need to use this as the starting point for two pages, so first save it as `members.php`. Then, save it once again as `author.php`. Close `members.php` because right now you need to focus on building the `author.php` file. So, in `author.php`, enter the following code just after the `<?php get_header(); ?>` tag.

```
<div>

<div>
  <h2><?php echo $curauth->company_name; ?></h2>
  <?php if( get_the_author_meta('street_address', $curauth->ID) != '')
:?>
  <?php echo $curauth->street_address; ?><br />
  <?php endif;?>
  <?php if( get_the_author_meta('city', $curauth->ID) != '') :?>
  <?php echo $curauth->city; ?>, CA
  <?php endif;?>
</div>

<div>
  <h2>Website/Contact Information</h2>
  <a href="<?php echo $curauth->user_url; ?>"><?php echo $curauth-
>user_url; ?></a><br />
  <?php if( get_the_author_meta('phone', $curauth->ID) != '') :?>
  Phone: <?php echo $curauth->phone; ?><br />
  <?php endif;?>
  <?php if( get_the_author_meta('aim', $curauth->ID) != '') :?>
  AIM: <?php echo $curauth->aim; ?><br />
  <?php endif;?>
  <?php if( get_the_author_meta('yim', $curauth->ID) != '') :?>
  Yahoo IM: <?php echo $curauth->yim; ?><br />
  <?php endif;?>
  <?php if( get_the_author_meta('jabber', $curauth->ID) != '') :?>
  Jabber/Google Talk: <?php echo $curauth->jabber; ?><br />
  <?php endif;?>
</div>

<div>
  <h2>About <?php echo $curauth->company_name; ?></h2>
  <?php echo $curauth->company_profile; ?>

<div>
  <?php userphoto($wp_query->get_queried_object()) ?>
</div>

</div>

</div>
```

The author-specific information retrieved in the header is used to build much of the content on this page. As was the case with the page title, these details are included by echoing $curauth->field_name; throughout the page, with field_name, once again, being replaced by the actual field that you would like to display.

As you will have noticed, some of these fields are wrapped in conditional statements while others aren't. The reason for this is that some of these fields are required while others aren't. If these non-required fields were not wrapped in conditional statements, then the text that's used to label them would appear even if nothing was entered by the registrant.

The code used on this page retrieves the **Company Name**, **City**, **Phone**, **Street Address**, and **Company Profile** custom fields that you added earlier during the configuration of Register Plus. It also includes a call to retrieve the user photo for that member. If you added any other custom fields during the configuration of Register Plus, and you would like them to appear on this profile page, then you will need to add them to this author page as well.

The process for displaying a custom field will depend upon whether you designated it as being required or not. If the field isn't required, then you will need to enter the following code. This code includes the conditional statement so that nothing will be displayed if the user doesn't enter anything into that particular field. You will, of course, need to replace both Field Name and field_name with the actual title that you used for that field. When replacing field_name be sure to only use lowercase text and an underscore rather than a space.

```
<?php if( get_the_author_meta('field_name', $curauth->ID) != '') :?>
Field Name: <?php echo $curauth->field_name; ?><br />
<?php endif;?>
```

Required fields need much less code in order to be displayed. For fields of this type, the following is all that's required. Once again, you will need to replace both Field Name and field_name with the title that you used when creating your custom field. You will also need to be sure, when replacing field_name, that it's entered in lowercase and that each word is separated by an underscore rather than a space.

```
Field Name: <?php echo $curauth->field_name; ?><br />
```

Once you've finished working on the authors.php file, save it and then upload it to your theme's folder.

Later on, when a profile page has been added to your site, it may not look like much. That's because you may need to make some additions to your stylesheet in order to get these member profile pages looking just right. For example, you will probably find that a new style must be created for the profile photo, so that the company profile text wraps around the image.

Special considerations when configuring WordPress for use with this project

In addition to all of the plugins that you have had to configure in the process of creating this site, there are also certain changes that you will need to make to the settings used by WordPress, so that your site will operate smoothly.

Allowing registrations

First of all, if the **Membership** setting in WordPress isn't enabled, visitors will be unable to register at your site. This is easily remedied by navigating to **Settings | General Settings** and then ticking the checkbox next to **Anyone can register**.

In creating this site, its purpose isn't to allow members to post messages. Instead, the only thing that you want them to be able to do is create and edit their profile. That means that **New User Default Role** should be left set to **Subscriber**. Otherwise the members at your site will be able to perform actions beyond what you want to allow them to do. With the **General Settings** properly configured, scroll to the bottom of the screen and then click **Save Changes**.

Improving the author permalink structure

Now, it's time to think about how the links on your site will be formatted. With their default setting, they won't be very memorable, which means that it will be difficult for the members of your site to share their profile pages with potential clients. Your site's links also won't be very search engine friendly in their current state.

To correct these problems, navigate to **Settings | Permalinks**. Once there, in the **Common Settings** area, choose the **Custom Structure** setting. Then, enter **/%postname%/** into the textbox next to that setting. Finally, click **Save Changes**.

Common settings

◯ Default	`http://example.com/?p=123`
◯ Day and name	`http://example.com/2010/05/21/sample-post/`
◯ Month and name	`http://example.com/2010/05/sample-post/`
◯ Numeric	`http://example.com/archives/123`
◉ Custom Structure	`/%postname%/`

Switching to a static home page

With your current settings, the front page of your website is acting as a blog. That means that, if you had published any posts, they would be appearing on the home page of your site. Since posts have no place on this site, you need to take steps to create a new, static home page.

Creating a template for the static home page

If you were to use the default template for your static home page, you would soon find that the title of the page is being displayed. To prevent the title from displaying on this page you will need to build a custom template file that will be used exclusively for your home page.

This template can easily be created by using the `page.php` file, found in your theme's folder, as a building block. So, open `page.php` in your text editor and then, at the top of the file, add the following.

```
<?php /* Template Name: Static Home */ ?>
```

Now, you will need to remove the code used to display the title of the page, so look for the section that includes `<?php the_title(); ?>`. The content included in this section will differ depending on your theme. For example, you may find that additional elements, such as the `<?php the_permalink(); ?>`, are also included along with the title template tag.

Once you locate that section, remove all of the code associated with the title. That means, if the permalink template tag is included in this section, you will need to remove it as well. Next, save this file as `statichome.php` and then upload it to your theme's folder.

Publishing the static home page

Now you need to publish a new page that will be used in place of the typical post-filled home page. So, click on **Page | Add New**. Name this page something like **Index** or **Home** and then, in the text area, enter any content that you would like to appear on your front page. You might, for example, want to include a paragraph or two explaining what your site is about and how it can benefit both businesses and potential clients.

From the **Template** drop-down menu, select **Static Home**. Next, in the **Discussion** section, both **Allow Comments** and **Allow trackbacks and pingbacks** on this page should be disabled. Finally, click **Publish**.

Now it's time to visit the **Reading Settings** screen, so click on **Settings | Reading**. At the top of the page you will see the **Front page displays** settings area. Tick the radio button next to **A static page** and then select the page that you just created from the **Front page** drop-down menu. Finally, click **Save Changes**. Having completed all of those steps, the home page for your local business directory will now display a static page.

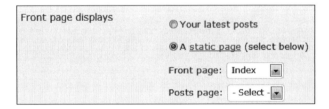

Preventing duplicate links in the navigation menu

Now that you have published your static home page you will see that a link to the page that you created has been added to the navigation menu on your site.

This link obviously shouldn't be displayed because it's causing your home page content to be accessible at two locations. Steps must, therefore, be taken to remove this link and that's where the **Exclude Pages** plugin, which is available at `http://wordpress.org/extend/plugins/exclude-pages/`, comes in.

Introducing Exclude Pages

As you might suspect from the name, this plugin allows you to exclude certain pages from your navigation menus. The plugin accomplishes this by adding an **Include this page in user menus option** to each page that's published on your site. This setting is enabled by default, but if you choose to disable it, a link to that page will no longer appear on the navigation menus.

Setting up and configuring Exclude Pages

After installing and then activating the Exclude Pages plugin, navigate to **Pages | Edit**. Next, select the page that you just created. Locate the **Exclude Pages** setting and then remove the checkmark next to **Include this page in user menus**. Click **Update** to save these changes. With that, the link to this page will no longer appear in your site's navigation menus.

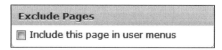

Removing author from the permalink

Even with the improvements that you've made to the permalink, it still isn't perfect. That's because the word author is included in the URL. This doesn't make sense since this is a local business directory where your members won't be writing any posts and, therefore, won't be authors. This problem can, however, be corrected with the help of the **WP htaccess Control** plugin found at `http://wordpress.org/extend/plugins/wp-htaccess-control/`.

Introducing WP htaccess Control

The WP htaccess Control plugin is designed to add custom rules to the `.htaccess` file created by WordPress as well as customize the author permalink. This plugin may include many features, but it's only the ability to customize the author permalink that you're interested in.

Setting up and configuring WP htaccess Control

Once the WP htaccess Control plugin has been installed and activated, a **WP htaControl** link will be added to the **Settings** menu. Click on that link to be taken to the **Wp htaccess Control** configuration screen. Once you arrive on this screen you will see several collapsible settings areas.

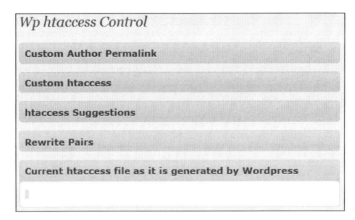

Since your one and only objective in using this plugin is to customize the author permalink, you can ignore all of these collapsible settings areas except for the one titled **Custom Author Permalink**. Click on that to reveal the **Author Base** setting. In the textbox, type the word that you would like to be used instead of author in the permalink. Depending upon the businesses that you're planning to feature, you might substitute author for something like plumbers or electricians. Once you've entered the word of your choosing, click **Save all changes**.

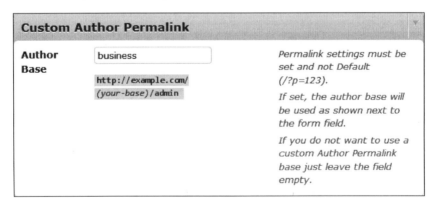

Creating a profile and adding a photo

It's now important that you create a member profile because, without first performing this step, it will be impossible to properly configure the **Members List** plugin that you will install next. That's because, if an account hasn't been added to the database, then some of that plugin's settings won't include the custom fields that you previously created during the configuration of the Register Plus plugin. You must also upload a profile photo during this process so that the fields associated with the User Photo plugin will be made available when configuring Members List.

Creating this profile will also serve another purpose since it will allow you to test the system to ensure that the registration process is functioning smoothly. So, visit your website's registration page and then sign up. As you do, be sure to complete all of the fields. The next step that you need to take will depend upon the verification options that you chose during the configuration of Register Plus. Once your account is verified, log in to the **Dashboard** and then visit the **Profile** page for this account. Scroll down to the **Additional Information** section and then upload an image to be used as a profile photo.

With these steps complete, you will have verified that visitors will be able to submit a business profile to your site. You will also be able to move on to the next step which is to add the Members List plugin to your site.

 After you finish building your local business directory don't forget to delete the test account that you created during this step.

Deluxe Widgets

1212 Any Place Ave.
Los Angeles, CA

Website/Contact Information

http://example.com

About Deluxe Widgets

 Deluxe Widgets has been manufacturing widgets since 1924. With that many years in the business, they have a wealth of experience in the industry. That means that you can rest assured that Deluxe Widgets will have exactly the right kind of widget that you need when you need it.

Displaying your members list

At this point businesses can sign up at your site and build their profiles, but you still don't have a centralized page where their listings can easily be found. That's why you must now build a members' page. To build this page you will need to use the Members List plugin found at `http://wordpress.org/extend/plugins/members-list/`.

Introducing Members List

With the Members List plugin you will be able to create a highly configurable page that displays the users on your site. Visitors to this page will be able to view businesses in a paginated list, search through the various businesses, and sort listings based upon certain criteria.

Setting up and configuring Members List

After the installation and activation of this plugin is complete a **Members List** menu will be added to the **Dashboard**. This menu contains three settings screens that you will need to visit in order to configure this plugin.

Settings

To begin, click on **Members List | Settings**. This will take you to the **Members Settings** screen where you will first need to choose the URL that you would like to use for your members' page. While this is perfectly fine with the default URL, you may change it to anything that you prefer.

The **Use a word other than "Members" on the front-end** setting is fine as is, but you can certainly change it, if you like. Next is the **Hide email addresses from anyone who is not logged in** setting, which should be left set to **no**, so that visitors will be able to see the email addresses of the businesses featured on your site.

The **Automatically hide new members** setting is currently set to **no** and should be left with that setting, so move on to **Number of viewable members at one time**. While the default of **10** is fine, you can raise of lower this number if your would prefer to display a different number of listings on each page. Keep in mind, however, that it's best not to display too many member listings on one page since load time may suffer as a result.

Next is **Sort the members list originally by**. This is set to **User Name**, but that isn't the best option since the user names used by these businesses won't even be displayed on this page. Instead, choose **company_name** from the drop-down menu. **Sort members list originally in this order** should be left at its default setting of **Ascending**.

Now, move on to **Meta fields to search by**. By default, your list of members is searchable by first name, last name, description, username, email address, and URL. You can also add additional fields to this text area to make those fields searchable as well. For example, you will probably want to include **company_name** and **city**. Anything else that you decide to add, however, will depend entirely upon your preferences and the custom fields that you previously created.

The last setting on this page is **Use gravatars?**, which is currently set to **yes**. This should be left as is, so click **Save Changes** before moving on to the second of these three settings screen.

Configure Mark-Up

Click on **Members List | Configure Mark-Up** to be taken to the **Configure Your Members List Mark-Up** settings screen. It's on this screen that you will be able to choose which fields will be shown on the members' page as well as perform various edits.

As you can see, the first setting on this page allows you to select fields from a drop-down menu which you can then include on the members' page. While you can certainly add as many fields as you like, it's best to keep the content shown on the members' page to a minimum. After all, if you display too many fields on this page, then your visitors will have no reason to click-through to each individual profile page.

The only piece of information that absolutely must be displayed on the members' page is company name. So, add that field by selecting **company_name** from the drop-down menu and then clicking **Add New Field**. Now, add any additional fields that you would like to appear on the members' page. For example, you might want to display the city field so that visitors will be able to easily browse for businesses that are located nearby.

Now, it's time to remove two fields that are being displayed by default. The members of your site should be represented by their business name rather than their user name, so that's the first field that you will need to remove. To do this, hover over **user_nicename**. Doing this will cause an **Edit** link and a **Remove** link to appear. Click **Remove** and this field will be deleted from your site's members' page. The email address for each business is also being shown, but it would seem better to display that piece of information only on the profile page, so repeat this process to delete that field as well.

Database Field	Field Name	Mark-Up
user_nicename Edit | Remove	user_nicename	<div class="tern_wp_members_user_nicename">%value% </div>

Now, drag-and-drop the company name so that it's placed at the top of the list. Any remaining fields that you've chosen to add may be displayed in any order that you prefer. So, drag-and-drop those fields until they're arranged to your liking.

Next, you need to edit the markup being used on the **company_name** field so that it's displayed more prominently than the other fields. To do this, first hover over **company_name** and then click **Edit**. This will cause both the **Field Name** and the **Mark-Up** sections of the **company_name** field to become editable. To make this change, you need to replace all of the markup located in the text area for this field with the following and then click **Update Field**.

```
<div class="tern_wp_members_company_name"><h3><a href="%author_
url%">%value%</h3></div>
```

Edit Members

Navigate to **Members List | Edit Members** to visit this plugin's last configuration screen. It's here that you will be able to prevent the administrator's account from being displayed on the members' page. To do this, first hover over your user name. This will reveal two links titled **Show** and **Hide**. Click the link titled **Hide** and then click **Apply**. Having done that, your account will no longer be displayed.

Username	Name	E-mail	Role	Displayed
hwallace Show | Hide	Heather Wallace	hwallace@example.com	administrator	no

Building the members' page

You've got everything in place to build a wonderful members' page. The only problem is that no one can see it. That's because you still need to build the members.php template file so that all of this information will be displayed.

Open the members.php file that you previously saved and then add the following line at the very top of that file:

```
<?php /* Template Name: Members */ ?>
```

Next, enter the following just after the `<?php get_header(); ?>` tag.

```
<div>
  <h1><?php the_title(); ?></h1>
</div>
<div>
  <?php $members = new tern_members;$members->members(array('search'=>
true,'pagination'=>true,'sort'=>true));?>
</div>
```

Now, save this file and then upload it to your theme's folder.

Publishing the members' page

Now it's time to publish the members' page to your site. Navigate to **Page | Add New** and, once there, enter a name for this page into the textbox. Next, from the **Template** drop-down menu, choose the **Members** template. Then, click **Publish**. The members' list for your site will now be available online at the URL that you specified during the configuration of the Members List plugin.

Editing the search and sort options

With the configurations of **Meta fields to search by** previously completed, your members are now searchable not only by the default fields used by the plugin but, also, using all of the custom fields that you specified. While this will make it quite easy for visitors to locate information, there's one problem. Take a moment to visit the members' page on your website and then click the drop-down menu located next to the search bar. As you can see, any custom field of two or more words contains an underscore between each word.

To hide the fact that the searchable fields aren't being displayed properly, you need to remove the drop-down menu. With it gone **All Fields** will become the default search behavior, which means that any search terms that your visitors enter will be checked against all fields.

To remove the drop-down menu, open `tern_wp_members.php` which is located in the `plugins/members-list` folder. Once this file is open, look for the following line and then delete it:

```
by '.$getOPTS->selectPaired($o,'by','by','','','All Fields',array($_
REQUEST['by'])).'
```

Now, with that problem solved, it's time to move on to the **Sort by** section of the screen. It doesn't really make sense for your sort options to include **Last Name**, **First Name**, and **Email** if those fields aren't being displayed on your members' page. It would be better to, instead, allow your users to search by fields such as company name, city, and what ever other fields you chose to include on this page.

To alter these **Sort by** links you will, once again, need to make some changes to the `tern_wp_members.php` file, so locate this line.

```
$a = array('Last Name'=>'last_name','First Name'=>'first_
name','Registration Date'=>'user_registered','Email'=>'user_email');
```

To remove the options for last name, first name, and email and, instead, display sort options for company name and city, you will need to replace that line of code with the one that follows.

```
$a = array('Company Name'=>'company_name','City'=>'city','Registration
Date'=>'user_registered');
```

If you would like to include any other fields among these sortable links, then you will need to enter them using the following format:

```
'Link Title'=>'field_name'
```

Now that these edits have been performed, don't close this file because you will be making additional changes to it in the next section.

Correcting the Members List compatibility issue

Take a moment to visit the members' page that you previously created. Everything seems perfect, but there's a problem lurking on that page. If you hover over the company name of the account that you created earlier you will see that the hyperlink is formatted like this `http://example.com/?author=2` That isn't ideal since you specifically installed the Wp htaccess Control plugin, so that you could remove any reference to author from the URL.

This problem occurs because Members List was written in such a way that it prevents Wp htaccess Control from doing its job. Luckily, António Andrade—the developer behind Wp htaccess Control—devised a way to correct this problem by performing two edits on the `tern_wp_members.php` file.

First, look for the following line:

```
$s .= '<a class="tern_wp_member_gravatar" href="'.get_
bloginfo('url').'/?author='.$u->ID.'">'."\n         ".get_avatar($u-
>ID,60)."\n    ".'</a>'."\n    ";
```

Once you've located that line, replace it with the following:

```
$s .= '<a class="tern_wp_member_gravatar" href="'.get_author_posts_
url($u->ID).'">'."\n         ".get_avatar($u->ID,60)."\n    ".'</a>'."\
n    ";
```

Next, find this line:

```
$s .= "\n          ".str_replace('%author_url%',get_bloginfo('url').'/
?author='.$u->ID,str_replace('%value%',$u->$v['name'],$v['markup']));
```

Once you've found it, replace it with the following line:

```
$s .= "\n          ".str_replace('%author_url%',get_author_posts_url($u-
>ID),str_replace('%value%',$u->$v['name'],$v['markup']));
```

Save this file and then upload it to the `members-list` folder. Then, return to your members' page to see the changes that you've made. As you can see, the search by drop-down menu is gone, the **Sort by** links have been customized and, when you hover over the company name, the URL displayed in the status bar will no longer include author. Instead, that word will have been replaced by the word that you entered when configuring the **Author Base** setting used by the Wp htaccess Control plugin.

Summary

During the creation of your local community directory several plugins were installed, some pages were created, a few edits were made, and many configurations were performed. With all of the time and effort that has been put into this project, you really should be proud of all that you've accomplished.

With this project complete, you must next concentrate on building your membership base. After all, very few (if any) businesses will want to join an empty directory and, without business listings, potential clients will have no reason to visit your site. So, your main objective will now be to encourage a few businesses to create profiles. Once those first few profiles are online, you should find that other businesses won't be so hesitant to join, and that your membership base will soon begin to grow.

In this chapter, you learned how to use a variety of plugins to build a directory where local businesses can submit company profiles. You also learned how to use custom templates to create a members' page, display the information collected during sign-up on a company profile page, and use a special template as the home page of your site.

In the next chapter, you will learn how to build a membership site where you will be able to sell subscriptions of various types, add content, configure membership options, and collect subscription fees using the payment processor of your choice.

9
Project 9: Building a Membership Website

There are many different methods for generating revenue online. For example, site owners can rely on affiliate marketing, CPM advertising, products sales, and so on. While all of these are perfectly viable options, there's one method that's especially attractive because it can provide a stable, reoccurring source of income. This revenue-generating method is operating a membership site. With a membership site, you will be able to rely on your earnings much more than some of the other online money making models because, with a membership base in place, you will be able to enjoy a steady, predictable income.

WordPress will, of course, be the backbone of this membership site, but it's the addition of **WishList Member**, available at `http://member.wishlistproducts.com/`, that makes this project possible. With this plugin, you will be able to transform an ordinary WordPress installation into an online membership site where members can sign-up for paid access to your content.

WishList Member can do quite a lot, so that means that a substantial amount of configuring will be involved to get your site up-and-running. Once the site is operational, however, virtually all that will be left for you to do is add content and occasionally perform administrative tasks.

In this chapter, you will learn how to:

- Activate WishList Member so that you can begin using it on your site
- Add a variety of membership levels for visitors to choose from
- Create various error, alert, and confirmation pages
- Hide members-only content from search engines

- Display a portion of your posts, so that visitors can get a sample of the content that your site has to offer
- Prevent your members from sharing their log in information with others
- Include a registration form on any post or page
- Customize the information included on your registration pages
- Manage the accounts of your members
- Add members to your site from the Wishlist Member administration area
- Import and export CSV files containing all of your site's members
- Send an email broadcast to either all or some of your members
- Ban certain people from joining your site based on their email or IP address
- Integrate a shopping cart, so that payments can be processed at your site
- Integrate an autoresponder, so that members are automatically added to your mailing list

Once this project is complete, you will have succeeded in creating a site that's similar to the one shown in the screenshot:

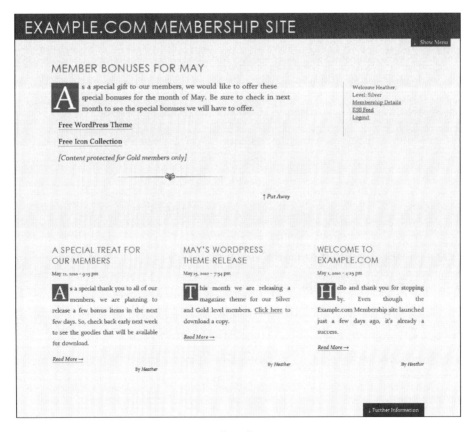

Introducing WishList Member

With this premium plugin installed, you will be able to create a robust membership site that can be run from within WordPress. This plugin is available in both single and multi-site license versions. If you only want to build one membership site, then the single license option is the way to go. If, instead, you want to build several membership sites, you will need to choose the multi-site license.

Here is just a sampling of the features that will be available to you regardless of which license you choose.

- Create unlimited membership levels that are available at various prices
- Offer free, trial, or paid membership levels
- Integrate several popular shopping carts
- Maintain complete control over the content that you would like to make available to your members. Specify that certain posts, pages, categories, and comments are only visible to certain membership levels
- Secure your RSS feeds so that only paying members will be able to read the material that's published at your site
- Offer memberships that last for days, weeks, months, or years
- Entice visitors to join your site by offering them a preview of the content that they will receive as a paying member

Activating WishList Member

After purchasing WishList Member you will receive an email that contains your WishList Member activation key as well as the URL where you can download the plugin. If you didn't download the plugin immediately after purchase, do so now. Next, unzip the ZIP file and then upload the `wishlist-member` folder to the plugins directory on your server. Now, from the **Dashboard**, click on **Plugins | Installed** and then activate WishList Member.

After activation, you will see that a **WL Plugins** menu has been added to the **DashBoard**. Before you can begin working through the configuration screens of this plugin, you will first need to activate it.

To activate WishList Member, click on **WL Plugins**. This will take you to the **WishList Products Key** screen where you will need to enter your activation key and the email address that you provided when you purchased this plugin. After you've entered both of these pieces of information, click **Save WishList Products Key**.

Please enter your WishList Products Key and Email below to activate this plugin

WishList Products Key * ☐ (This was sent to the email you used during your purchase)

WishList Products Email * ☐ (Please enter the email you used during your registration/purchase)

[Save WishList Products Key]

If the activation was successful, your screen will refresh so that it now displays the WishList Member **Dashboard** along with an alert message, located at the top of your screen, that informs you that your license information was saved. If this message doesn't appear (or you encounter any other difficulties during the activation process) contact the WishList Member support team for assistance. If, however, everything went smoothly, you will be able to access all of the settings screens and proceed with the configuration of this plugin. Before you begin working on these settings, however, there's still one more thing that you need to do.

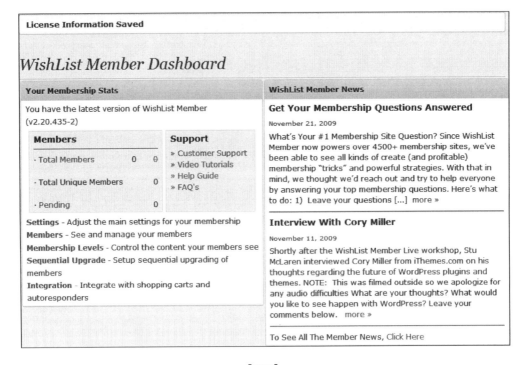

License Information Saved

WishList Member Dashboard

Your Membership Stats

You have the latest version of WishList Member (v2.20.435-2)

Members		**Support**
· Total Members	0 0	» Customer Support
		» Video Tutorials
· Total Unique Members	0	» Help Guide
		» FAQ's
· Pending	0	

Settings - Adjust the main settings for your membership
Members - See and manage your members
Membership Levels - Control the content your members see
Sequential Upgrade - Setup sequential upgrading of members
Integration - Integrate with shopping carts and autoresponders

WishList Member News

Get Your Membership Questions Answered

November 21, 2009

What's Your #1 Membership Site Question? Since WishList Member now powers over 4500+ membership sites, we've been able to see all kinds of create (and profitable) membership "tricks" and powerful strategies. With that in mind, we thought we'd reach out and try to help everyone by answering your top membership questions. Here's what to do: 1) Leave your questions [...] more »

Interview With Cory Miller

November 11, 2009

Shortly after the WishList Member Live workshop, Stu McLaren interviewed Cory Miller from iThemes.com on his thoughts regarding the future of WordPress plugins and themes. NOTE: This was filmed outside so we apologize for any audio difficulties What are your thoughts? What would you like to see happen with WordPress? Leave your comments below. more »

To See All The Member News, Click Here

Publishing event-specific pages

When you begin configuring WishList Member, there will come a time, when you reach the **Configuration** screen when you will need to specify where you would like your visitors to be directed when various events occur on your site. For example, for the **Non-Member** setting, you will be able to choose to either direct non-subscribers to a published page or a specific URL when they click on the **Register** link that's located in the **WishList Member** widget or when they attempt to access members-only content.

While it's best to choose the external URL option for some of these settings, others require special pages. That means that you need to create a selection of pages prior to configuring the first few settings found on this screen. These pages should be published now so that they will be available for use when you're ready to begin configuring those settings.

To publish these various pages, you will need to navigate to the **Add New Page** screen, so click on **Pages | Add New**.

Non-Members page

The first page that you're going to create will be shown to non-members when they attempt to access content in your members' area or when they click the **Register** link found in the **WishList Member** widget.

First, enter **Register** as the title of this page. Then, in the text area, enter information about becoming a member of your site. Now, provide links to each of the available membership levels. In the **Discussion** area of the screen, remove the checkmarks from both settings. Finally, click **Publish**.

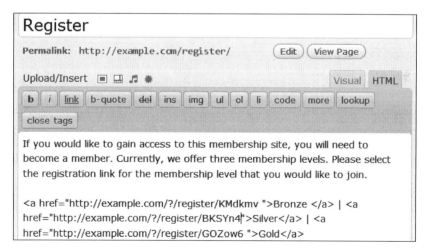

While the **Non-Members** page has been created, there are still several more that you need to publish, so proceed with this process by next publishing the **Wrong Membership Level** page.

Wrong Membership Level page

The **Wrong Membership Level** error page will come in handy if a member tries to access content that's not available to their membership level. In that event, they will see this page which will alert them that the content that they're trying to access isn't available to them.

To create this page, navigate to **Pages | Add New** and then enter **Upgrade** as the title for this page. Next, in the text area, enter a message to alert your members that they will have to upgrade to a higher membership level in order to view this protected content. In the **Discussion** area of the screen, remove the checkmarks from both settings. Prevent non-members from accessing this page by scrolling down to the **WishList Member** section of the screen and then ticking the checkbox next to **Yes, protect this content (members only)**. Then, click **Publish**.

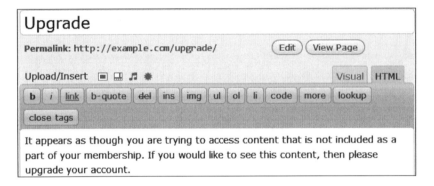

Membership Canceled Page

Now you need to publish the page that will be displayed if a member cancels their subscription or their payment method fails. So, once again, click on **Pages | Add New** and then enter **Access Denied** as the title of this page. Then, in the text area, add the text that you would like to display on this page. For example, you might want to mention that there appears to be a problem with the member's payment and that they should contact support to resolve the issue. In the **Discussion** area of the screen, remove the checkmarks from both settings. In the **WishList Member** area, enable the **Yes, protect this content (members only)** setting. Finally, click **Publish**.

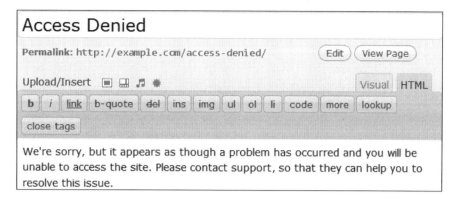

After Registration page

Now, you need to publish the page that members will be directed to immediately after registration. Click **Pages | Add New** and then enter **Successful Registration** as the title for this page. You should next enter a welcome message for your new members. For example, you could include helpful information designed to get them started with their newly purchased membership. In the **Discussion** area of the screen, remove the checkmarks from both settings. Scroll down to the **WishList Member** section of the screen and then tick the checkbox next to **Yes, protect this content (members only)**. Then, click **Publish** to save this page.

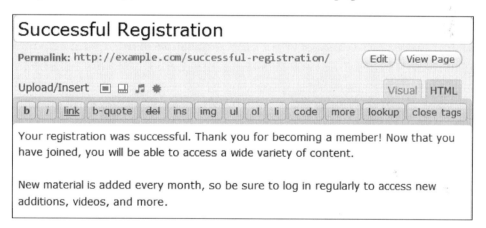

Custom Unsubscribe Confirmation page

The last page that you need to create is the **Custom Unsubscribe Confirmation** page. This page will be displayed to your members if they unsubscribe from the email broadcasts sent via WishList Member or if they cancel their membership to your site.

To create this page, click **Pages | Add New**. Once there, enter **Unsubscribed** as the title for this page. In the text area, you will need to enter an appropriate message. In the **Discussion** area of the screen, remove the checkmarks from both settings. For example, you could confirm that their cancellation has been processed and then thank the member for previously subscribing. In the **WishList Member** settings area, tick the checkbox next to **Yes, protect this content (members only)**. Finally, click **Publish**.

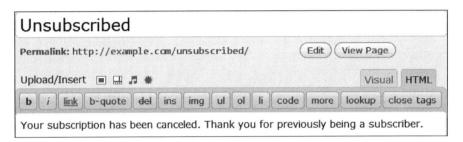

Setting up and configuring WishList Member

The WishList Member **Dashboard** is similar in design to the WordPress **Dashboard** in many ways. For example, both provide a set of stats, display excerpts of the latest news and information, and link to various settings screens.

> **WishList Member Notice:** No Membership Levels added yet. <u>Click here</u> to add a new membership level now.

As you work to ready your site for launch, you will need to visit several of these settings screens, so that you can perform various configurations. As soon as you navigate to any other screen, an alert will appear at the top of the page to inform you that you haven't added any membership levels yet. Since you won't be able to configure some of the other settings until membership levels have been added, you should take care of that right now.

Adding membership levels now will mean that you will be visiting the WishList Member configurations screens out of order, since you will be navigating to the **Membership Levels** area before any of the others. You will, however, return to the screens that you've skipped over and configure those settings at a later time.

Membership Levels

To visit the **Membership Levels** settings screen, click on **WL Plugins | WL Members | Membership Levels**. Once you arrive at this screen, you will see the **Add New Membership Level** area. It's in this area that you will need to enter the data required to create your membership levels.

For this example, you will create three different membership levels called Bronze, Silver, and Gold. You should begin by adding the Bronze level membership.

First, enter **Bronze** into the **Level Name** textbox. **Grant Continued Access** should remain disabled because, if this feature where enabled, then individuals who cancel their membership would still be able to access the content that was provided during their time as a subscriber.

Next is **Role**, which should be left set to **Subscriber**. You may change the editable portion of the **Registration URL** or you can leave it as is. With your present settings, your registration page will include an alert that will instruct existing members who arrive at that page to log in to their account. If you prefer that this message not be displayed, tick the checkbox next to **Disable Existing Users Link**. Otherwise, leave this setting unchecked.

Leave both the **After Login** and the **After Registration** drop-down menus set to **Default**. In the **Access to** section, leave all of the selections unchecked. If you would like to offer access to your site on a subscription basis, first enter a number into the **Length of Subscription** textbox and then select either **Days**, **Weeks**, **Months**, or **Years** from the drop-down menu. If you would prefer to charge members a one-time fee for continued access rather than offer a subscription, then tick the **No Expiry Date** checkbox instead. Click **Save Settings** to add this membership level to your site.

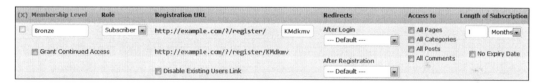

After clicking **Save Settings**, your screen will refresh and your newly created Bronze level membership will appear at the top of your screen. Just below that, you will see the **Add New Membership Level** area. This time, however, there will be a drop-down menu included in this section that you can use to copy the settings from an existing membership level to another membership level. Now that the Bronze membership level has successfully been created, add the Silver membership level to your site.

In the **Add New Membership Level** area, type **Silver** into the **Level Name** textbox. Then, tick the checkbox next to the **Copy an Existing Membership Level** setting while leaving the drop-down menu set to **Bronze**. Now, click **Save Settings**.

The screen will, once again, refresh and your site will now include both Bronze and Silver membership levels. Now, it's time to add the Gold membership level.

In the **Add New Membership Level** area, type **Gold** into the **Level Name** textbox. Then, tick the checkbox next to the **Copy an Existing Membership Level** setting while leaving the drop-down menu set to **Bronze**. Now, in the **Access to** section of the screen, tick the checkbox next to every option. This will give Gold members access to all of the content on your site. Now, click **Save Settings**.

Once you've finished adding each of these membership levels, your screen should look like this.

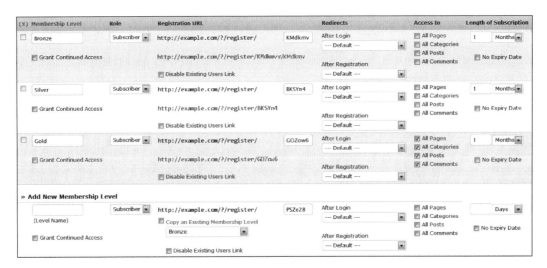

With that process complete, your site now has three membership levels and you can now move on to the configuration of some of WishList Member's other settings. While the **Membership Levels** area does contain two additional configurations screens, you should turn your attention elsewhere and return to them later on. The **Settings** area is the next place that you need to visit as you configure WishList Member, so go ahead and click on **Settings**.

Settings

The screen that you've arrived at is actually the first of four configurations screens found in this area. If you look to the right side of your screen, you will see that there's a sub-menu that will take you to each of the other settings screens located in this area of the WishList Member plugin.

Configuration   Email Settings   Registration Page   Advanced

Configuration

First, click the drop-down menu located next to the **Non-Members** setting and then select **Register**. The **Wrong Membership Level** setting is next. Here you will need to choose **Upgrade** from the drop-down menu. For the **Membership Cancelled** setting, choose **Access Denied** from the drop-down menu. With that, all of the error pages have been configured.

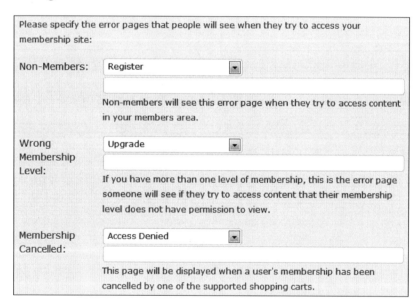

Now it's time to configure the **After Registration Page**, so click the drop-down menu located next to this setting and then choose **Successful Registration** from the list. Next, is the **After Login Page** setting. Rather than selecting a page from the drop-down menu you will, instead, need to choose **Enter an external URL below**. Next, enter the URL for the home page of your membership site into the textbox. That way, after members log in to your site, they will be able to see the latest content that's available. For **After Logout Page** once again select **Enter an external URL below** from the drop-down menu. Then, in the textbox, enter the home page of your membership site. Finally, for the **Custom Unsubscribe Confirmation Page**, select **Unsubscribed** from the drop-down menu.

Please specify the page to which a newly registered member will be redirected to:

After Registration Page: Successful Registration ▾

Newly registered members will see this page after they register.

Please specify the the page to which a a member will be redirected to when he/she logs in:

After Login Page: Enter an external URL below ▾

http://example.com

Members will see this page after they login.

Please specify the the page to which a a member will be redirected to when he/she logout:

After Logout Page: Enter an external URL below ▾

http://example.com

Members will see this page after they logout.

Custom Unsubscribe Confirmation Page: Unsubscribed ▾

With all of these page-related configurations complete, you can now move on to the other settings found on this screen. **Pending Period for New Registrations** is next. What this setting does is place newly registered members into a pending period for a certain number of days. With this pending period in place you will be able to verify that each new sign up is, in fact, a paying member, which will help you to avoid fraudulent registrations. If you would like to institute a pending period, enter the number of days that you would like it to last into the textbox. If you would rather not verify member registrations, then enter don't enter anything into the textbox.

Both the **Minimum Password Length** and **RSS Secret Key** settings are already configured. Since both are fine as is, move on to the group of radio buttons located below these settings. First up is **Only show content for each membership level**, which is currently set to **No**. This, however, should be changed to **Yes**. Otherwise visitors to your website will be able to view content that's only supposed to be made available to members of a certain level.

Only show content for each membership level: ⦿ Yes ◯ No

Next is the **Hide protected content from search results** setting. Since you obviously don't want random visitors to be able to access your protected content via the search engine results, this should also be set to **Yes**.

Hide protected content from search results: ⦿ Yes ◯ No

Now you will come to the **Protect all content after the "more" tags** setting. What this does is allow you to display a portion of your posts, so that visitors can get a sample of the content found in the protected area of your site. All of the content that you enter after the `<!--more-->` tag, however, will only be visible to registered members. Non-members who try to access the rest of the post will be taken to the non-member error page that you created earlier. This feature is already set to **Yes**, which is ideal, so move on to the **Do you want to automatically protect content by inserting the "more" tag if the "more" tag is not inserted into any post?** setting. This is set to **No** which really is the best option since this configuration allows you to decide, on a post-by-post or page-by-page basis, when you would like to offer a teaser. **Default Protection** is next and it should be set to **On**.

Default Protection ⦿ On ◯ Off

The **Text to display for content protected with private tags** section doesn't need any changes, so turn your attention to the **Default Login Limit**. It's very likely that at least a few of the members of your site will share their login information with others. You can, however, take measures to prevent these non-members from accessing your site with the use of this setting. This setting ensures that an individual may only log in from a certain number of IP addresses on any given day. Since your users might access your site from home, work, or school it's best to set this feature to **3**. Allowing them access from that many IPs should be more than enough to accommodate legitimate site usage by your members.

Default Login Limit: 3 IPs per day
Enter 0 (zero) or leave it blank to disable

Next is the **Login Limit Message**. This will be displayed if a member tries to log in from a fourth IP address in one day. This message is perfectly fine, so turn your attention to the last few settings found on this screen.

Notify admin of new user registration is set to **Yes**, but you can change this to **No** if you would rather not receive email notifications when new members register. **Prevent duplicate shopping cart registrations** should remain disabled because some WishList Member plugin users have reported registration issues when this feature was enabled. **Members can update their info** is set to **Yes**, which is fine. If you would like to try and earn affiliate commissions by promoting WishList Member on your site, then leave **Show Affiliate Link in Footer** set to **Yes**. Otherwise set this option to **No**.

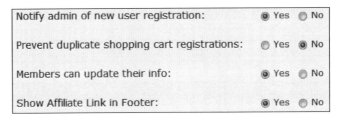

If you chose to promote WishList Member on your site, you will need to enter your affilaite ID into the **Affiliate ID** textbox. If you haven't joined their affiliate program, right-click on **Sign Up Now** to open this link in a new browser window. Doing this will take you to the **Affiliates** section of the WishList Member site located at `http://wishlistproducts.com/affiliates/`. On this page, you will need to complete the registration process to become an affiliate and to receive your ID. Once you have your affiliate ID, return to the WishList **Configuration** screen and then enter it into the **Affiliate ID** textbox.

Once all of your configurations on this screen are complete, click **Save Settings** before proceeding to the **Email Settings** screen.

Email Settings

Click on **WL Plugins | WL Member | Settings | Email Settings** to visit the next screen that you need to configure. In the **Sender Name** textbox, enter the name that you would like to use for email messages sent by WishList Member. Next, in the **Sender E-mail** textbox, enter the email address that you would like to include in these messages.

The remainder of this screen is devoted to the messages that will sent at registration, when login details are lost, and to the admin when a new member registers. These messages are already very well written, so there really isn't any point in rewriting them.

If you do decided to make any edits, be sure to use the handy links located next to each of the text areas, so that dynamically generated, member-specific information can be inserted by WishList Member. Once you've finished making changes on this screen, click **Save Settings**.

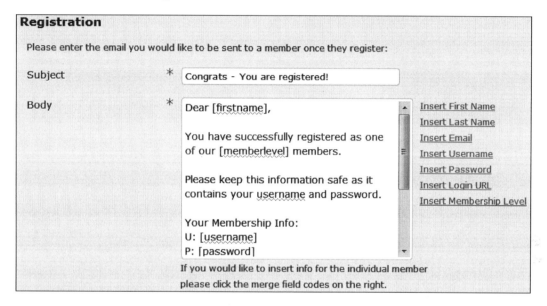

Registration Page

Before you visit the **Registration Page** settings screen, where it's possible to customize the content that's displayed along with the registration forms that will appear on your site, it's best to first take a moment to learn how **Registration Merge Codes** can be used to add registration forms to posts and pages.

If you would like to include a registration form on one of your posts or pages, then you can do this by using a Registration Merge Code. For example, suppose that you were writing a post in which you talk about the benefits of the Gold membership level. To link to the registration page for that membership level, you would simply need to include [register_gold] somewhere in the post. Including the registration form for any of your other levels is as simple as replacing gold with the name of that other membership level.

Now that you know how these forms can be included on your site, you should next navigate to the **Registration Page** settings screen. So, click on **WL Plugins | WL Member | Settings | Registration Page**. Now, choose **Bronze** from the **Membership Level** drop-down menu. After the screen refreshes, you will see two text areas where you can add HTML that will appear both before and after the registration form.

You certainly don't need to add anything to either of these boxes, but it's a good idea for you to familiarize yourself with this settings area in case you should ever want to make additions to any of your registration pages. So, if you would like to add additional content to your Bronze registration form, do so now. To make changes to any of your other registrations pages, just select the appropriate membership level from the drop-down menu and then enter whatever you like into the text areas. Once you've finished on this screen, and saved any changes that you may have made, you can move on to the **Advanced** settings area.

Advanced

The **Advanced** settings screen is the last one that you need to visit in the **Settings** area of the WishList Member plugin, so click on **WL Plugins | WL Member | Settings | Advanced** to visit this page.

The first thing that you will see when you arrive at this page is the **CSS Code** settings area. In this section, you can apply your own styles to three separate areas. The first is the **WishList Member Sidebar Widget**. While no changes are required here, you can enter your own CSS into the text area if you would like to apply certain styles to the **WishList Member** sidebar widget. Next are the **Login Form Merge Code CSS** and the **Registration Form CSS** settings areas. Once again, no changes are required in these areas, but you're free to add your own CSS if you wish.

The **Registration Instructions** configuration area is next. In the **New Member Registration** and the **Existing Member Registration** sections you can edit various instructions that will be provided to your site's visitors. While no edits are required, you can make changes to this text if you wish. If you do choose to perform edits in this section, be sure to make use of the available merge codes so that WishList Member can insert dynamically generated information into your text.

If you performed any edits on this screen, click **Save Settings** to save your changes. Otherwise, click on **WL Plugins | WL Member | Members** to visit the **Members** screen.

Members

When you need to manage the members on your site, you will have to visit the member management area of WishList Member. Here you can add members, upgrade/downgrade subscription levels, import members, export members, send an email broadcast, and even blacklist certain people from registering on your site.

Manage Members

Manage Members is the first configuration screen that you will see. Once your site has an active membership base, you will be able to perform a variety of actions from this screen. For example, you will be able to do things like search for specific members, move a member to a different membership level, and delete a member from the database as well as perform many other administrative tasks related to your members and their accounts.

It's a good idea to test out these features before your site has been populated with paying members. That way you will be able to get a feel for how all of these controls work so that you're well-versed in their usage before your site goes live.

Adding a new member from the WishList Member admin area

While you could try out these controls on your own administrator account, it's best not to use it for testing. Instead, you can use the **Add New Member** form, located at the bottom of the screen, to create a fictitious member account on your site. Once this member account has been created, you can then use it to test the controls provided on this screen.

To create this account, you must first enter a user name for this member into the **Username** textbox. Next, enter a name for this member into the **First Name** textbox. In the **Last Name** textbox, enter a last name for this member. Now, enter a genuine email address that you have access to into the **E-mail** textbox. Create a password for this account and then type it into both of the textboxes located in the **Password** area. The **Membership Level** drop-down menu can be left set to **Bronze**, so go ahead and click **Add Member**.

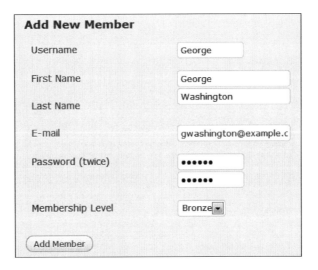

Once your screen refreshes, you will see that the information about this new member has been added to your screen. At this point it's possible for you to perform various actions on this member's account in order to familiarize yourself with the member management controls provided on this screen. After you've become comfortable with the member management process, you can then move on to exploring and configuring the remaining settings provided by this plugin.

	Name	Username	E-mail	Member Since	Status	Sequential	Membership Level
☐	George Washington	George	gwashington@example.com	05/30/2010	Active	On	Bronze

Import

With the features found on the **Import** page, it's possible to import members into your site. This will certainly prove to be useful if, for whatever reason, you ever need to restore your membership site. Since, at this point, you don't have any members to import, you should just take a look around this screen, so that you can familiarize yourself with the way that this process works.

To visit the **Import** screen, click on **WL Plugins | WL Member | Members | Import**. Should you ever need to import a CSV file containing a list of members, here is the process that you will need to follow.

From the **Select CSV File** section click **Browse**. Then, locate and select the file that you would like to import. On the **Membership Level to Import to** drop-down menu, select which membership level to assign to these imported members. For example, if your file is filled with Silver level members, you would need to select **Silver** from the list. For the **How to Handle Duplicates** setting, **Do not import duplicate usernames or emails** should remain selected to ensure that redundant data is not added to your database. The **Default Password for New Users** textbox should be left blank. Depending upon your preferences, **Notify New Users via Email** can be set to either **Yes** or **No**. The importation process can then be initiated by clicking **Import Members**.

The data from your CSV file won't import correctly unless it's formatted as follows:

- **UserName**, **FirstName**, **LastName**, and **Email** columns are required. An optional **Password** column may also be included
- CSV files that you plan to import should be saved as a Unix file using UTF-8 encoding
- A comma should be used as the delimiter and each piece of information should be surrounded with double quotes

If you're importing a CSV file that you previously exported from WishList Member it will already be formatted properly and should import with no problem.

After your file has been imported, a message will appear at the top of your screen with details about the various elements of the importation process.

```
10 new users imported.
0 duplicates ignored.
0 errors encountered.
10 total rows processed.
```

Export

Now that you've taken a look at the **Import** screen, it's time to become acquainted with the **Export** feature. To access this screen, click on **WL Plugins | WL Member | Members | Export**. In this area, you can export all of your site's member details in a CSV file. This is an important action that should be performed often so that you will always have an up-to-date backup of your membership base in case anything should ever happen and you need to restore your site.

While you can export all of your members in one CSV file, there are two reasons why it would be better to, instead, separately export a file for each membership level:

1. If your site acquires a large number of members, then exporting the entire membership base in one file could put quite a strain on your server.

2. Exporting your members based upon their membership level will allow for easier importing since you will be able to easily restore your members to their appropriate membership level.

When the time comes that you want to export your members you will need to first select a membership level from the **Membership Level** drop-down menu. For this example, suppose that you want to export a backup of your Silver level members. To do that, you just need to select **Silver** from the drop-down menu and then click **Export Members**. Once the **Save** dialog box appears you can then save the file to your computer's hard drive.

Email Broadcast

If you ever want to send a message out to either some or all of your site's members, you can easily do that from the **Email Broadcast** screen. To see how the process works, visit this screen by clicking on **WL Plugins | WL Member | Members | Email Broadcast**.

Just because your site doesn't currently have any real members, that doesn't mean that you can't send an email broadcast to see how this feature works.

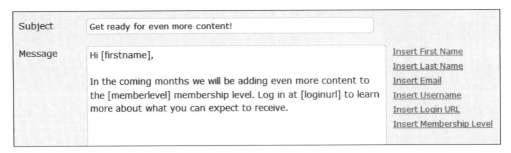

To get started creating your first email broadcast, first enter a title for your message into the **Subject** textbox. In the **Message** text area, enter a brief message. As you create this message, be sure to use the links provided on the right side of the text area to insert dynamically generated information. If you want to include a signature with your message, enter it into the **Signature** text area.

In the **CAN SPAM** area, you must provide a mailing address before this message can be sent. If you're unfamiliar with the CAN-SPAM Act or you're uncertain why this information is required, then visit Wikipedia at `http://en.wikipedia.org/wiki/CAN-SPAM_Act_of_2003` to learn more about this piece of legislation.

In the **Membership Level** settings area, you can choose to send this message to one or more of your membership levels. For the purposes of this example, tick the checkbox next to **Select/Unselect All Levels**. In the **Include** section, leave both **Pending Members** and **Canceled Levels** deselected.

Now, click **Preview Message** to see what your email broadcast will look like. If you want to make changes, click **Go Back and Edit**. Otherwise, click **Send Message to Members**. After this message has been sent, you will be able to see what it looks like because a copy will have been sent to the email address that you provided earlier when you added a fictitious member to the site.

Blacklist

Now head on over to the final configuration screen found in the **Members** area by clicking on **WL Plugins | WL Member | Members | Blacklist**. If, during the administration of your site, you should ever find it necessary to ban someone from registering, this is where you will do it.

When it comes to blacklisting, you have a few options. You can either add a specific email address to the **Email Blacklist** or you can block an entire domain by entering `*@example.com`. The `example.com` domain would, of course, need to be replaced with the actual web address that you would like to ban. The same method applies to the **IP Blacklist** field where you can either entire a specific IP address that you would like to blacklist or a partial IP address followed by an asterisk to prevent that entire block of IP addresses from accessing your site. How you choose to manage this part of your site will depend upon your own individual circumstances and preferences.

Since there's no need to perform any actions in this area at this time, move on to the **Sequential Upgrade** section of WishList Member.

Sequential Upgrade

Click on **WL Plugins | WL Member | Sequential Upgrade** to visit the **Sequential Upgrade** screen. You won't be making any changes to the default settings found here, but it's still a good idea to familiarize yourself with the functionality provided by these settings in case you ever want to enable this feature.

What the **Sequential Upgrade** settings area does is allow you to configure your site so that members in certain membership levels are either moved or added to a different membership level after a specific number of days. With the default settings found on this screen, none of the members on your site will be automatically upgraded after any length of time.

As you may have noticed, when you created your fictitious member account, sequential upgrade was turned **On** for that member. That may be confusing, but rest assured that your members aren't going to be automatically upgraded. If you should ever change the settings in the **Sequential Upgrade** area, however, members with **Sequential** set to **On** may then be subject to the changes that you make on this screen.

Integration

Integration is the last settings area found in WishList Member and this section is divided into two screens. In one, you will be able to integrate your payment processor while, in the other, you can integrate an autoresponder with your site.

Shopping Cart

To get started with the integration process, click on **WL Plugins | WL Member | Integration | Shopping Cart**. Here you will first need to select your shopping cart provider from the **Select System** drop-down menu. Doing this will reveal integration information specific to the payment processor that you've selected. The information provided on this screen is quite detailed, so just follow the step-by-step onscreen instructions to integrate the shopping cart of your choice into your membership site.

Making a test purchase

After you've finished setting up your shopping cart you must next ensure that the payment process is working properly. To do this, you first need to change the price of your membership levels to a nominal fee. You don't, after all, want to charge yourself a large sum as you conduct this test.

When it comes time to provide an email address for this new membership registration be sure that you don't enter one that's already in use on your membership site as this will cause the test to fail. Once you reach the payment stage of this process, the steps that you need to take will depend upon which payment processor you've chosen to use.

If you're using **PayPal** as your payment processor you will need to use a funding source and an email address that isn't attached to your PayPal account.

If **Clickbank** is being used to process payments on your site, then visit the *Creating a Payment Link* page on their website, which can be found at `http://www.clickbank.com/help/vendor-help/vendor-basics/creating-a-payment-link/`. There you will learn how to make a test purchase when using their service.

If you've elected to use **1ShoppingCart**, **Cydec**, or some other payment processor on your site, then you will need to contact their support staff in order to learn about the process that should be used when making a test payment.

After you've completed the sign up process, navigate to **WL Plugins | WL Member | Members**. On that page check to see if the account that you just created has been added to your list of members. Then, log in to the account for your payment processor where you will need to check to see if the payment was successful. If everything went smoothly, you can return your membership fees to their normal amounts and then delete this newly created member from your site.

If your member account wasn't created or the payment didn't go through, consult the integration instructions provided by WishList Member to ensure that each step was properly completed. If you find that the instructions were followed correctly, then you will need to contact the support staff at either WishList Member or at your payment processor.

Autoresponder

As mentioned, WishList Member allows you to integrate an autoresponder into your membership site. Now, you may be unfamiliar with what an autoresponder is and what it can do. Basically, an autoresponder is a program that makes it possible for you to automatically send messages to people. So, by integrating WishList Member with an autoresponder, you could set up a prewritten sequence of messages that would then be automatically sent to the members of your site.

When it comes to integrating autoresponders, WishList Member offers you a few choices. However, while they provide options for **AWeber**, **AutoResponse Plus**, and **GetResponse**, only the first two are viable options. That's because, as of WishList Member v2.20.435-2, GetResponse integration is still in Beta. So, at this point in time, it hasn't been fully tested and it isn't being fully supported by the Wishlist Member support staff. For that reason, if you're planning on integrating an autoresponder with WishList member, it's best to go with either AWeber or AutoResponse Plus since both have been much more thoroughly tested.

When choosing which of these two autoresponders to use, you will also need to decide if you want to use one that's hosted (AWeber) or one that must be installed on your server (AutoResponse Plus.)

Integrating AWeber

To begin the AWeber/WishList Member integration process, you first need to navigate to **WL Plugins | WL Member | Integration | AutoResponder**. Once there, select **AWeber** from the **AR Provider** drop-down menu. Then, click **Set AutoResponder Provider**. Clicking that button will cause your screen to refresh. Once it does, a new settings area will appear where you can configure settings specific to AWeber. As you can see, it's possible to integrate a list for each of your membership levels. You should begin by integrating an AWeber list with your Bronze level membership.

In the first textbox located in the **AWeber List Name** column you will need to enter the name of the list that you want to associate with this membership level. For this example, suppose that you've created three lists at AWeber named bronzenews, silvernews, and goldnews. That means, to associate the bronzenews list with the Bronze level membership, you would enter **bronzenews@aweber.com** into the Bronze **AWeber List Name** textbox.

Now it's time to specify the **Safe Unsubscribe Email** that will be associated with this list, but, before you do, you should first learn what this feature does. When you configure the **Safe Unsubscribe Email** setting a message that contains special commands will be sent to AWeber if someone wants to unsubscribe from your list. When AWeber receives this email from the address that you specified in that field, it will interpret the commands and perform the required action, which will be to remove that subscriber from future mailings. Now that you know what that setting does, you can go about configuring it.

In the first of the **Safe Unsubscribe Email** textboxes enter an email address that's specific to your domain. For example, you could enter an email address similar to **bronze-unsubscribe@example.com**. You will, of course, need to replace example.com with your own domain name. To save these changes, click **Update Autoresponder Settings**.

Membership Level	Aweber List Name (ex: listname@aweber.com)	Safe Unsubscribe Email
Bronze	bronzenews@aweber.com	bronze-unsubscribe@example.com

Now it's time to log in to your AWeber account where you need to perform some additional configurations. Navigate to `http://aweber.com`, log in to your account, and then click **My Lists**. On this screen, click the link for the list that you want to integrate with your Bronze level membership.

Email Marketing & Analytics   (+ Create a New List)
Click the list you wish to edit: Back Up & Export All Active Lists

bronzenews (Deactivate)   Unsubscribes: 0

Active Subscribers: 0

Setup: 34%

Scroll down to the **Notifications** area of the screen and then, in the **Name** textbox, type **Unsubscribe Email Address**. In the **Email** textbox, type the email address that you previously entered into the Bronze **Safe Unsubscribe Email** textbox. Click **Add** and then click **Save List Settings**.

Notifications Receive an email every time a new subscriber is added to your list.

Enter your name and email below:

Unsubscribe Email Addre: | bronze-unsubscribe@example.com | ADD

Before this integration is complete, you must still configure one more setting in AWeber so that their system knows that you're using WishList Member in conjunction with their service. To do this, hover your mouse over **My Lists** and then select **Email Parser** from the drop-down menu. Scroll down until you reach the **Memberships Sites and Podcasting Tools** section of your screen. Once there, tick the checkbox next to **WishList Member**. Having done that, your Bronze level membership and AWeber have now been integrated.

Now that your Bronze level membership has been integrated with AWeber, you can work on integrating your remaining membership levels. To perform these integrations, simply repeat the process that you used to integrate an AWeber list with your Bronze level membership.

Integrating AutoResponsePlus

In order to integrate AutoResponse Plus with WishList Member you need to have first installed the AutoResponse Plus software on your server. This software can be obtained from the AutoResponse Plus website at `http://www.autoresponseplus.com/`. Once you have that software installed and operational, you can then proceed with this integration process.

To begin integrating these two applications, you need to click on **WL Plugins | WL Member | Integration | AutoResponder**. When you arrive at this integration screen, you must then select **AutoResponsePlus** from the **AR Provider** drop-down menu. Next, click **Set Autoresponder Provider**. This will cause your screen to refresh. When this happens, a new settings area will appear, so that you can continue with the integration process.

In the **ARP Application URL** textbox, you need to enter the web address where the `arp3-formcaprure.pl` file is located on your server. Next, in a new browser window, log in to your installation of AutoResponsePlus. It's here that you need to locate the autoresponder that you would like to integrate with your Bronze membership level. Once you've decided which autoresponder will be associated with the Bronze membership level, you must next determine the autoresponder ID that has been assigned to that list. To do this, move your mouse so that it hovers over any of the links located in the **Actions** column that correspond to that particular autoresponder. Now, look at the URL displayed in your status bar. At the end of that URL you will see `id` followed by a number. Once you determine that number, return to the WishList **Autoresponder Integration** screen and then enter it into the **Autoresponder ID** textbox that corresponds to the Bronze membership level.

Now, just repeat this process for each of your remaining membership levels. Once you've finished, click **Update Autoresponder Settings** to save these changes.

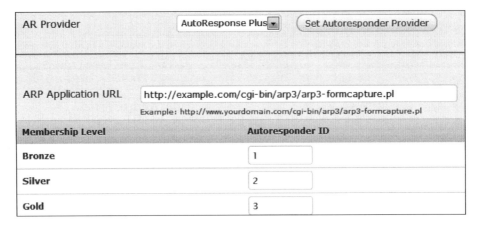

Disabling comments

While comments certainly have their place on WordPress sites, they aren't very well-suited to a membership site. When you publish pages and posts containing content, videos, audio, downloads, and so on, it's highly unlikely that you will want your members to add comments. For that reason, it's best to completely disable the commenting feature in WordPress.

To disable comments sitewide you will need to click on **Settings | Discussion**. Doing that will take you to the **Discussion Settings** screen. In the **Default article settings** section, located at the top of the screen, look for the **Allow people to post comments on new articles** setting. Remove the checkmark next to that setting and then click **Save Changes**.

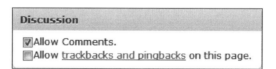

Keep in mind, with this feature disabled, that it's still possible for you to override that setting and allow comments on a case-by-case basis. When writing a page or post, all you need to do is tick the checkbox next to **Allow Comments** which can be found in the **Discussion** section of the screen.

Providing access to your site

Your membership site is nearly complete, but there's still one more piece of the puzzle that needs to be put in place for it to be fully-functional. At this point, you need to add the **WishList Member** widget to one of your site's widetized areas.

With this widget in place, your visitors will have access to a registration link and your members will be able to log in and out of their accounts. To place this widget on your site, navigate to the **Widgets** screen by clicking on **Appearance | Widgets**. Once there, drag the **WishList Member** widget from the **Available Widgets** section of your screen over to the widgetized area of your choosing. While this widget does have a selection of configurable options, it will operate just fine with its default settings left in place.

With the **WishList Member** widget in place, you can now turn your attention to adding and managing content.

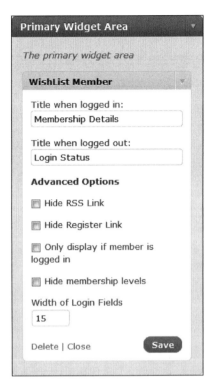

Adding and managing content

Now that the technical aspects of your site are configured and ready to go; it's time to start adding content to your site. After all, without content there wouldn't be any incentive for people to join your membership site.

Adding content

The process for adding content to your membership site is nearly identical to the one normally used in WordPress for adding posts and pages. The only difference is the fact that a **WishList Member** settings area has been added to both the **Add New Post** and the **Add New Page** screens. These extra settings will, of course, need to be configured as part of the post/page creation process.

So, now it's time to add some content so that you can see exactly how the process works. For the purposes of this example, you will be publishing a post that's intended for Silver and Gold members only.

Navigate to **Posts | Add New**. Once there, enter a title for your post and then type some content into the text area.

 You can include Merge Codes to personalize the text of your message. A full list of the available Merge Codes is provided in the **WishList Member** section of your screen.

In the **Categories** area click **Add New Category,** and then type the name of the category, into the textbox, where you would like to place this post. Click **Add** and then deselect **Uncategorized**.

If you like, you can add **Post Tags** and a **Featured Image**. Now, turn your attention to the **WishList Member** settings area. In the **Do you want to protect this content?** section of the screen choose **Yes, protect this content (members only)**. Next, in the **Select the membership level that can access this content** area, tick the checkbox next to **Silver**.

As you can see, this content is already being made available to Gold members because of the default settings that you configured earlier in the **Membership Levels** settings area. Finally, click **Publish**.

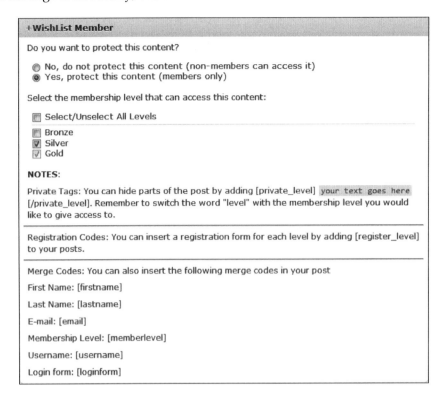

With that a post will now be published to your site that's only viewable by Silver and Gold members. As you can see, the process of creating a post isn't that different to normal. With the configuration of only a few additional settings, you will be able to specify exactly who will have access to the content that you publish on your site.

Private tag protection

With private tags, you can add yet another level of protection to your content. Private tags make it so that any content located between these tags is only visible to the membership level that you specify.

You can write another post to see exactly how this feature works. For this example, suppose that you want to create a post that includes special bonuses for the members of your site. Further suppose that you want to offer some of these bonuses to all members and make one of them available only to Gold members.

To begin, navigate to **Posts | Add New**. On this screen, enter a title for your post and then type some content into the text area. As you type this content into the text area, be sure to include three links. Now, you're going to use private tags to make it so that one of those links is only accessible to Gold members. To do this, surround the last of the three links with these private tags.

```
[private_gold] [/private_gold]
```

Your post should now look similar to the one shown in the following screenshot:

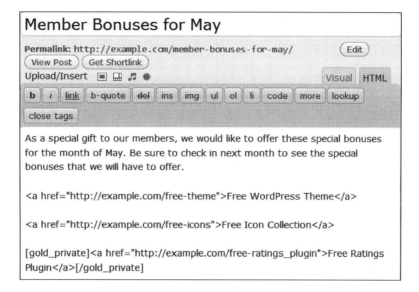

Now, scroll down to the **WishList Member** configuration area and then enable the **Yes, protect this content (members only)** option. Also, in the **Select the membership level that can access this content** area, tick the checkbox next to both **Bronze** and **Silver**.

Scroll back to the top of your screen and then click **Publish**. If either a Bronze or Silver member accesses this post, this is what they will see.

While this example illustrated how to make it so that a portion of content is viewable by Gold members only, you can do the same thing for any of the other membership levels on your site. All you need to do is insert the name of the membership level into the private tag. So, opening and closing Bronze private tags would look this `[private_bronze] [/private_bronze]` while opening and closing Silver tags would be formatted like this `[private_silver] [/private_silver]`.

Managing content

As you just saw, as you added the previous post to your site, it's possible to protect your content on a post-by-post or a page-by-page basis. In WishList Member there is, however, another way to manage content. To use this method, you will need to visit the **Membership Content** screen, which is located in the **Membership Levels** area of WishList Member. Navigate to that screen now by clicking on **WL Plugins | WL Member | Membership Levels | Membership Content**.

When you arrive at this screen, you will see a drop-down menu that contains four options. There are a few ways to manage content from this screen which you will take a look at now so that you will have experience with this area of WishList Member when your site goes live.

Content Protection

First, select **Content Protection** from the drop-down menu. Doing this will cause your screen to refresh and reveal all of the posts currently published on your site. This area will also include links to your pages and categories so that you can manage the protection for them as well. To get a feel for how this works, you should walk through the process used to manage the protection on your posts.

To begin, tick the checkbox next to **Date**. This will cause all of your posts to become selected. Then, click **Set Protection**.

Having done that, any posts that where not already protected will now have protection enabled. That means that non-members won't be able to access any of these formerly unprotected posts. In addition, Gold level members will be able to access these posts while Bronze and Silver level members won't.

The process for changing the access settings on your pages and categories is exactly the same as the one that you just used for posts. To perform these changes, however, you would need to click on either the **Categories** or the **Pages** links that appear on the **Membership Levels** screen.

Membership Level protection

Now that you've seen how Content Protection works, you can now take a look at what happens if you select a specific membership level from the drop-down menu.

So, choose **Silver** from the drop-down menu. Once again the screen will refresh to reveal all of the posts published on your site. Tick the checkbox next to **Date** and then click **Grant Access**.

With this process complete, your Silver level members will now have access to the all of the posts on your site. Selecting Bronze or Gold from the drop-down menu instead will similarly allow you to grant those members access to some or all of your site's posts.

Once again, the steps required to change the access settings on your pages, categories and comments is exactly the same as the one that you just used for posts. To manage the protection for any of these you will need to click on either the **Categories**, **Pages**, or **Comments** links that appear on the **Membership Levels** screen.

Now that you know how the controls on this screen work, take a moment to configure these settings so that the **Wrong Membership Level**, **Membership Canceled**, **After Registration**, and **Custom Unsubscribe Confirmation** pages that you published earlier are all viewable by your Bronze, Silver, and Gold level members.

Moving Membership Levels

There's just one more place that you need to visit in WishList Member and that's the **Move Membership Levels** screen. To reach that screen, click on **WL Plugins | WL Members | Membership Levels | Move Membership Levels**.

In this area you can either move or add all of the members in one membership level into a different membership level. Your site may not have any paying members, but that doesn't mean that you can't take a look around and become acquainted with how this process works so that you will be able to easily perform this action later.

Moving members to another membership level

Suppose that you decide to retire the Bronze level membership. That would mean that you would need to place all of your Bronze level members into a different membership level. The process of moving these members really is quite simple. All you need to do is select **Silver** from the drop-down menu located in the **Bronze** area of the screen and then click **Move**. When you perform this action with a full membership base, all of your Bronze level members will be elevated to a Silver membership.

Adding members to another membership level

Once your site is up-and-running, you might, for whatever reason, want to add all of the members from one membership level to another membership level so that they have a dual membership. If, for example, you wanted to add all of your Silver members to the Gold level membership, here is how you would go about doing that.

First, select **Gold** from the drop-down menu located in the **Silver** section of the screen. Then, click **Add**. With that, all of your Silver members would become Gold members as well.

Summary

Your membership site is now completely configured, but you can't go out and start looking for members just yet. Before you try to build your membership base, there are still a few things that you need to do.

First, be sure to delete any test posts or pages that you created during the configuration of this plugin. Next, delete the fictitious member that you created earlier (if you haven't already done so). Also, delete the member account that was created as part of the test that you conducted to ensure that your payment system was operating properly. Finally, double-check that you returned your subscription fees to their normal rates after you finished testing the payment system on your site.

Once all of that's complete, you can then turn your attention to filling your membership site with content. After creating a stockpile of content, you can then begin marketing your membership site, so that people will know exactly what it has to offer.

In this chapter, you learned how to use the WishList Member plugin to build a membership site from which you will be able to sell subscription-based access to various types of content.

Now that you've had a chance to work on all of the projects found in this book, you should next take a look at *Appendix A*. In it you will learn about a small collection of plugins that can be used to improve just about any website that was built with WordPress.

A
Plugins Suited to Several Projects

The projects that you completed as you worked your way through this book are fully-functional as is, but it's still possible to make them even better. Additional features and functions can be added to your projects just by installing the collection of plugins included in this appendix. Here you will find plugins that will help you fight spam, backup your data, perform maintenance without inconveniencing your visitors, and prevent registered users from accessing certain sections of WordPress's backend.

Introducing Akismet

If you plan to use comments and/or trackbacks on your website, then the **Akismet** plugin is a must since this plugin will severely reduce the amount of time that you have to waste sorting through spam. It does this by checking the comments and trackbacks that are submitted to your site against the Akismet web service. If you don't want to completely rely on the judgment of this plugin, then you can review the comments that it flags by going to the **Comments** section of your admin area.

Setting up and configuring Akismet

The Akismet plugin is included with every installation of WordPress, so you can just visit your **Plugins** screen to activate it. Once Akismet has been activated, a message will appear at the top of the **Plugins** screen to alert you that this plugin won't be operational until you enter your **Akismet API key**.

Akismet is almost ready. You must enter your Akismet API key for it to work.

Now, depending upon your situation, you will either need to create a new Akismet API or retrieve a previously created key that you might have forgotten.

Retrieving a previously-created API Key

If you previously obtained an API key, but have now forgotten it, then you can retrieve it by visiting `http://wordpress.com`. Once there, log in to your account and then click on **My Dashboard | Profile | Personal Settings**. When you arrive at this page your API key will appear right at the top of the screen.

Creating a new API Key

If you don't have an API key, then you will need to visit the Akismet website at `http://akismet.com/get/` to create one. Once there, either choose a subscription type or, if you run a hobby or personal site, select the free option. Next, complete the form to receive your API key.

Configuring Akismet

Now it's time to enter your API key on the **Akismet Configuration** screen. So, click on **Plugins | Akismet Configuration**. In the **Akismet API Key** section of your screen is the textbox where you need to enter your API key. Underneath that textbox is an option that allows you to automatically discard spam comments on posts older than a month. Tick the checkbox to enable this setting, so that your site will never become cluttered with a backlog of spam comments. Now, click **Update options** to save these changes.

It should only take a few seconds for your API key to be verified and, once it is, your site will then be protected from becoming inundated with spam.

Project suitability

The Akismet plugin is well-suited for usage on any of the sites featured in this book on which comments and/or trackbacks will be enabled.

Introducing WP-DB-Backup

When it comes to their websites, many site owners fail to follow those sage words of advice offered by the Boy Scouts. That's because they just aren't prepared. For many, if their site went offline, all of their data would be lost. This is certainly a scenario that you don't want to befall you. With all of the time and effort that you've put in to the creation of these sites, it really is in your best interest to prepare for the worst so that your data are never lost.

With that in mind, the **WP-DB-Backup** plugin, available at `http://wordpress.org/extend/plugins/wp-db-backup/`, is absolutely essential. What this plugin does is allow you to easily backup your core WordPress database tables as well as other tables that are located within the same database. With this backup, you will always be prepared in case something unfortunate occurs.

Setting up and configuring WP-DB-Backup

After installing and activating this plugin, navigate to **Tools | Backup** to be taken to the **Backup** screen.

The **Tables** section is the first settings area that you will see. In the **These core WordPress tables will always be backed up** area, you will see all of the tables that will be included in your backup by default. In this area, you can choose to exclude both spam comments and post revisions from your backups. Excluding both of these is a good idea, so go ahead and tick the checkboxes next to each table.

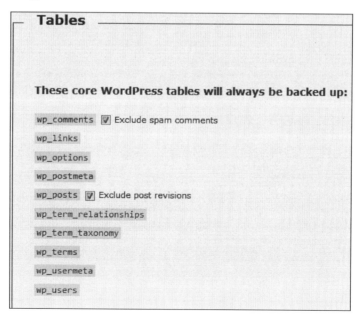

In addition to those core tables, you will also see optional tables that you may choose to include in your backup. These are displayed in the **You may choose to include any of the following tables** area of your screen. The wp_commentmeta table, for example, is listed in this area. Depending upon your site, you may also see other tables listed here as well. Tick the checkbox next to each of the tables in this section that you determine should be included in your backup.

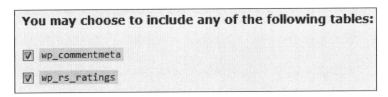

The settings found in the **Backup Options** section of this settings screen are only applicable if you're planning to create an immediate backup of your database. If that's the case, then you can choose **Save to server**, **Download to your computer**, or **Email backup to**. The option that you choose will depend upon your own preferences.

The **Scheduled Backup** settings area provides you with the ability to schedule backups of your site. These sets of features are, by far, the most useful ones provided by this plugin because they allow you to create regular backups with ease. In the **Schedule** settings area, choose how often you would like to receive backups of your site. While you may choose any of the available options, weekly backups should be sufficient.

In **Tables to include in the scheduled backup** area you will, once again, need to select the tables that you think it would be wise to backup, in addition to the core tables that will be saved by default.

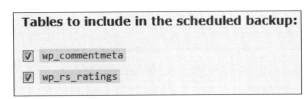

Finally, enter your email address into the **Email backup to** textbox and then click **Schedule backup**.

Email backup to: hwallace@example.com

Project suitability

The WP-DB-Backup plugin is well-suited for usage on all of the sites featured in this book.

Introducing WP-reCAPTCHA

Akismet certainly does a great job of dealing with spam that has already been submitted, but that function is only one part of the overall spam-preventative measures that you should have in place to protect your sites. The second plugin that you need to use in order to win your battle against spam is **WP-reCAPTCHA**.

This plugin, which is available at `http://wordpress.org/extend/plugins/wp-recaptcha/`, works by displaying an image that includes distorted words that your visitors must type in correctly. Using the settings provided by this plugin, this image can be configured to display on the comment form as well as the registration page.

Because of the methods that WP-reCAPTCHA uses to generate their CAPTCHA images, it's much less likely that spammers will be able to use OCR reading spam bots to bypass the protection offered by this plugin.

WP-reCAPTCHA is used by some very well-known sites, such as **Facebook**, **Twitter**, and **StumbleUpon**. Its spam-prevention capabilities are even being employed by a few U.S. government websites. If these sites are confident enough in the protection offered by WP-reCAPTCHA, then there really isn't any reason why you shouldn't entrust your site to it too.

Setting up and configuring WP-reCAPTCHA

After installing and activating WP-reCAPTCHA, a message will appear at the top of the plugins screen to inform you that this plugin won't function until you provide reCAPTCHA API keys.

reCAPTCHA is not active You must <u>enter your reCAPTCHA API key</u> for it to work

If you already have reCAPTCHA API keys associated with this site, then click on **Settings | reCAPTCHA** and, then enter them into the textboxes found in the **reCAPTCHA Keys** settings area. If you don't have reCAPTCHA API keys for this site, then you will need to create them before you can begin using this plugin.

Creating new API keys

To create these keys, you need to visit the **reCAPTCHA** site at `http://recaptcha.net`. ReCAPCTHA is now a part of Google, so, if you already have a Google account, you can use that user name and password combination to create the API keys for this domain. If you don't have a Google account, then you will need to create one before proceeding.

Either way, click on **My Account**. If you already have a Google account, log in now. If you don't have an account with Google, click on **Create an account now** and then complete the sign up process.

Once you've logged into the reCAPTCHA website, navigate to the reCAPTCHA key creation screen by clicking on **My Account | Add a New Site**. Next, type the URL of your site into the **Domain** textbox. The **Enable this key on all domains (global key)** setting should remain disabled, so just click **Create Key**.

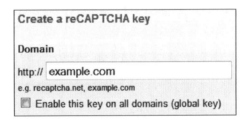

After your information has been submitted, you will be taken to a page that contains both the public and private keys that have been associated with your domain. Copy both of these keys to your text editor, so that you can enter them into the appropriate textboxes on your website.

Return to the admin area of your website and then click on **Settings | reCAPTCHA**. At the top of the screen, you will see the **reCAPTCHA Keys** area. In the **Public Key** textbox, enter the public key for this domain. Then, in the **Private Key** textbox, enter the private key.

Configuring the remaining reCAPTCHA settings

With those two keys entered, you can now concentrate on configuring the remaining settings found on the **reCAPTCHA Options** screen. The **Comment Options** settings section is next. The first setting found here is **Enable reCAPTCHA for comments** which is enabled. This should be left as is, so take a look at the next setting.

If you enable the **Hide reCAPTCHA for registered users who can** option, a reCAPTCHA won't be shown to the type of users that you choose from the drop-down menu. There doesn't seem to be much point in requiring users of a certain level to type in a reCAPTCHA since you will, mostly likely, trust that they won't spam your site. So, enable this setting by ticking the checkbox. The drop-down menu that accompanies this setting is currently set to **All registered users**, but that's a bit too lenient. Instead, it would probably be best to choose **Publish Posts**.

The **Theme** setting is next and it's here that you can choose the color used for the background of the reCAPTCHA image that will be shown on your website. So, choose your preferred color from the drop-down menu.

The last setting found in this area is **Tab Index**, which is currently set to **5**. This setting allows you to specify the location of the reCAPTCHA image in the tabbing order of the submission form. While this should be fine at its default, you may need to return to this screen later and make adjustments to that number until you find the appropriate setting for your site.

The **Registration Options** area is next. Since you hardly want your site to be inundated with spam registrations, you should activate the **Enable reCAPTCHA on registration form** setting. A **Theme** setting is, once again, found in this area, so select your preferred reCAPTCHA color from the drop-down menu before moving on to the next set of configurations.

<table>
<tr><td>Registration Options</td><td>☑ Enable reCAPTCHA on registration form.
Theme: White ▾</td></tr>
</table>

No changes need to be made to the settings found in the **Error Messages** and **General Settings** areas, so move on to the **MailHide** section of your screen. In this area you can enable settings that will protect the email addresses displayed on your blog from being harvested by spammers.

Before you begin to configure these settings, you will need to first generate another set of public and private keys for usage with MailHide. To do this, right-click on **key generation service** and then open that link in a new browser window to be taken to `http://mailhide.recaptcha.net/apikey`. The screen that you arrive at will contain your public and private MailHide keys.

Copy both of these keys to a text document and then return to the reCAPTCHA settings screen. Once there, enable each of the settings found in the **Enable MailHide email obfuscation for** section of your screen. Then, enter the public key that you just generated into the **Public Key** textbox. Next, the private key that you just created should be entered into the **Private Key** textbox.

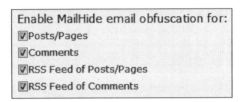

In the **Visibility Options** area, enable the **Show full email addresses to registered users who can** setting. Then, choose your preferred setting from the drop-down menu. Once again, **Publish Posts** is probably ideal. The default method of hiding email addresses is fine, so skip the remaining configurations found in this area and, instead, click **Update Options**.

Project suitability

Since some of the sites found in this book already have reCAPTCHA built-in, or use a CAPTCHA method of their own, there's no need to install this plugin on those sites. Also, a CAPCHTA feature doesn't have any place on some of the other sites that you've created throughout the course of this book. The WP-reCAPTCHA plugin is, however, well-suited for usage on all of the following sites:

- Project 1: Migrating a Static Website to WordPress
- Project 4: Building a Local Classified Ads Website
- Project 5: Building a Consumer Review Website
- Project 9: Building a Membership Website

Introducing Maintenance Mode

At some point or another there's going to come a time when you need to perform maintenance on your site. When that time comes, the functionality of your site will probably suffer in some way until the maintenance has been completed. This will leave your visitors confused and inconvenienced since they will have no idea that the problem is being caused by maintenance that you're performing behind the scenes. Rather than inconveniencing your visitors, instead, install the **Maintenance Mode** plugin, which can be found at `http://wordpress.org/extend/plugins/maintenance-mode/`.

With this plugin installed, a screen will be displayed that will alert visitors that your site is temporarily down for maintenance. While visitors will be shown this splash screen, normal access to the frontend will still be possible for those logged in as administrators.

When your site is placed into maintenance mode, visitors arriving at your site will see a screen similar to the following:

Setting up and configuring Maintenance Mode

After installing and activating this plugin, navigate to **Settings | Maintenance Mode**. **Activate/Deactivate Maintenance Mode** is the first area that you will see on this screen. The settings found here can be ignored for now, but, when you want to activate or deactivate maintenance mode, this is where you will need to go.

In the **Message** section you will find the text that will be shown to visitors when you place your site into maintenance mode. This message is fine as is, so you can move on to the **Splash Page Theme** option.

This setting causes the plugin to use either the default theme, the WordPress login page, or the 503.php file from your site's theme as the basis for the maintenance page. If you choose the **Use 503.php from theme folder** option, and your theme doesn't include a 503.php file, then the plugin will use the default theme as a substitute. So, from the drop-down menu, choose the option that you prefer. The **Access to blog front-end and administration (back-end)** settings area is next. In this section you can specify who can access both of these areas of your site once its been placed into maintenance mode. The default settings found here should be fine, so go ahead and move on to the next settings section. In the **Paths to be still accessable** area you can enter paths for pages that you would like to still remain available even while your site is in maintenance mode. Nothing needs to be entered during this initial configuration since the pages, if any, that you want to remain available will, most likely, change on a case-by-case basis depending upon what kind of maintenance you're performing on your site.

The last option found on this screen is located in the **Miscellaneous** area. Here you will find the **Apply HTTP header '503 Service Unavailable' and 'Retry-After <backtime>' to Maintenance Mode splash page** setting. Tick the checkbox next to this setting to enable it on your site. With this setting enabled, any search engine crawlers that visit your site while its offline will know exactly when they should come back to look for updates.

All of the configurations that can be performed at this point have been completed, so click on **Save Changes**.

Revisiting the Maintenance Mode settings screen

When you want to place your site into maintenance mode, you will need to revisit this screen. In the **Activate/Deactivate Maintenance Mode** portion of your screen, first tick the radio button next to **Activated**.

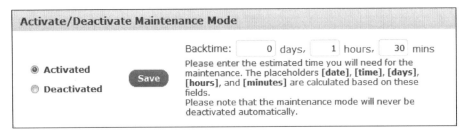

Next, in the **Backtime** textboxes, enter the amount of time that you anticipate this maintenance will last.

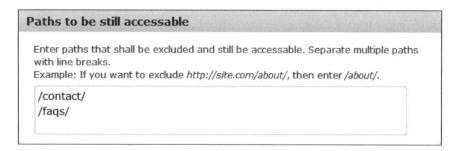

Finally, in the **Paths to be still accessable** text area, enter the paths for any pages that you want to be exempted from maintenance mode, so that they will still remain available to visitors. Once those steps have been completed, click **Save Changes**.

 Once you've finished working on your site, don't forget to visit the **Maintenance Mode** settings screen to deactivate maintenance mode. Once that's done, your site will, once again, be available to visitors.

Project suitability

The Maintenance Mode plugin is well-suited for usage on all of the sites featured in this book, except Project 8. That's because Maintenance Mode conflicts with the Register Plus plugin, which is used during the creation of the Local Business Directory site.

Introducing WP Hide Dashboard

If registrations are open on your site, then the **WP Hide Dashboard** plugin, found at http://wordpress.org/extend/plugins/wp-hide-dashboard/, will prove to be a beneficial addition. That's because a user assigned to the role of **Subscriber** can do more than just log in to the backend of WordPress and edit their profile. As a registered member of your site, they can also access certain areas of the **Dashboard** that it's completely unnecessary for them to ever visit.

This problem can easily be remedied, however, with the WP Hide Dashboard plugin. This plugin works by removing both the **Dashboard** and **Tools** menus as well as the **Help** link found on the **Profile** page. That way, when these users log in, they will arrive at their **Profile** page and be unable to navigate to any of the other screens located within the backend of your site. These changes will only apply to users who have been assigned to the role of **Subscriber**. All other users will still be able to use the **Dashboard** normally.

To use this plugin, nothing more is required than to install and activate it. Upon activation, all of the features built into WP Hide Dashboard will be put in to place without any configuration. After activation, when a subscriber-level user logs in, their screen will look similar to the following:

Project suitability

The WP Hide Dashboard plugin is well-suited for usage on all of the sites featured in this book.

Summary

As this appendix illustrates, with WordPress plugins, it's possible to make a great website even better. While this appendix highlighted five recommended plugins, you should by no means feel as though these are the only additional plugins that you could install on your sites. That's because there are so many plugins on offer that provide non-essential and yet beneficial features.

Now that you've finished creating the projects featured in this book, and have further improved them by installing the plugins mentioned in this appendix, you should next visit the **Plugin Directory** found at `http://wordpress.org/extend/plugins/`. There are many more plugins out there that offer an incredible selection of features and most of them can be found in the Plugin Directory. So, take some time to browse through this incredible collection. As you do, you will be sure to find a plugin or two that you just can't resist adding to your sites.

B

Installing Themes and Plugins

If you're new to WordPress, the concept of installing themes and plugins may be foreign to you. The methods used to add themes and plugins to an installation of WordPress are, however, quite easy, so you shouldn't have any trouble getting started.

In this appendix, you will find instructions that will guide you through the process used to install themes from the WordPress **Free Themes Directory** and plugins found in the WordPress **Plugin Directory**. Instructions are also provided for how to install themes and plugins that haven't been added to either of those two directories.

Adding new WordPress themes

When it comes to adding new themes to your site, there's more than one way to go about it and the method that you chose will depend upon the theme that you want to use.

Installing a theme from the Free Themes Directory

In WordPress, it's possible to install a theme from the WordPress Free Themes Directory, located at `http://wordpress.org/extend/themes/`, with just a few clicks. To do this, click on **Appearance | Themes**. At the top of the screen, you will see two tabs that are labeled **Manage Themes** and **Install Themes**. You're currently on the **Manage Themes** screen, so click on **Install Themes**.

On this page, you can search for themes by keyword, author, or tag. You can also click the **Featured**, **Newest**, and **Recently Updated** links to browse though the themes found on those screens.

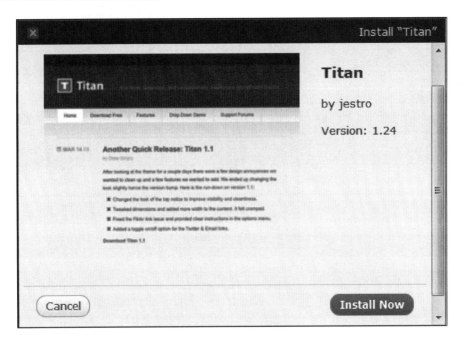

When you've found a theme that you would like to use on your site, click its **Install** link. Clicking that link will cause a pop-up window to appear that contains **Cancel** and **Install Now** buttons. Click **Install Now**. After clicking that button, WordPress will install your chosen theme. Once the installation process is complete, all that's left for you to do is click **Activate**.

Uploading and installing a theme

If you want to use a premium theme or a free theme that hasn't been added to the WordPress Free Themes Directory, then you will have to upload it so that it can be installed by WordPress. This may sound like a daunting task, but it's really quite simple.

Once again, you will need to navigate to **Appearance | Themes** and then click on the **Install Themes** tab. This time, however, click the **Upload** link located just above the search box. Now, browse your computer to locate the ZIP file that contains your theme. Once you locate the file, select it and then click **Install Now**. WordPress will, once again, attempt to install your theme. After WordPress has successfully installed your theme, click **Activate**.

> If the theme that you would like to install isn't in a ZIP file, then you need to upload it to the `wp-content/themes` directory on your server using either an FTP program or the file manager provided by your web host. After the theme has been uploaded, visit the **Appearance | Themes** screen to activate your theme.

Adding additional plugins

Once again, there are different ways to go about adding plugins to your site and the method that you need to use will depend upon which plugin you would like to install.

Installing a plugin from the WordPress Plugin Directory

Plugins found in the WordPress Plugin Directory, which is located at `http://wordpress.org/extend/plugins/`, can quite easily be added to WordPress on the **Install Plugins** screen. To reach this screen, click **Plugins | Add New**. On this page, you can search for plugins by keyword, author, or tag. In addition, you can also click the **Featured**, **Popular**, **Newest**, and **Recently Updated** links to browse though the plugins found there.

Once you've located a plugin that you would like to add to your site, click **Install Now**. When the pop-up box appears to ask you if you're sure that you want to install the plugin, click **OK**. WordPress will then work to install the plugin on your site. Once it's finished, you will be presented with an installation results page. On this page, click **Activate Plugin**.

Uploading and installing a plugin

If you would like to use a plugin on your site that can't be found in the WordPress Plugin Directory (because it's either a premium plugin, or because the developer hasn't submitted it for inclusion), then you will have to use a different method to add it to your site.

In that case, the plugin must be uploaded before WordPress can install it. To do this, click on **Plugins | Add New**. Next, click the **Upload** link found near the top of the **Install Plugins** screen. Now, browse your computer to find the ZIP file that contains the plugin that you would like to add to your site. After you've located and then selected the file, click **Install Now**. WordPress will then work to install your chosen plugin. When you arrive at the installation results screen, click **Activate Plugin**.

As was the case with themes, if the plugin that you want like to add to your site isn't in a ZIP file, then you need to go about things a bit differently. In this instance, you need to use either an FTP program, or the file manager provided by your web host, to upload the plugin's folder to the wp-content/plugins directory on your server. Once the plugin has been uploaded, visit the **Plugins** screen to activate it on your site.

Summary

As you can see, it's quite easy to add themes and plugins to WordPress even if you're a complete beginner. With the right theme and plugins, you will be able to customize the appearance and functionality of WordPress, so that you can transform your site into something truly spectacular.

Index

C

Thank you for buying
WordPress 3 Site Blueprints

About Packt Publishing

Packt, pronounced 'packed', published its first book "*Mastering phpMyAdmin for Effective MySQL Management*" in April 2004 and subsequently continued to specialize in publishing highly focused books on specific technologies and solutions.

Our books and publications share the experiences of your fellow IT professionals in adapting and customizing today's systems, applications, and frameworks. Our solution based books give you the knowledge and power to customize the software and technologies you're using to get the job done. Packt books are more specific and less general than the IT books you have seen in the past. Our unique business model allows us to bring you more focused information, giving you more of what you need to know, and less of what you don't.

Packt is a modern, yet unique publishing company, which focuses on producing quality, cutting-edge books for communities of developers, administrators, and newbies alike. For more information, please visit our website: www.packtpub.com.

About Packt Open Source

In 2010, Packt launched two new brands, Packt Open Source and Packt Enterprise, in order to continue its focus on specialization. This book is part of the Packt Open Source brand, home to books published on software built around Open Source licences, and offering information to anybody from advanced developers to budding web designers. The Open Source brand also runs Packt's Open Source Royalty Scheme, by which Packt gives a royalty to each Open Source project about whose software a book is sold.

Writing for Packt

We welcome all inquiries from people who are interested in authoring. Book proposals should be sent to author@packtpub.com. If your book idea is still at an early stage and you would like to discuss it first before writing a formal book proposal, contact us; one of our commissioning editors will get in touch with you.

We're not just looking for published authors; if you have strong technical skills but no writing experience, our experienced editors can help you develop a writing career, or simply get some additional reward for your expertise.

WordPress 2.7 Complete

ISBN: 978-1-847196-56-9 Paperback: 296 pages

Create your own complete blog or web site from scratch with WordPress

1. Everything you need to set up your own feature-rich WordPress blog or web site

2. Clear and practical explanations of all aspects of WordPress

3. In-depth coverage of installation, themes, syndication, and podcasting

4. Explore WordPress as a fully functioning content management system

5. Concise, clear, and easy to follow; rich with examples

WordPress MU 2.8: Beginner's Guide

ISBN: 978-1-847196-54-5 Paperback: 268 pages

Build your own blog network with unlimited users and blogs, forums, photo galleries, and more!

1. Design, develop, secure, and optimize a blog network with a single installation of WordPress

2. Add unlimited users and blogs, and give different permissions on different blogs

3. Add social networking features to your blogs using BuddyPress

4. Create a bbPress forum for your users to communicate with each other

Please check **www.PacktPub.com** for information on our titles

1676870R0017

Printed in Great Britain
by Amazon.co.uk, Ltd.,
Marston Gate.